CASTLES *of* *the* NORTH

CANADA'S GRAND HOTELS

PROJECT PRODUCERS

BARBARA CHISHOLM
RUSSELL FLOREN
ANDREA GUTSCHE

LYNX
IMAGES

Lynx Images would like to extend its grateful thanks to the Canadian Studies Program, Department of Canadian Heritage, for its financial support.

Project Producers: Barbara Chisholm, Russell Floren, and Andrea Gutsche
Cover and inside design: Andrea Gutsche, Lynx Images Inc.
Editorial Assistance: Joan Campbell
Cover photograph: Banff Springs Hotel, c.1920. Whyte Museum of the Canadian Rockies
Previous page: Fireplace in the Riverview Lounge of the Banff Springs, 1927, Glenbow Archives
1st Edition: June 2001

Printed and bound in Canada by Transcontinental Printing Inc.

Canadian Cataloguing in Publication Data

Chisholm, Barbara, 1962-
    Castles of the North: Canada's Grand Hotels

Includes bibliographical references and index.
ISBN 1-894073-14-2   Book
ISBN 1-894073-15-0   Video
ISBN 1-894073-16-9   Book/video package

1. Hotels – Canada – History. I. Title.

TX910.C2C494 2000   647.9471'01
C00-932384-8

CASTLES *of* *the* NORTH

CANADA'S GRAND HOTELS

EDITED BY
BARBARA CHISHOLM

WRITTEN BY

BARBARA CHISHOLM
FRANCES BACKHOUSE
RAY DJUFF
JOHN LINDSAY
DAVID MACFARLANE
FRANCE GAGNON PRATTE
TERRY REKSTEN
HARRY M. SANDERS
ROBERT W. SANDFORD
ADRIAN WALLER
WILLIAM WEINTRAUB

CONTENTS

CASTLES OF THE NORTH

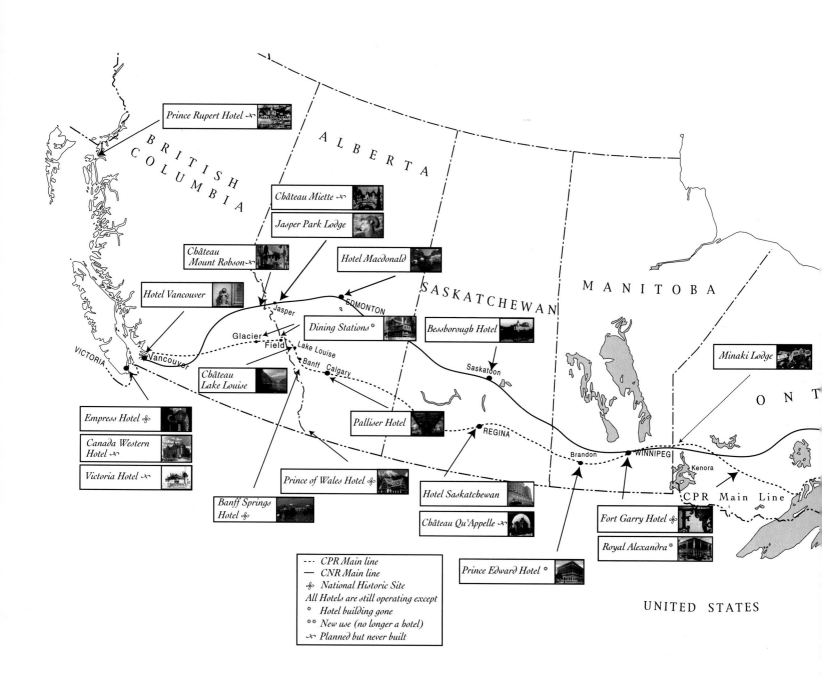

Prince Rupert Hotel

BRITISH COLUMBIA

ALBERTA

Château Miette

Jasper Park Lodge

Château Mount Robson

Hotel Vancouver

Hotel Macdonald

SASKATCHEWAN

MANITOBA

Jasper

EDMONTON

Glacier

Dining Stations *

Bessborough Hotel

Field

Lake Louise

Banff

Calgary

Saskatoon

Minaki Lodge

Vancouver

VICTORIA

Château
Lake Louise

Empress Hotel ❧

Canada Western
Hotel ☙

Victoria Hotel ☙

Palliser Hotel

REGINA

Brandon

WINNIPEG

Kenora

ONT

Prince of Wales Hotel ❧

Hotel Saskatchewan

Banff Springs
Hotel ❧

CPR Main Line

Château Qu'Appelle

Fort Garry Hotel ❧

Royal Alexandra *

Prince Edward Hotel *

- - - CPR Main line
——— CNR Main line
❧ National Historic Site
All Hotels are still operating except
❋ Hotel building gone
❋❋ New use (no longer a hotel)
☙ Planned but never built

UNITED STATES

THE GRAND HOTELS OF CANADA

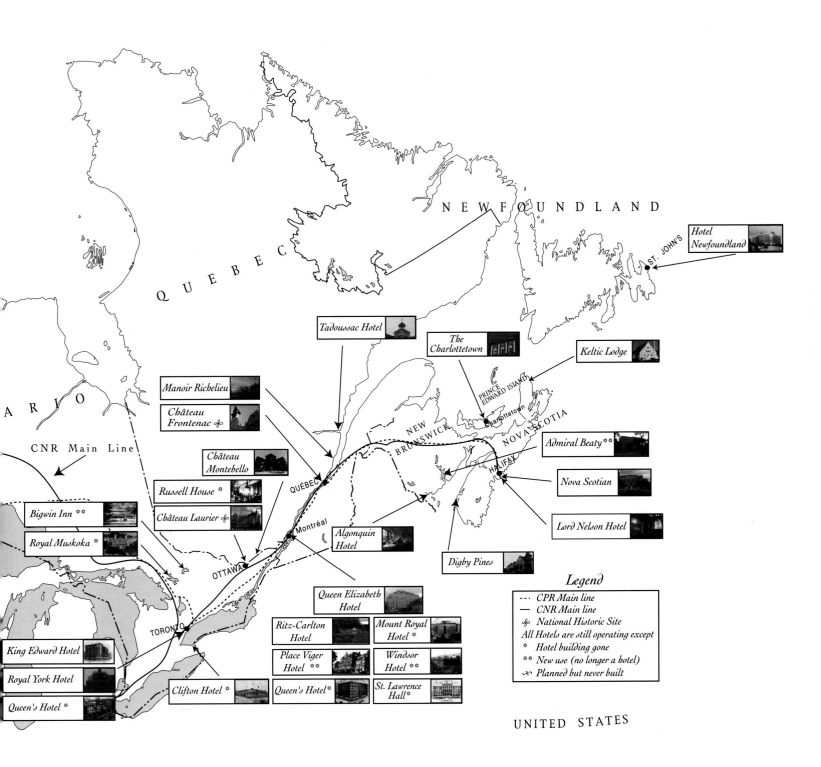

NEWFOUNDLAND

QUEBEC

ST. JOHN'S

Hotel Newfoundland

Tadoussac Hotel

The Charlottetown

Keltic Lodge

Manoir Richelieu

Château Frontenac ✿

ARIO

PRINCE EDWARD ISLAND

CNR Main Line

NEW BRUNSWICK

NOVA SCOTIA

Admiral Beaty ✳✳

Château Montebello

QUÉBEC

HALIFAX

Nova Scotian

Russell House ✳

Château Laurier ✿

Bigwin Inn ✳✳

Montréal

Algonquin Hotel

Lord Nelson Hotel

Royal Muskoka ✳

OTTAWA

Digby Pines

Legend

- --- CPR Main line
- — CNR Main line
- ✿ National Historic Site

Queen Elizabeth Hotel

All Hotels are still operating except

TORONTO

Ritz-Carlton Hotel

Mount Royal Hotel ✳

✳ Hotel building gone

King Edward Hotel

Place Viger Hotel ✳✳

Windsor Hotel ✳✳

✳✳ New use (no longer a hotel)

Royal York Hotel

↶ Planned but never built

Queen's Hotel ✳

Clifton Hotel ✳

Queen's Hotel ✳

St. Lawrence Hall ✳

UNITED STATES

The opulent rotunda of the old Hotel Vancouver. Grand hotels transport guests from the everyday to a richer, more exotic world.

INTRODUCTION

Try to imagine Quebec City without the Château Frontenac's striking silhouette, Victoria without the Empress anchoring the Inner Harbour, or Banff without the Banff Springs. Canada's historic grand hotels are national icons. They are located at the centre of our cities and in this country's beautiful wilderness settings. From the 1890s through to the 1960s, if an event of social consequence was taking place, it was taking place at one of the hotels.

Six of Canada's grand old hotels have been declared National Historic Sites and many others are recognized as municipal heritage buildings. Built by the railways, the early hotels enticed the country's first tourists. Yet today, as cities have grown up around them, it is easy to pass by these familiar landmarks without noticing their magnificence or considering their historic role. These hotels hold marvellous stories about their construction, their guests and staff, changing eras and social mores.

What do we mean by the designation "grand hotel?" It is not just size, although many were enormous. What makes a hotel "grand" is its exceptional service offered in a building of architectural merit. Splendid public halls, like the ballroom in Quebec City's Château Frontenac, were fit for royalty. And royalty came—the King and Queen of Siam, with a 56-person entourage and five hundred pieces of luggage, and in 1939, King George VI and Queen Elizabeth, the first reigning British royal couple to visit Canada. The hotels attracted heads of state, dignitaries, celebrities and moneyed people from around the globe. Events of international importance happened here, such as the Quebec Conferences between Winston Churchill and Franklin D. Roosevelt during World War II. And the hotels were the sites of other thrilling moments, like the 1964 arrival of the Beatles at Toronto's King Edward when 3,500 screaming fans waited outside to catch a glimpse of the Fab Four, registered at the hotel as the Nurk Twins.

For urban residents, the hotels were *the* place to go in town. No other place had the splendour so evocative of European court life. As A. Rogatnick said in the article "Canadian Castles Phenomenon of the Railway Hotel" in *The Architectural Review* of 1967, the grand hotel allowed people "to pose in the elegant costume of an age of social classes, which suggested that those who entered the ballrooms of the palace were invited guests of rank, gentlemen and ladies of importance, squires rather than peasants." The hotels were at the heart of their communities. During World War I, for example, the Palliser in Calgary accommodated military balls for departing officers, and served as the headquarters of the Patriotic Fund. The hotels had it all—afternoon tea, conventions and balls, Christmas and Easter celebrations, and supper dances featuring the big bands (even during the war years when, in

In young western cities, the grand railway hotels towered over the surrounding city blocks, appearing as if they had been dropped there from the sky.

Vancouver, the windows had to be blacked out at night in accordance with wartime regulations).

The locations of railway stations and grand hotels affected the patterns of growth in many Canadian cities. When William Cornelius Van Horne of the Canadian Pacific Railway (CPR) chose to situate the first Hotel Vancouver at Georgia and Granville Streets, away from the city's core, his critics thought him crazy—until Vancouver grew toward the hotel and the intersection became the commercial heart of town. A railway's grand hotel always meant a huge boost to a city's prospects for economic development. Opening day hyperbole was unrestrained. In 1935, local Saskatoon businessmen welcomed the Bessborough Hotel in the *Star-Phoenix*, "The opening of the Bessborough is another indication that Saskatoon is in the front line of progress and another expression of belief in her future greatness."

The city hotels played other useful roles. Many were important commercial centres, with entire floors set aside for sample rooms in which travelling salesmen could show their lines. The hotels also filled a good portion of their rooms with permanent residents. In

the 1950s, the Royal York had 500, and at the Château Laurier, many senators and members of parliament lived at the hotel. The Château Laurier had suites of unmatched elegance, but on the sixth floor, it also offered dormitories for those who could not afford a room. The Royal York even had its own hospital, which may have come in handy during one particularly anarchic Grey Cup celebration, when the refined Tudor Suite was converted into a temporary police station to deal with the hundred overzealous fans arrested that night.

"A CITY WITHIN A CITY"

Behind the scenes, many of the services the hotel needed were procured within its very walls. Self-sufficient, they had their own upholstery and carpentry shops, printers, silver re-plating rooms and power generation facilities. And they had armies of staff to do the countless tasks required to create the experience of seamless service. The *Star-Phoenix* offered an inventory of the specialized kitchen jobs upon the opening of Saskatoon's Bessborough in 1935: "night chef, second cook, garde manger, swingman, fry cook, roast cook, butcher, vegetable cook, vegetable boy, fireman, pot washer, staff cook, head still room girl, pastry chef, baker, assistant pastry chef, pastry pot washer...." One catering manager at the Royal York described using a string to line up goblets to set them perfectly for Queen Elizabeth II.

General managers, who often took a suite in the hotel, maintained strict order and were feared by most employees. One maintenance worker recalled that, in the early years, simply looking the general manager in the eye while passing in a hallway was cause for swift dismissal. At the Banff Springs, only front-of-house staff were allowed to go near the entrance or lobby on pain of severe reprimand and potential firing. The rule books were comprehensive. Flawless service and grooming were expected of every member of the staff. One was to serve guests with warm hospitality and a courteous and helpful manner. The words "but" and "no" were off limits. One was to be poised, decorous, tactful and discreet, and was never to tell stories about the guests.

The staff aimed to go to any lengths to satisfy requests. In these matters, quirky was expected. In *No Ordinary Hotel: the Ritz-Carlton's First Seventy-five Years*, Adrian Waller relates the story of a waiter who broke a man's fall as he toppled from a balustrade. Picking himself up, the waiter gave a slight bow from the waist, and politely enquired of the man whether someone would be joining him. Also at the Ritz-Carlton, Room Service Manager Peter Ryles arrived at work on March 16, 1964 to the news that Richard Burton and Elizabeth Taylor were planning to be married in the Royal Suite… in a few hours. Opera soprano Lily Pons ordered filet mignon—for her dog. And at the Château Laurier, Rudolph Nureyev requested an extra-large bed for dance practice. Hotel staff have served the whims of guests from Howard Hughes, who took up half of the eighth floor of the Ritz-Carlton for his retinue, to John Lennon and Yoko Ono who, in preparation for their week-long bed-in, had all of the furniture—except a bed—stripped from their 17th-floor suite.

Demanding though their work can be, staff have dedicated 40, and sometimes 50 years to their hotels. At the Château Frontenac in Quebec City, many have a proprietary feeling about the place. Their families have worked here for generations. Bellman Roger Martel's two uncles worked a combined 105 years at the Château. At least 30 members of Lionel Verret's extended family have worked at the Château. He recently retired after 54 years of service.

If you ask hotel staff members what they like about their jobs, most will reply that they love working with people. For 37 years, Royal York switchboard operator Beatrice Blucher handled 500 calls a day with a smiling voice. And across the country at the Hotel Vancouver,

A salesman shows his new line in one of the Royal York's sample rooms, 1963

Frances Kay, a manual elevator operator, greeted countless guests with warmth during approximately 118,000 elevator trips over her long career. While employees have witnessed enormous changes at the hotels—the job of manual elevator operator disappeared years ago—they continue to pride themselves on providing the best possible service to guests. The desire to exceed expectations is timeless.

GRAND BEGINNINGS

Canada's first grand hotel, indeed one of the first in North America, was Montreal's Windsor Hotel. It made its appearance in 1878, proclaiming itself to be "the Dominion's first, biggest, and best." A beautiful Second Empire building the size of an entire city block, it was considered a palace. Luxurious interior appointments set new standards in opulence for hotels in the country. The amenities were unheard-of (but still, there were only three bathrooms per floor!). For the first time, shops were located right in the hotel, prompting a newspaper to report that "under one roof, every comfort and convenience of life can be found." By offering exceptional service in such an impressive setting, the Windsor

Canada's first grand hotel, the Windsor, opened in Montreal in 1878.

transported guests from the everyday to a richer, more exotic world. It was a fantasy fulfilled.

THE CANADIAN PACIFIC EMPIRE

It was the Canadian Pacific Railway (CPR) that became best known for building Canada's "dream-castles." In 1885, it completed the transcontinental rail line linking Canada from coast to coast—a monumental feat. Still another daunting job lay ahead: encouraging the use of this new "Imperial Highway." In such a young country, there was little demand for the railway line. To increase passenger traffic (and so to see a faster return on the investment), CPR president William Cornelius Van Horne envisioned a chain of grand hotels that would link the country along the rail line. Van Horne wanted hotels grand enough to rival the Ritz in Paris and in London. He wanted to build them in Canada's most beautiful wilderness locations and in its biggest cities. Yet his sweeping vision of luxurious hotels had modest beginnings.

In 1886–87, the company built three rustic Swiss-style chalets in the Rocky and Selkirk Mountains: Mt. Stephen House, Glacier House, and Fraser Canyon House. Not originally planned as hotels, they were dining stations, meant to replace the railway dining cars which were too heavy to climb the steep mountain grades (and too dangerous on the descent). Yet the magnificent surroundings left such an indelible impression on Victorian travellers that many wanted to return for longer visits. And so began a series of expansions and improvements that transformed the dining stations into small resort hotels.

Van Horne also wanted a hotel in Vancouver, the railway's western terminus. Designed by Thomas Sorby, the same architect who built the dining stations, the hotel fell short of grand. Critics likened it to a "glorified farmhouse" and a desperate memo from a hotel commissioner to the CPR's assistant president in 1890 begged for help in dealing with the "rats and cockroaches [that] have got complete possession of the house, and are in fact a regular plague."

These early buildings were far more humble than what Van Horne envisioned. He wanted a castle in the mountains. Van Horne figured that the "Canadian Alps," as the CPR promotional engine dubbed the Rockies, could attract the same kind of people who had toured the Swiss Alps with Thomas Cook since 1863. These were tourists with the means to travel anywhere their hearts desired. For this kind of clientele, nothing short of luxury in the wilderness would do. So, for his next hotel, Van Horne chose a site at the confluence of the Bow and Spray Rivers at Banff with a "million dollar view." He commissioned architect Bruce Price to create a "monumental architecture" befitting the splendour of the Rockies and accommodating the worldliness of its guests. Price's building, constructed of wood in a combination of styles,

When William Van Horne (inset) chose this site (at Georgia and Granville Streets) for the 1887 Hotel Vancouver, critics thought he was crazy... until the intersection became the commercial heart of town.

including Scottish baronial and French château, was impressive enough for Van Horne to proclaim the Banff Springs "the finest hotel on the North American continent." Over the years, the wooden building was transformed into a stone baronial castle. The first in Canadian Pacific's grand hotel empire, it remains Canada's most historic and most famous resort hotel. The Van Horne and Price collaboration would span several years, establishing Price as a major architect and the CPR as the builder of some of the world's finest hotels.

THE CANADIAN CHÂTEAU

Van Horne's next project was a castle in Quebec City. It was here that transatlantic passengers landed and began the rail trip west. Once in Vancouver they could transfer to Canadian Pacific's steamship line to the Orient. As with the Banff Springs, Van Horne wanted the Quebec City hotel to rival any luxury establishment in Europe. Again, the proposed location was dramatic and inspiring—the site of an earlier French fort overlooking the St. Lawrence, and towering over the old section of the city.

Architect Bruce Price's Château Frontenac (1893) did not disappoint him. Modelled after early

French chateaux, the majestic brick and stone structure with its towers, turrets and cornices, captured the popular imagination. Fortress-like and solid, it exuded strength while the interior was infused with worldliness and opulence.

The Château Frontenac's success inspired Canadian Pacific to use this "château style" in subsequent hotels. Price designed the Place Viger Hotel in Montreal (1898), a combined hotel and railway station, after the British model. Then, in 1908, the Empress opened in Victoria. Although less ornate than the Château Frontenac, the new CPR hotel, designed by Francis Mawson Rattenbury, had the same steep roof and dormers. *The Colonist*, a local newspaper, declared that the Empress made the "Western gateway of the great transcontinental system a fitting companion to the historic pile on the heights of Quebec."

The first of Canada's château-style hotels, the Château Frontenac, opened in 1893.

AROUND THE WORLD WITH THE CPR: THE MARKETING OF CANADA

In the Victorian era, British tourists travelled in style. As Edmund Swinglehurst wrote in *The Romantic Journey*, they "wanted and expected to find themselves treated in a manner suitable to an Englishman's station in the world, to be provided with a decent, comfortable room and board, deferential service, and the English newspapers at breakfast." The great success of the Banff Springs and CPR's other grand hotels was due largely to promotional campaigns designed to attract wealthy visitors to Canada. "If we can't export the scenery," said Van Horne in his now-famous remark, "we'll import the tourists." To draw people to the Rockies, the CPR advertised them as "50 Switzerlands in One."

In addition to the train line across the country, the CPR had developed steamship lines, including the luxurious Pacific Empresses, ships that crossed the Pacific between Canada's west coast and Asia. Posters proclaimed "Around the World with the CPR" and "Fastest to the Orient," enticing travellers to see the world in comfort. CPR publicity portrayed Canada as a place of unparalleled scenic beauty, its transcontinental train akin to the Orient Express.

Van Horne was as involved in marketing as he was in planning the hotels. He approved advertising slogans, hired photographers and artists, and sometimes even oversaw the art direction. He gave well-known photographer William MacFarlane Notman his own railway car from which to capture the beauty of the wilderness. But because photography tended to diminish the majesty of the mountains, Van Horne preferred to use painters, who were free to render the landscape even more impressive, mystical, and vivid than it was.

Van Horne's campaign to "import the tourists" was enormously successful. With its "Imperial Highway" spanning the nation, its steamship lines circling the globe and its magnificent hotels inviting the world to visit, Canada assumed a new and impressive place on the world stage.

Canadian Pacific continued to add to its network of grand hotels. To keep up with demand, it expanded its mountain resorts, the Banff Springs and the nearby chalet at scenic Lake Louise. In 1905, it purchased the Algonquin, an early resort in the pleasant East Coast resort town of St. Andrews, New Brunswick. Soon the CPR's city hotels, in particular, moved to more contemporary forms of architecture that showed an American influence. As early as 1906, Winnipeg's Royal Alexandra (1906) was a simple box with a flat roof and classically-inspired details. The Palliser, built in 1914, was similarly restrained.

THE RAILWAYS COMPETE

The Grand Trunk Railway (GTR) and its subsidiary, the Grand Trunk Pacific (GTP), were eager to emulate the CPR's success. Van Horne's counterpart was Charles Melville Hays. Hays was equally determined to complete a transcontinental line to the West and to establish his own string of luxury hotels along the route. The first GTR hotel, a showpiece for the nation, was the Château Laurier, which opened in Ottawa in 1912. For the Laurier, the Grand Trunk's architects borrowed the château style—the steep copper roof and dormers—from Canadian Pacific, but added gothic detailing to the exterior limestone in deference to the adjacent Parliament Buildings.

In 1913, the Grand Trunk Pacific opened the Fort Garry in Winnipeg and, in 1915, the Hotel Macdonald in Edmonton. Like the Château Laurier, these grand hotels had Indiana limestone walls and steep copper roofs, stylistic elements that identified them as Grand Trunk, already a Canadian symbol of first-class accommodation. However, not all of Hays' ambitious plans came to fruition. The huge cost of laying track across the continent crippled the Grand Trunk Pacific. Along with many other Canadian rail lines, it suffered from over-competition and difficult years, and was heading towards bankruptcy. As a result, GTP's plans for future château-style hotels were cancelled (see pp. 280-281).

CANADIAN NATIONAL RAILWAYS AND CN RADIO

After World War I, the Federal government nationalized the troubled railways. The Grand Trunk, Grand Trunk Pacific, Canadian Northern and many smaller lines were amalgamated to form Canadian National Railways (CNR). The CNR's first president, Sir Henry Thornton, was an untiring, driving force in its early years. Thornton oversaw 22,000 miles of track and left an indelible mark on the hotels under his control. Like his predecessors, he was enthusiastic about expanding the railways' network of luxury hotels and ensuring exceptional standards of service. The CNR built the Charlottetown and the Nova Scotian (overlooking Halifax's harbour) in an elegant, restrained Georgian style. After Newfoundland's confederation with Canada in 1949, the CNR took over management of the Hotel

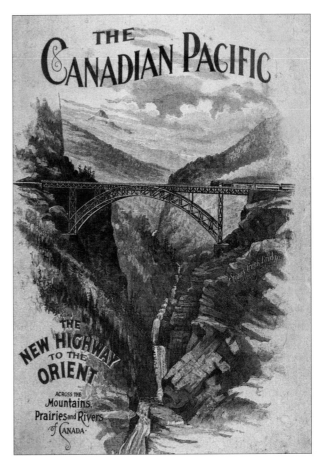

An early CPR advertisement ran: "You shall see mighty rivers, vast forests, boundless plains, stupendous mountains and wonders innumerable; and you shall see all in comfort, nay, in luxury."

Newfoundland in St. John's. For wilderness resorts, Thornton was a proponent of rustic bungalow camps that fit into the surrounding landscape, but offered luxurious services inside. CNR's wilderness resorts included Jasper Park Lodge in Jasper National Park and Minaki Lodge in northern Ontario.

But Thornton's unique contribution to Canada's grand hotels, and to the country as a whole, was his appreciation of radio's potential. To entertain passengers on its transcontinental trains, the CNR created its own Radio Department in 1923, and established the first coast-to-coast radio network in North America. In radio's infancy, Thornton installed receivers

The Château Laurier was built in the château style, which soon rose in the national imagination as a distinctly Canadian form of architecture.

on a number of passenger trains and had radio stations built along the entire cross-country route in order to maintain a strong signal. As radio entertainment became popular, Sir Henry insisted on good orchestras and performers for his pioneering network. What more logical place to broadcast such entertainment than from a grand hotel? Shows could be performed in front of live audiences, and the signal could be sent from a rooftop broadcasting studio. One of the key radio studios was located in the Château Laurier, the CNR's flagship hotel in Ottawa. Politicians and other public figures would stroll over from Parliament, take the elevator up to the studio and broadcast their messages directly to the Canadian people. These broadcasts were a tremendous boon to the Château Laurier, to Winnipeg's Fort Garry, and to other CNR hotels. Thornton's CN Radio

network would later become the Canadian Broadcasting Corporation.

MORE THAN THE RAILWAYS

Like the railways, other transportation companies quickly saw the benefit of operating grand hotels. In Quebec, the Richelieu and Ontario Navigation Company (later Canada Steamship Lines) ran two resorts along its popular cruise route down the St. Lawrence: the Tadoussac Hotel, near the mouth of the Saguenay River, and the Manoir Richelieu (1899) at Murray Bay (La Malbaie), a popular summer destination. Grand resorts including the Royal Muskoka (1901) and Bigwin Inn (1920) also sprang up on inland lakes.

In the country's two financial hubs, Toronto and Montreal, the business elites created their own exclusive and more intimate hotels in the downtown core as an alternative to the railway hotel: Toronto's King Edward opened in 1903, and the Ritz-Carlton in Montreal in 1912.

In those same cities, the optimistic 1920s saw the appearance of two enormous hotels. Montreal's Mount Royal Hotel (1922) was a splendid establishment, offering a stunning array of services. The Mount Royal, with its 1,046 rooms, claimed to be the largest hotel in the British Empire. After 1929, that claim no longer held true when Canadian Pacific opened the still more massive Royal York in Toronto.

The crash of 1929 came just months after the Royal York opened its doors and soon the hotel's extravagance seemed out of step with the times. Its staff began to work for tips alone. These were difficult years for all of the grand hotels. Many shut entire floors or closed down altogether. Construction of the new Hotel Vancouver, begun in 1929, came to an abrupt halt, leaving a haunting steel skeleton on the city skyline. The major era of grand hotel building in Canada was nearing a close. Even still, some hotels were built during the 1930s. The exclusive log resort along the Ottawa River, now known as the Château Montebello, was completed in 1930 by a construction force of 3,000, in an astounding four months. In Saskatoon, Canadian National's last château-style hotel, the Bessborough, rose on the horizon.

In 1939, ten years after it was started, the new Hotel Vancouver was completed just in time to honour King George VI and Queen Elizabeth during their royal tour of Canada. After World War II, extravagance fell out of style. The new middle-class traveller arrived by private automobile instead of railway car. The grand old hotels, with their cavernous and formal spaces, were out of favour. Vacationers were more mindful of cost. Many of them preferred the new motor hotels and chose more adventurous and rustic destinations. Aircraft quickly replaced trains and steamships as the most desired means of travelling long distance, delivering a near-fatal blow to the hotels.

DECLINE—AND RENEWAL

In 1958, the bold new Queen Elizabeth convention hotel burst onto the Montreal scene, the first of many new hotels boasting amenities the older hotels could not provide. Attempts were made in the 1960s and 1970s to "modernize" the historic grand hotels. Travertine pillars in lobbies were boarded up, low false ceilings were constructed to hide originals trimmed with intricate plaster mouldings, while brown and orange shag carpeting was used to cover marble floors. Some attempts to popularize the hotels reached extreme levels—for a time both the Hotel Macdonald and the Royal York offered topless dancing in their entertainment lounges.

And these were the lucky hotels. Several others were damaged in fires, were demolished or were converted to new uses. The Mount Royal Hotel in Montreal is now a shopping concourse. Only a small portion remains of the coffered ceiling from its once-famous Rotunda. Of the hotels that have survived, many have recently experienced astonishing renewal and are once again at the centre of it all.

Painstaking restorations have returned the spirit of several important hotels, making it possible once again to appreciate their distinct beauty. These mammoth buildings now have many hidden and abandoned spaces. Below the sub-basement of the Empress, one can actually see the giant concrete pylons upon which the entire hotel sits. And an abandoned print shop can be found high up in a tower of the Fort Garry. One of the most intriguing spaces lost to time lies under the giant roof of the Hotel Vancouver—the abandoned CBC transmitter room—still with its old equipment and dials, and sporting the old CBC crest on its door. Toronto's King Edward has the greatest secret of them all: the abandoned Crystal Ballroom on its top floor, its floor-to-ceiling windows offering a spectacular view of the city.

Canada's grand hotels are constantly in transition. They have mirrored the growth of the country, its ups and downs, its changing fashions. These architectural and historic treasures deserve to be protected and enjoyed for years to come.

(Above) CBC crest on the door of the abandoned transmitter room, Hotel Vancouver. Every Saturday night, the fledgling Canadian Broadcasting Corporation broadcast live performances to eager audiences across the country. Canadians were glued to their radios listening to Dal Richards and his Orchestra "from the Panorama Roof high atop the Hotel Vancouver," and to Mart Kenney's live show, "Sweet & Lo" from the Royal York's Imperial Room. CBC's weekly broadcasts provided the music and levity Canadians needed. Everyone was tuning in.

RESORTS

Alpine Club of Canada climbers at the President range in Yoho National Park, British Columbia, 1930. Challenging the summits proved an irresistible draw. As expressed by writer Lafcadio Hearne in 1890, "we are nearly five thousand three hundred feet above the sea—but we are still walled up to heaven." (Opposite page) Tea on the terrace of the Banff Springs Hotel overlooking the splendid Bow Valley, c.1920

To The

MOUNTAINS

Dining room at Glacier House. At Glacier House, the CPR offered the same excellent standards as were enjoyed on their trains: starched linens, gleaming silverware, sumptuous meals and the best European wines. (Right) Glacier House staff, c.1914

DINING STATIONS

British Columbia

Illecillewaet Glacier. Hard to pronounce. Harder still to spell. Yet from the late Victorian era through the Edwardian years, it was a name well known to those with time, money and a sense of adventure who searched the world for exotic locales that could be explored from the lap of luxury. In this case, the luxury was provided by Glacier House—a hotel that rose from humble beginnings to become, briefly, one of the finest mountain resorts in Canada. Illecillewaet Glacier still drapes the flanks of Mount Sir Donald, but of the hostelry that stood at its foot, nothing remains but crumbling foundations.

One hundred and thirty-seven kilometres to the east, in the town of Field, was another grand mountain hotel that flourished at the turn of the century. Mount Stephen House had much in common with Glacier House. Built by the CPR and opened in the winter of 1886–87, both offered similar amenities and served the same affluent clientele. Both also owed their existence to the mountains that surrounded them. For the builders of the CPR, the soaring peaks and plunging valleys of the Rocky and Selkirk mountains were a formidable hurdle. Two of the greatest challenges between the prairies and the Pacific coast were steep, narrow, avalanche-prone Rogers Pass and the abrupt descent into Kicking Horse Valley.

Across most of the country, first-class passengers on the CPR took their meals in deluxe dining cars, but the "Big Hill" in Kicking Horse Valley, and other precipitous grades through the mountains, made it necessary to remove these heavy cars on the run between Calgary and Vancouver. Of course, the travellers could not go hungry, so dining stations were established. The first of these were Mount Stephen House at the base of the Big Hill, Glacier House at Rogers Pass and Fraser Canyon House at North Bend.

All three were built on a plan drawn up by architect Thomas Sorby. A central block, three storeys high, was flanked by two wings, one double-storied and the other single. The ground floor was mostly occupied by dining rooms and kitchen facilities.

GLACIER HOUSE
Location: Glacier Station, B.C.
1887: Opened in January
Initial Owner: CPR
Architect: Thomas Sorby
Style: Swiss chalet
Number of rooms when opened: 15
Number of storeys when opened: 3
1890–92: Construction of 32-bedroom "first annex"
1897–98: Addition of billiard and recreational building
c. 1900: Addition of bowling alley and observation tower
1904: Construction of 54-bedroom "second annex"
Architect: F.M. Rattenbury
1925: Closed
1929: Demolished
Named After: Illecillewaet Glacier

MOUNT STEPHEN HOUSE
Location: Field, B.C., in the Kicking Horse Valley
1886: Opened in October
Initial Owner: CPR
Architect: Thomas Sorby
Style: Swiss chalet
Number of rooms when opened: 15
1901–02: Addition to increase rooms to 100
Architect: F.M. Rattenbury
1953: Demolished
Named After: Mount Stephen

FRASER CANYON HOUSE
Location: North Bend, Fraser Canyon, B.C.
c. 1887: Opened
Initial Owner: CPR
Architect: Thomas Sorby
Style: Swiss chalet
Early 1900s: Burned to the ground; rebuilt
1897: Expansion by Edward Maxwell
Current Status: Demolished

Mount Stephen House was dominated by the brooding presence of its namesake mountain, which towered 2,400 metres above the hotel. (Opposite page) Mount Stephen House in later years.

Upstairs were 15 small bedrooms, half for staff and the rest for anyone who wished to stay on and see more than a fleeting meal stop would allow.

Edward Roper, an English tourist who stopped at Mount Stephen House shortly after it opened, described it as "one of the most strikingly handsome hotels in Canada" possessed of "every provision for comfort and enjoyment, except a sitting-room"—an oversight that he found absurd. But the company's general manager, William Cornelius Van Horne, had grander plans. Having instructed Sorby to design the dining stations in a Swiss chalet style, with shingled upper storeys and bracketed, widely overhanging eaves, he set out to promote the Rocky Mountains and the neighbouring Selkirks as the "Canadian Alps" and "fifty Switzerlands in one."

Van Horne's sales pitch was aimed at the wealthy, well-educated elite of Great Britain, Europe and North America, who had embraced the concept of tourism with a vengeance since its introduction earlier in the century. By the late 1800s, they had refined the art of leisurely travel in foreign countries and developed an insatiable appetite for

adventure in exotic lands. Inspired by the homage paid to the wilderness by authors such as Henry Thoreau and John Muir and the scientific writings of Charles Darwin and others, many of these Victorian travellers were enchanted by the idea of venturing into the untrammelled wilderness and studying nature firsthand.

At Glacier House, the foremost attraction was Illecillewaet Glacier. It "pours seemingly out of the sky in a magnificent cascade," wrote one eloquent visitor, "and descends into the valley towards the hotel as a massive, fissured tongue, most often silvery white in appearance but sometimes tinted a lovely greenish blue." The opportunity to walk to the toe of the glacier, 2.4 kilometres from the station over a rough trail, tempted many a traveller to book a room and stay overnight. But while the chance to marvel up close at the immensity of the frozen mass was enough for many, for others it was just a beginning. Alpinism, or mountain climbing, had recently emerged as a popular sport and its devotees were always looking for new summits to conquer.

The first true mountain climbers to use Glacier House as a base were Reverend William Spotswood Green, an esteemed member of the Alpine Club of London, and his cousin, Reverend Henry Swanzy. In 1888, the pair spent six weeks exploring the area, often sleeping under canvas, but returning between excursions to the comforts of fine food and hot baths. No doubt they also looked forward to the hotel's soft beds, but these, they discovered, could not be taken for granted. On one occasion they arrived back from an overnight jaunt to find their rooms occupied and their two spare tents pitched on the lawn for additional guests.

(Above) Swiss mountaineering guides Edward Feuz and Christian Häsler, 1899.

23

After that, a sleeping car was brought in and parked on a siding to house the overflow, and construction soon began on a 32-bedroom annex. When the expanded hotel opened in 1892, meal prices remained at 75 cents, but room rates rose from one dollar a night to three. For this, guests expected the best and got it, including steam heat, running water and electric lights.

While Glacier House was to become a mecca for serious alpinists, it was also the place where many novices got their first taste of the sport. The Vaux family of Philadelphia was typical. Having fallen completely in love with the Selkirks and Rockies during a railway tour of western Canada in 1887, George Vaux Sr. and his three adult children, George Jr., William and Mary, became regular visitors to Glacier House from 1894 on. In 1897, their stay coincided with that of two other habitués, Dr. and Mrs. J. H. Stallard. Experienced and enthusiastic mountaineers, the Stallards soon had the younger Vauxes ascending some of the easier routes and eyeing the more challenging ones. In subsequent years, the Vauxes combined mountaineering with an extensive and highly regarded study of Illecillewaet and other glaciers in the area.

Dr. Stallard's introduction to climbing had been in Switzerland, where he had been impressed by the skill and professionalism of the trained, licensed guides found at every alpine resort. Stallard was largely responsible for convincing the CPR to hire guides for their own mountain hotels. In 1899, Edward Feuz and Christian Häsler journeyed from Switzerland to Glacier House and became the first professional climbing guides available for public hire in North America. By 1900, there were four Swiss guides on staff and the year after that, six. Guides were also soon stationed at the CPR's other mountain hotels, but the largest contingent was always at Glacier House.

The guides' clients invariably sang their praises. One satisfied customer reported that:

> The grave and sedate guide…had my life hanging at the end of his rope several times that day and I should not hesitate to trust it there again…. He will stand and chop holes in the ice at the top of a 500-foot precipice with nothing but a few inches of ice between him and the next life, looking as if it were nothing out of the ordinary, and a novice at the end of his rope liable to slip and give him a send-off through the Styx at any minute. I used to think these men earned their money easily, but I have changed my mind entirely.

In 1904, the discovery of an extensive limestone cave system not far from the hotel added another attraction for the adventure-minded. Ladders and handrails were installed and visitors were led by lamplight through the dark maze of tunnels and chambers to the cavernous "Judgement Hall" and the eerie ice sculptures of "The Witch's Ballroom." Glacier House also offered more sedate entertainment, including excursions on horseback, billiards, bowling in the indoor alley and badminton or croquet on the lawn. "An invalid unable to stir a dozen steps could enjoy a summer here," opined one fan, waxing poetic about the "winsome grandeur" of the views from the hotel.

When the growing popularity of Glacier House dictated the need for further augmentation of the facilities, the CPR enlisted the talents of Francis M. Rattenbury, the architect who had designed the British Columbia Legislative Buildings. Completed in 1904, the new, three-storey extension brought the number of guest rooms to ninety, but because of the heavy winter snows, the two annexes were only open from May to October.

(Above) Glacier House guides, waiters and Chinese cook, 1899. (Below) Removing snow from Glacier House roof, 1925.

Meanwhile, Mount Stephen House, which was gaining a following of its own, had also undergone major structural changes. Like Glacier House, it offered everything from challenging ascents for experienced mountaineers (with or without the assistance of the Swiss guides) to moderate rambles for the less ambitious. One unique attraction, accessible by a relatively easy route, was the Mount Stephen fossil bed, where a rockslide had exposed a large area of shale, each slab marked with the delicate tracings of trilobites and other ancient creatures. Mount Stephen House was also an ideal jumping-off point for exploring the Yoho Valley, famous for its waterfalls. Excursions to Yoho required at least a couple of days, but saddle and pack ponies, tents, porters and cooks could all be hired at the hotel.

When it became evident that Mount Stephen House could no longer meet the demand, Rattenbury was commissioned to replace it with something bigger and better. The CPR called the stately and sprawling new resort "an entirely new hotel," but the historical record is unclear as to whether the original buildings were actually torn down or simply incorporated into the new design. Like the second annex at Glacier House, the new Mount Stephen House included many elements of the Queen Anne Revival style, such as offset towers, steep hipped roofs and tall chimneys. Opened in 1902, it could accommodate one hundred guests in suites with private baths. It also featured a large billiard hall and a darkroom for developing photographs. Prior to the expansion, photographers probably used the wine cellar for this purpose, as they did at Glacier House. Now the cellar could be dedicated to storing the excellent vintages that were served with the hotel's superior cuisine. Edward Roper would have been pleased to know that the need for a sitting room had also been addressed.

The pre–World War I period was the heyday of Mount Stephen House and Glacier House. But their demise was imminent. Ironically, the mountainous terrain that had prompted the CPR to build dining stations in these two locations was also a key element in the decisions that led to their closing. In 1914, the CPR was still promoting Mount Stephen House as "a favourite place for tourists, mountain climbers and artists," but in 1918, it turned the hotel over to the YMCA as a hostel for railway workers. From then on, the hotel went into a decline that ended with its demolition in 1953.

We can only speculate why the hotel was jettisoned, but it is notable that its downfall coincided with the rise of the CPR's Emerald Lake Chalet. The latter, located eleven kilometres from the Field train station, had originally been a rough mountain camp, but its canvas-roofed log cabins were soon replaced by a small, refined lodge. The serene beauty of Emerald Lake contrasted markedly with the forbidding environs of Mount Stephen House. By the second decade of the century, Mount Stephen House had also ceased to be essential as a dining station. In 1909, the Big Hill had been tamed by two spiral tunnels that moderated the grade and doubled the hauling capacity of locomotives travelling over the Kicking Horse Pass.

Engineering improvements to the line played an even more important role in determining the fate of Glacier House. Although snowsheds protected the railway from the major avalanche paths on its route through Rogers Pass, a large crew was required to clear the tracks outside the sheds. The CPR carried on with this expensive arrangement until 62 workers were buried alive in a particularly disastrous snow slide. Fearing further loss of life, the company decided to build an eight-kilometre-long tunnel through the worst of the slide zone. The Connaught Tunnel, completed in 1916, increased the safety and efficiency of the line, but it left Glacier House cut off from the railway that had nourished it for thirty years.

Henceforth, passengers who wanted to stay at Glacier House had to disembark several kilometres away and pay extra to be driven to and from the hotel. Climbers and mountain-lovers still came despite a reduced operating season of June to September, but the revenues they brought in failed to cover the cost of maintenance. So, in the fall of 1925, the hotel was declared permanently closed.

In 1926, the CPR offered to sell the entire complex to Edward Feuz, Jr. (son of the hotel's first Swiss guide) for one dollar, but the young man, more interested in mountaineering than business, declined. The empty wooden buildings were increasingly viewed by the CPR as a liability, especially after fire struck both Château Lake Louise and the Banff Springs Hotel. Finally, a demolition order was issued. By the time the first snow fell on Illecillewaet Glacier in 1929, Glacier House was only a memory.

(Above) Fraser Canyon House at North Bend, 1898. (Left) Inazo Nitobe and family on trail near Glacier House, 1898. The prime attraction was the Illecillewaet Glacier, which "pours seemingly out of the sky…."

Banff Springs Hotel, the "dream-castle" in the wilderness

BANFF SPRINGS HOTEL

Banff, Alberta

William Cornelius Van Horne was a man of great ambition, determination, business acumen—and stout dimensions. Undoubtedly, it was the latter attribute that was most apparent to the three young men who cinched a rope around his ample girth in the summer of 1885 and lowered him 20 feet into an underground cave in the Rocky Mountains, in which they had discovered a mineral hot spring. What they should have been paying closer attention to, however, was Van Horne's appraisal of their find. "These hot springs," declared the general manager of the Canadian Pacific Railway upon emerging from the steamy cavern, "are worth a million dollars."

Franklin McCabe and the McCardell brothers, William and Thomas, had built a cabin by the cave. They hoped this would give them squatters' rights to any development potential, but the government refused to recognize their proprietary claim. Discouraged about their prospects for profiting from the hot, sulphurous waters, they jumped at the opportunity when Van Horne offered them $675 apiece to renounce their tentative hold on the site.

Although Van Horne greatly underestimated the value of the hot springs, he was correct in calculating that they were a worthwhile investment. But his idea was not for the CPR to own this resource. Since 1883, he had been lobbying the federal government to set up a system of protected natural areas that would enhance tourism opportunities. He was particularly interested in the mountains of western Canada, where he envisioned building luxury resort hotels. These hotels, he hoped, would alleviate the railway company's financial burden.

BANFF SPRINGS HOTEL

Location: Confluence of Bow and Spray Rivers, Banff, Alberta

Initial Owner: CPR

Architect: Bruce Price

Style: Combination French château, Swiss chalet and Scottish baronial

1888: Opened in June

Number of storeys when opened: 5

Principal Material: Wood

1914: 11-storey central tower added

Architect: W.S. Painter

1926: Fire destroyed north wing

1926–28: North wing replaced, south wing added

Architect: J.W. Orrock

Principal materials: Concrete and steel, faced in Mount Rundle stone

Prominent Guests: Marilyn Monroe, Jack Benny, Benny Goodman, King George VI and Queen Elizabeth

Named After: The town, park and hotel are named after Banff, near the Scottish birthplace of Lord Strathcona. His financial backing was essential to completing the CPR, and he was given the honour of driving the "last spike." The "Springs" refers to the hot springs around which Banff National Park was formed.

Sikh bodyguards of the Duke of Cornwall, 1901. When royalty travelled, it was not unusual for their entourage to occupy thirty rooms.

A few months after his descent into the Banff cave, Van Horne got his wish. A federal order-in-council established a 26-square-kilometre reserve around the hot springs, within which the government proposed to lease out bath house sites while maintaining control of the design of buildings and the operation of businesses. Officially, this reserve was for "the sanitary advantage of the public," but Van Horne and the politicians knew that the real purpose was to deal with the debt that the CPR and the government had run up in building the national railway. As Prime Minister John A. Macdonald remarked, "These springs will recuperate the patient and recoup the treasury."

Once the Banff Hot Springs Reserve had been decreed, Van Horne personally selected the site for the hotel: high on a prominence above the junction of the Bow and Spray rivers, close to the upper hot springs and blessed with magnificent views. Then he hired a prestigious New York architect, Bruce Price, to realize his vision of a castle in the wilderness. Price's design drew most heavily on the architecture of sixteenth-century châteaux from France's Loire Valley, but it also incorporated traditional Tudor and Swiss elements. With its steep hipped roofs, pointed dormers, turrets, tiered verandas, bay windows and cedar shingle and stone exterior, the five-storey building was both aristocratic and complementary to the surrounding landscape.

Work on the hotel was well underway when Van Horne arrived in 1887 on a tour of inspection. He took one look and exploded in rage. The building had been erected back to front! Instead of the kitchens facing the plain, green flanks of Sulphur Mountain, they looked out on the splendid panorama of the Bow Valley and the distant Fairholme Range—the view intended for the paying guests. It was far too late to reverse this error, but Van Horne, who would one day be knighted and adopt the motto *Nil Desperandum* (Never Despairing), quickly shifted from anger to action. Snatching up a piece of paper, he briskly sketched a rotunda to be built in front of the kitchens, thus salvaging the favoured vista.

The Banff Springs Hotel opened in June 1888 and accommodated 1,503 visitors during its first season. Charging $3.50 a night, at a time when railway workers earned a daily wage of about $1.50, the CPR was clearly targeting an elite clientele. With characteristic lack of modesty, Van Horne pronounced it the "finest hotel on the North American continent." A more objective commentator, Baedeker's 1899 travel guidebook, rated it as one of the five best hotels in Canada and, notably, the only top-tier contender west of Ottawa.

Boys on Tunnel Mountain across the Bow River from the early Banff Springs Hotel, 1900–10.

Besides accommodations for 280 guests, the new hotel also contained a large dining room, a ballroom and more intimate spaces for relaxing and socializing, including smoking and billiards rooms for the gentlemen, and parlours and a reading room for mixed company. Most striking was the octagonal lobby at the centre of the hotel—a five-storey open space surrounded by overhanging balconies on every floor. The Great Hall may have impressed most new arrivals, but one regular guest, the nephew of CPR president George Stephen, refused to pass through the lobby. Instead, the reclusive gentleman always used his bedroom window to enter and exit the hotel, an idiosyncrasy only tolerated because of his connections.

From the very beginning, Van Horne had modelled his vision for the Banff Springs Hotel on the exclusive spa resorts of Europe and the United States. The opportunity to bask in the glow of high-society glamour while taking the waters was a winning combination in places such as Baden-Baden, Saint Moritz and Saratoga Springs, and the CPR intended to make the most of the liquid assets

Waitresses in the Banff Springs' kitchen, 1924. Guests who left $50,000 deposits for three-month stays expected flawless service.

flowing just outside its back door. Early hotel promotions trumpeted the hot springs' curative properties, noting that they were particularly effective in treating rheumatism, gout, diabetes, Bright's disease, chronic dyspepsia and liver conditions. Dr. R. G. Brett, who ran The Sanatorium—a nearby hotel-hospital with bathing facilities—made similar claims. He also bottled water from the hot springs and sold it as "Banff's Lithiated Mineral Water."

The therapeutic waters that filled the Banff Springs Hotel's pool were piped 240 metres down from where they bubbled out of Sulphur Mountain. Unfortunately, plumbing problems sometimes caused the flow to cease. When this happened, the hotel staff would covertly fill the pool with hot water and add sulphur from bags kept hidden for just such emergencies. The guests were none the wiser.

Within years of its opening, visitors flocked to the Banff Springs Hotel from every corner of the world. The one thing they had in common was their affluence, which overcame most differences of culture and language. But that didn't stop the European and British nobility with their old money from poking fun at the ways of their Yankee nouveaux riches acquaintances. According to one snooty commentator:

The spectacular view of the Bow River
Valley from the Riverview Lounge has
proven to be an irresistible draw, attracting visitors from around the world.

Mount Stephen Hall lent an air of baronial elegance and splendour to gatherings, c.1930.

Some of [the Americans] are very plain people, and tell the story of how they became rich with much naïveté, disowning the idea of their possessing any special faculty (in which the hearer is disposed to agree with them) and confessing also that they don't know what to do with their money now they've got it, which also seems easily understandable.

Despite their money, however, would-be patrons were increasingly being turned away for lack of rooms. In 1910, nearly four hundred people without reservations had to settle for beds in railway sleeping coaches at the Banff station. Finally, the CPR decided it was time to stop trying to tack additions onto an inadequate building.

Walter S. Painter, chief architect for the CPR since 1905, set to work. His design for the new Banff Springs Hotel honoured Price's original concept, but was more reminiscent of a seventeenth-century Scottish baronial castle than a Loire Valley château. His plans also dictated a shift to steel and concrete, rather than the outdated wood construction of the original edifice.

In the fall of 1911, the centre portion of the old hotel was torn down and rebuilding began. The next summer, guests were greeted with a new entrance and lobby and a redesigned, three-tiered bathing area. Lowest and furthest from the hotel was a semicircular pool of cold fresh water. The second terrace held the hot mineral pool, Turkish and Russian baths and one hundred individual change rooms. On the uppermost terrace were private sulphur baths, cooling chambers and rooms dedicated to the ministrations of the hotel's Swedish masseur.

Over the next two winters, construction efforts focused on an eleven-storey central tower faced with limestone from nearby Mount Rundle. The Italian stonecutters and Scottish masons Painter brought in for the job found the limestone brittle and difficult to split, but they proved equal to the challenge and the Painter Tower was unveiled to great acclaim in the spring of 1914. Much to everyone's surprise, however, in the following years the gunmetal hue of the freshly quarried rock gradually matured to the warm, rich brown seen today.

(Above) The nearby Cave and Basin pool. During WWI the Cave and Basin was converted to an internment camp housing up to 600 prisoners. (Below) Image from an early Banff Springs Hotel menu. During the annual "Indian Days" celebration, Stoney Indians entertained the hotel guests.

(Left) Byron Harmon taking motion pictures from a rock promontory above the Illecillewaet Valley, n.d. (Above) Actors Vivienne Osborne and Gaston Class and the cast of Sergeant Cameron of the Mounted filmed near Banff, c.1920. (Lower left) Marilyn Monroe stayed at the Banff Springs while filming River of No Return.

Inside the new tower, all was elegance and refinement. Persian carpets, dark wood panelling, elaborate chandeliers to cast a gentle radiance on the European furnishings and costly paintings—no expense had been spared. The creative force behind all this was Kate Reed, wife of the CPR's Director of Hotels and a recognized authority on art and antiques. Her impeccable taste was ideal for making the rich and famous feel at home.

Among the elite company in August 1914 were the Duke and Duchess of Connaught, brother and sister-in-law of King Edward VII of England. For this, their second visit to the Banff Springs Hotel, the royal couple had reserved 22 of the 300 bedrooms in the Painter Tower, plus ten more in one of the old wings. Regrettably, their planned fortnight of leisure and wilderness diversions was cut short when world affairs intervened. Returning from a canoeing jaunt one afternoon, the Duke was greeted by a solemn contingent of Mounties. Great Britain, they told him, had just declared war on Germany.

The Duke's departure on an eastbound train a few hours later marked the beginning of a hiatus for the hotel, a lull that would last until after World War I drew to a bloody close in 1918. The hotel continued to operate during

Feeding a bear cub, c.1925, something strictly prohibited today.

this period, but business slowed and the endless grim tidings from Europe affected the mood of staff and guests alike.

In contrast, the 1920s and 1930s were decades of giddy pleasure and careless extravagance, as short-skirted flappers with bobbed hair and brash young men in white flannels made the hotel their own. For most guests of this era, the Banff Springs Hotel was not a stop on a longer journey. It was a seasonal home away from home. Arriving with letters of credit worth $50,000 and mountains of luggage, couples would settle in for two or three months. The hotel manager's job was to ensure that these long-stay visitors did not become bored, far from the bright lights of New York, London and Paris.

The hot springs continued to be among the main attractions. So did the surrounding mountains and rivers. Guides, horses and canoes were available to hotel patrons who wished to scale the peaks, walk or ride the trails, or challenge the white water of the rivers. The guides themselves—intrepid Swiss mountaineers, plain-talking cowboys, former trappers and prospectors who knew the country like the backs of their leathery hands—were as much a part of the entertainment package as the excursions themselves. Guests also played tennis on the hotel courts, or golfed, initially on a nine-hole course built in 1911. In 1927, at the cost of one million dollars, world-renowned golf course designer Stanley Thompson redesigned the greens and doubled the number of holes.

The CPR also sponsored two special events that were held each summer. Banff Indian Days had originated in 1889, when floods washed out sections of track in the Rockies and left passengers stranded. In a bid to keep his guests' minds off their disrupted travel plans, the hotel manager arranged a performance by some local Stoney Indians. By the 1920s, this spontaneous affair had grown into an annual multi-day event that featured a parade of costumed natives on horseback, followed by exhibitions of traditional singing, dancing and athletic games. Banff's second major summer event through the twenties and thirties was the Highland Gathering and Scottish Music Festival, which enjoyed the patronage of Britain's Prince of Wales.

When eminent personages like the Prince of Wales stayed at the Banff Springs, it always caused a stir, but musician Benny Goodman managed to create more excitement than most when he made his first visit in the late 1930s. Goodman wrote to the hotel management saying that he would like to come to Banff, but only if he could fly in. The town had no landing strip, so the CPR immediately arranged to have one built. When Goodman's plane inaugurated the runway, the entire community was in attendance to witness the event. With promotional opportunities like this, it's no wonder the hotel hired a publicity agent to keep the press informed about the comings and goings of celebrity guests.

When the hotel again filled to overflowing in the 1920s, it was time for another expansion. Painter had left the CPR, so another architect, J. W. Orrock, was called in to update his prewar plans. The old north wing was scheduled for demolition in the fall of 1926, but a fire that destroyed the old wood-frame structure in April advanced the timetable. Fortunately, the hotel was still closed for the winter and damage to the centre block was reparable. Orrock's new north wing was completed by the spring of 1927 and the south wing was ready one year later.

(Above) Admiring the view of the Banff Springs from Surprise Corner above Bow Falls, October 1929.

Like the Painter Tower, the new sections were faced with Mount Rundle limestone. The stately splendour of the exterior was easily matched inside. Thirty-two select guest suites were sumptuously decorated in a variety of styles, including Italian, Georgian, Tudor, Jacobean, Swiss, Empire, Art Déco and "modernistic." Lavish accents used throughout the public rooms included oak panelling, stained glass, decorative plasterwork and marble fountains. Intricate, cast-bronze doors graced the entrance to the Alhambra Dining Room. Huge, arched windows looked out from the Riverview Lounge. Fossil-rich Tyndall stone created unexpected beauty on stairs and window ledges. The most spectacular space in the new hotel was Mount Stephen Hall. Inspired by fifteenth-century Gothic architecture, this two-storey room was embellished with grilled balconies, a cloistered walkway, carved ceiling beams, leaded glass windows and a Bedford lime flagstone floor.

Then, in 1942, with the world once more embroiled in battle, the CPR decided to suspend its resort operations in the Rockies. The closure lasted only

Lobby, Banff Springs Hotel, 1924

three years, but there would be no going back to the Golden Age of the prewar period. Leisure habits had changed and for a while it seemed that the Banff Springs Hotel was destined for obsolescence. The turning point came in 1969, when the CPR decided to keep the hotel open through the winter for the first time in its history. With this bold experiment, Banff entered the era of four-season tourism. Its future secured, extensive renovations were undertaken to restore the aging structure to its former glory.

The well-to-do Victorian globetrotters who gave Van Horne's wilderness castle its first business in 1888 would be amazed if they could see it today, but they would applaud the fact that the Banff Springs Hotel was declared a National Historic Site on its hundredth birthday. And on closer inspection they would realize that the elements that made them love the original version—its air of distinction, and its spectacular mountain setting—still endure.

Swiss guide Rudolph Aemmer pointing out the mountain features from Chalet Lake Louise, c.1920. (Opposite page) Postcard of Château Lake Louise, c.1925.

CHÂTEAU LAKE LOUISE

Lake Louise, Alberta

"It is undoubtedly the finest scenery of the kind on the CPR at present," wrote an early guest about the Lake Louise Chalet, forerunner to today's Château of that name. But, he went on to complain in his letter to CPR vice-president Thomas George Shaughnessy,

> The road there is atrocious and the mosquitoes at the house on the lake beyond any I ever saw…. The reason is that the house is surrounded by a peat bog full of water, like a sponge. It should not take much to obviate this—some draining and filling. As it is, life is a burden there and will be for five or six weeks.

Today, both the bog and the mosquitoes are long gone and the hotel that stands on the shores of Lake Louise would be unrecognizable to the guest who wrote that letter. The loveliness of its setting, however, remains incomparable. In spring, silt-laden meltwater turns the lake a milky turquoise. Then, as summer progresses, it becomes an azure mirror reflecting the surrounding peaks. The timbered lower slopes of the flanking mountains are swathed in dark green, while their imposing heights are a study in grey and white. And at the far end of the lake, framed by a V of trees, the glittering ice of Victoria Glacier tumbles down the precipitous face of a massive head wall.

The Stoney Indians had long known this spot when they brought the first non-native to what they called "the lake of little fishes" in 1882. That privileged

41

(Above) This first chalet was built in 1890 by the CPR on the shores of Lake Louise. Guests at Banff were enticed to take the excursion to Lake Louise.

man was Tom Wilson, a 23-year-old Ontario-born adventurer who packed supplies for crews building the Canadian Pacific Railway. Curiosity and a rudimentary command of the Stoney language gained him a guided excursion to the lake one day when it was too wet to move supplies. Wilson later recollected that after he and his escort arrived at their destination, "we sat and smoked and gazed at the gem of beauty beneath the glacier." They were among the last to have the opportunity to appreciate the spot as pure wilderness.

In 1886, a couple of CPR officials had a fishing shack built at the foot of the lake for their own pleasure, and a rough trail was cleared from Laggan, the closest station on the line. In 1888, two members of the Alpine Club of London, Reverend William Spotswood Green and Reverend Henry Swanzy, followed this trail to investigate climbing opportunities in the area. "I was quite unprepared for the full beauty of the scene," wrote Green upon returning to Britain. "Nothing of the kind could possibly surpass it."

On their way home, the mountaineering clergymen stopped in Montreal to meet CPR president William Van Horne and report on all they had seen, remarking particularly on the untapped potential of Lake Louise. Shortly afterwards, Van Horne sent instructions west to have a small chalet built on the lake, to provide meals for day-trippers from Banff and overnight accommodation for the occasional climbing party.

(Left) After the first chalet burned down, a second Chalet Lake Louise was completed in 1894. This image, taken in 1894, shows Lady Aberdeen, wife of Canada's Governor General drawing on the chalet steps. So many guests were arriving that a second storey was built onto this chalet. Conditions were far from deluxe. As one early visitor commented, "it appears my dollar paid for only half the bed."

(Above right) Chalet Lake Louise as designed by Thomas Sorby. Photo, c.1904. Hotel manager Jean Mollison kept cows at the lake to provide guests with fresh milk and cream.

(Middle) Rattenbury's mock-Tudor chalet, built between 1900–12

(Left) Built between 1912–13, Walter Painter's concrete wing overshadowed F.M. Rattenbury's mock-Tudor chalet.

View of Château Lake Louise after the 1925 addition of a concrete nine-storey wing that replaced F.M. Rattenbury's wooden structure. One unkind critic compared the new wing to a prison.

A one-storey log cabin with kitchen, dining room, bar and a few bedrooms, was erected in 1890. The few hardy souls who made their way there on foot or on horseback did not seem to mind roughing it, which was good because early in the summer of 1893, the cabin burned down, and canvas tents had to suffice for the rest of the season. But the fire was a blessing in disguise, since the replacement chalet was built farther back from the lake, on less boggy ground. The new single-storey, wood-frame building was completed by the spring of 1894, and a second level was added the following year, bringing the guest capacity to about 15. Employees were consigned to a scattering of tents and outbuildings.

One of the first managers of the expanded establishment was Jean Mollison, a young Scottish immigrant who had begun her CPR career in 1888 as a housekeeper at the Banff Springs Hotel. From there she had been transferred to two smaller railway hotels—Fraser Canyon House and Glacier House—where she gained valuable experience and confidence. Although only 25 years old, Mollison did not hesitate to take matters in hand when she arrived at Lake Louise in 1895 and found "the entire white staff" drunk. She fired them all on the spot, then wired a request for Cantonese stewards from one of the company's steamships to be sent out as replacements. Her judgement was well respected and this was done immediately.

In 1895, Lake Louise's growing international reputation as a mountaineering destination brought 20 members of the Appalachian Mountain Club to the Chalet. Among them was Philip Stanley Abbot, widely acclaimed as "the most experienced alpinist among American lovers of the sport." Abbot's climbs that year

(Right) Lake Louise Chalet fire, 1924. Guests are surrounded by their possessions which were rescued by hotel staff. Most staff lost their own effects in the blaze.

whetted his appetite and he returned the following summer with three capable companions. Their goal was to be the first to ascend Mount Lefroy, one of the most prominent peaks in the area.

The quartet nearly succeeded, but 23 metres below the summit, disaster struck. Abbot was in the lead and had unroped while he tried to determine a route around an obstacle. He had just announced that he had found a good lead, when suddenly the rock he was standing on gave way. His horrified companions watched him hurtle through the air, strike the ice below and roll rapidly down the steep slope. It took three hours for them to reach their badly injured friend and he died in their arms shortly thereafter. Recreational mountain climbing had claimed its first victim in North America.

One year to the day after Abbot's death, the first ascent of Mount Lefroy was achieved. The honour went to a group of Abbot's associates—all of them skilled climbers—who had mounted the expedition as a tribute to their lost comrade. They were accompanied by Peter Sarbach, a highly regarded Swiss mountaineering guide. Sarbach had been brought to North America especially for this climb and after it was completed he spent the rest of the summer leading members of the group up other peaks in the Rocky and Selkirk mountains.

There were many who saw Abbot's death as evidence that mountaineering was inherently dangerous and should be discouraged. The CPR sided with the defenders of the sport, but worried that further accidents linked to its hotels could give the company a bad name. So, inspired by Sarbach's efforts, they brought two alpine guides from Switzerland and stationed them at Glacier House on a trial basis. Novice and expert climbers alike were enthusiastic about this new service. Since successful climbers made happy guests who would stay longer and return often, additional Swiss guides were hired and distributed amongst the mountain hotels. Lake Louise received its first contingent in 1901.

In 1890, the Lake Louise Chalet had hosted only fifty registered guests through the whole summer. Less than a decade later, that number might arrive in a fortnight, many of them being relegated to tents because of the lack of rooms. In an effort to cope with the overflow, Thomas Sorby was commissioned to

(Above) Philip Stanley Abbot, 1890. Abbot fell to his death while attempting to climb Mount Lefroy in 1896: the first known fatality in North American mountaineering. After the accident, the CPR imported Swiss guides to lead recreational climbers. Chalet Lake Louise's first manager, Willoughby Astley, was in the party that helped recover Abbot's body.

Staff pose in front of the celebrated vista of Lake Louise and Victoria Glacier, c.1950. According to Jon Whyte in
Lake Louise: A Diamond in the Wilderness, *that still lake was quite active during World War II. Château Lake
Louise was closed during the war when, in 1943, scientists came to test an ice that "wouldn't melt"—a mixture
of spruce pulp and ice. Apparently, Lord Louis Mountbatten imagined creating floating iceberg aircraft carriers.*

expand the hotel. He elongated the existing building by adding a wing on either side, but the new facility was obsolete almost before it was finished. In 1899, the CPR decided that a complete overhaul was in order.

The architect chosen to prepare the Lake Louise Chalet for the new century was Francis Rattenbury, a CPR favourite. He began by designing a three-storey block perpendicular to the Sorby building. The character of this addition, with its corner turrets and decorative bargeboards, was largely Victorian. Rattenbury's subsequent extensions and enlargements leaned toward the mock-Tudor style, relying heavily on half-timbering for the facade.

By 1912, guest numbers had risen exponentially. Walter Painter, already hard at work modernizing the Banff Springs Hotel, was given the task of creating an annex for the Lake Louise Chalet. In a marked departure from the work of his predecessors, he designed an austere concrete edifice with smooth, unadorned exterior walls, a flat roof and a tower at each end. The wide verandas that had been a feature of every incarnation of the hotel to date were replaced with private balconies and a flat-arched pseudo-loggia that framed the huge windows of the dining room. Architecturally, the annex bore some resemblance to an oversized Italian Renaissance villa, but none at all to the CPR's other mountain hotels. Reactions were mixed.

Some visitors praised the spaciousness of the addition and the modern elegance of its interior. Others were nostalgic for what had been lost. One habitué, British Member

(Above) Barber shop at Chalet Lake Louise, c.1910. (Right) Boatman at Chalet Lake Louise, 1906. The CPR hired Chinese boatmen to propel guests around the lake. Yen, the gardener and pastry chef for the chalet, kept a slab of marble in the boathouse where he could roll out pastry dough.

Visitors enjoying the spectacular view of lake and mountains.

of Parliament L.S. Amery, commented that "the great hotel is the last word in comfort; but I couldn't help regretting the little log chalet over which Miss Mollison presided." Although the popular manager had retired in 1908 because of deteriorating eyesight, Amery still fondly recalled the days when she had often "delighted a small handful of guests with her singing of old Scottish airs."

Nor was the new architecture the only change. In the early years a horse-drawn wagon had provided transportation to and from the train station. But modernization and an increasingly refined class of guests called for a more comfortable and convenient mode of travel. By 1913, a narrow-gauge tramline was in place, reducing the trip from 90 minutes to 20. Laggan was now so closely allied with the hotel that the station and the town that had grown up around it were both renamed Lake Louise.

Mountaineering enthusiasts continued to be drawn to Lake Louise, but the Chalet was no longer just for robust outdoorsmen and women. Those who preferred more staid activities could walk along well-groomed shoreline trails or hire a boat—and, if they wished, a Chinese boatman—to cruise the lake. Many were content to venture no further than the hotel grounds, from which they could photograph, paint or simply admire the famous panorama of water, forest, rock and ice, brightened by naturalized Icelandic poppies in the foreground.

But it was excitement for all on July 3, 1924. Early that afternoon, a blaze broke out in the staff quarters in the north wing of the Rattenbury addition. Fire spread rapidly through the wooden building, but fast-acting staff managed to isolate

Georgia Englehard climbing with guide Ernest Feuz, 1931. As a child, Englehard thought mountain climbing was "idiotic," yet she later became such a proficient alpinist that it was said of her, "What she needs is a mountain goat, not a guide." Englehard climbed Mount Victoria many times, including during the filming of She Climbs to Conquer.

the concrete Painter Wing by lowering metal fire screens between the two buildings and chopping down the connecting archway. The employees made a noble effort and successfully saved all of the guests' personal effects, as well as a great deal of hotel property, but had no time to rescue any of their own possessions. Within hours after the fire sirens had first sounded, the old Rattenbury hotel was reduced to a smoking ruin. In spite of the traumatic events of the day, however, dinner was served at six o'clock, with the orchestra playing in the background as usual, and the scheduled evening ballroom dance went ahead from 9 to 11.

Almost immediately, the CPR began preparing to rebuild. Barott and Blackader, the Montreal firm awarded the contract to augment the surviving structure, drew up plans that reflected Painter's Italianate vision rather than reverting to neo-Tudor or Victorian styles. The only modifications were a row of dormer windows below the roofline and covered arcades along the lakefront side. The remodeled hotel would have nearly 400 bedrooms, half of them facing the lake.

(Below) At 110 ft. long and 40 ft. across, Lake Louise's pool was the second largest in Canada when it was built in 1926.

49

Director Ernst Lubitsch and cameraman during filming of Eternal Love *on the Victoria Glacier, Lake Louise, 1928.*

Excavations for Barott and Blackader's nine-storey wing started on September 1, 1924, and it rose quickly through the winter, despite frigid temperatures, heavy snows and the remoteness of the building site. Nine months later the revitalized hotel opened under a new name that signalled a complete departure from its rustic roots.

Even more than its predecessors, the Château Lake Louise was conceived as a haven of luxury in the midst of wilderness. The opulence inside matched the natural grandeur outside. The CPR also extended the mantle of civilization into the surrounding landscape by building tea rooms and rest houses at popular hiking destinations to revive cold and weary adventurers before they embarked on the return journey. And no one had to worry about whether they would be presentable after a day of exploring the mountains, since the hotel's numerous amenities included a beauty parlour and barber shop.

The twenties and thirties were lively, glittering decades at the Château, made all the more exciting when movie stars were in residence. Mary Pickford and Douglas Fairbanks visited Lake Louise, and in the mid-1920s, Mary Astor came to star in *The Silent Partner*. When *Eternal Love* was being shot on location at Lake Louise in 1928, female guests and staff swooned at the sight of John Barrymore by the swimming pool or in the dining room.

In 1939, the social whirl was brought to an abrupt halt by the outbreak of World War II. The Château was closed until after the hostilities ended in 1945, and when it reopened, high times were replaced with hard times. The guests still came, but they stayed for shorter periods and spent less money. By the mid-1960s, there was talk of selling off the venerable hotel or even tearing it down.

Ultimately, it was the mountains that saved the Château Lake Louise, just as they had brought the original chalet into being. As North Americans embraced the sport of downhill skiing, it became feasible to transform the hotel

Hauling camera equipment to location. The two men on the right are guides, E. Feuz Jr. and Rudolph Aemmer.

into a year-round resort beginning in 1974. This lasted until 1979 when winter operations were suspended. After a 65-million-dollar makeover, the hotel reopened in 1988. In 1997, Canadian Pacific Hotels revived the mountain guide tradition, and once again, guides lead excursions through the mountains. For those whose appreciation of the peaks is more passive than active, they can indulge in the long tradition of admiring "the finest scenery of the kind" from the comfort of the lounge at Château Lake Louise.

(Inset) Mary Astor ski-joring at Lake Louise during the filming of The Silent Partner, c.1924.

Porters met guests at the train station and also took them on excursions through the mountains.

JASPER PARK LODGE

Lac Beauvert, near Jasper, Alberta

In the early 1920s, Jasper National Park was a remote wilderness. But even in the weak winter light, Henry Thornton, president of the Canadian National Railways, was immediately impressed by its breathtaking beauty. One was definitely in the mountains but not hemmed in as one was in Banff or Lake Louise. There was also wildlife. Deer and the occasional elk wandered right through the town and bears sauntered down the main street in summer.

After touring railway facilities in town, Sir Henry was conducted to a tourist camp that the railway owned on the shores of Lac Beauvert. Called Tent City by the locals, it did have a few, though quite inadequate, buildings, but amidst the glory of those timeless peaks, first class rail passengers were indeed staying in tents.

Pre-World War I plans for luxury hotels in Jasper National Park had come to naught (see Château Miette, p. 280). What emerged during the war was a tourist camp with ten large sleeping tents and a cook tent. Though it was a huge success in the summer of 1915, the camp closed at the end of the season and did not open again until the war was over. In 1921, the new Canadian National Railways (an amalgamation of the former Grand Trunk Pacific and 148 failed northern railway operations) bought Tent City. When it re-opened in June 1922 with new bungalow cabins, it was called Jasper Park Lodge.

Henry Thornton, who recognized Jasper Park's potential to attract international tourists to Canada, called for immediate expansion and an upgrade to exceptional quality. The CNR's chief architect, John Schofield, a follower of the English garden city movement, argued that this beautiful site in the Athabasca Valley should be altered as little as possible. In order for it to blend in with its

Jasper Park Lodge had humble beginnings as "Tent City" on the shores of Lac Beauvert in 1915.

Jasper Park Lodge was designed to blend in with its magnificent surroundings. Shown here is the second lodge, opened in 1953 after the first one burned down the previous year.

JASPER PARK LODGE

Location: Lac Beauvert, near Jasper, Alberta

1915: Tent City opened June 15

1921: CNR took over Tent City

1922: Jasper Park Lodge log bungalows opened in June

1923: Main lodge opened

Architect: Godfrey Milnes (working with John Schofield)

Style: Rustic bungalow camp

Principal Materials: Peeled log and field-stone

1942-45: Closed during WWII

1952: Main lodge burned down July 15

1953: New lodge opened

1988: Bought by CP Hotels & Resorts

2000: Outlook Cabin burned down

Prominent Guests: King George VI and Queen Elizabeth, the Duke of Kent, Sir Arthur Conan Doyle, Bing Crosby, Marilyn Monroe, Prime Ministers Mackenzie King and Pierre Trudeau

Named After: The National Park and town of Jasper are named after Jasper Hawes, a trader who worked at the North West Company supply post Jasper House during the heyday of the fur trade.

---

surroundings, he recommended moderate-sized cabins around a main building rather than a massive resort hotel of the kind favoured further south by Canadian Pacific.

This approach suited Thornton, who liked the idea of using simple materials—logs and fieldstone—and traditional methods to create luxury in a rustic setting. The rotunda of the main lodge used exposed log trusses, burled columns, and bent-stick brackets to great effect; and the cabins built of logs distinguished Jasper Park Lodge from the other railway resorts in the Rockies. Here, visitors were never more than a few steps away from the wilderness they had come to enjoy. Moreover, because the resort's cabins were scattered through forests of pine and Douglas fir, it never felt crowded even when it was full.

During the winter of 1922–23, the CNR constructed a grand new central building and a cluster of outlying bungalows. Designed by Godfrey Milnes, the new lodge was touted as the largest single-storey log building in the world. The main building was rustic—peeled logs on a fieldstone foundation—and low to the ground to blend in with the lakeside surroundings.

The wide valley and grand views made Jasper a perfect place to build a golf course. When the CNR took over Jasper Park Lodge, they commissioned a

(*Left*) By 1925, Jasper Park Lodge had over fifty log structures. The rustic simplicity of this resort made the lodge an exotic destination in the 1920s. (*Below*) Dominated by a grand stone fireplace, the main hall of the first lodge was filled with specially designed wicker furniture.

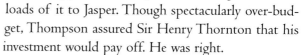

Waitresses at Jasper Park Lodge. In later years, to work at the Lodge over the summer carried great prestige. Students were recruited from universities in eastern Canada and thousands applied for summer jobs as waitresses, chambermaids, bus boys and chauffeurs. (Below) Shirley Abbey's late pass.

well-known Canadian golfer and golf course architect, Stanley Thompson, to design one. The site was cleared of boulders and trees in the summer of 1923 by a crew of two hundred men and fifty horse teams. When it became obvious that the soil was too thin for growing the thick grass necessary for a course, the railway bought some good farmland, stripped off the topsoil and transported trainloads of it to Jasper. Though spectacularly over-budget, Thompson assured Sir Henry Thornton that his investment would pay off. He was right.

The course officially opened in July, 1925, with Earl Douglas Haig, commander in chief of the British forces in World War I, hitting the first ball. It was instantly hailed as the best mountain course in the world. Few others provided a habitat for elk, deer and bears. (On Earl Haig's first hole, in fact, one of the balls was carried off by a black bear.) Nor did many other groundskeepers need to hire help to turn off the sprinklers that the bears were in the habit of turning on!

Henry Thornton played golf with the same enthusiasm he played the competitive railway game. One afternoon just after the completion of the course, Thornton hit a ball into a clump of trees. His position was hopeless. He could pick up the ball or lose who knows how many strokes ploughing his way out. The other players stopped to watch what he would do. Sir Henry hesitated a moment, then made up his mind. It was no good being president of the CNR for nothing. He spoke to his caddy who headed off at a run and soon returned with two men carrying a cross-cut saw. A few minutes

later a large tree crashed to the ground. There was one less tree in Jasper National Park, but Sir Henry won his hole.

In the 1920s and 1930s trail riding was very popular. The Lodge kept about three hundred horses and employed some fifty people to lead excursions—from half-hour "evening steak rides" to a nearby lake, to six-week pack trips along the "Glacier Trail" to Lake Louise. The hotel also hired Swiss guides for those wishing to go mountain climbing and had a fleet of cars and drivers available to take guests to scenic sites such as Mount Edith Cavell. Jasper Park Lodge even ran "bear-watching buses."

In 1927 and 1928, the central lodge was expanded and more bungalows were built around the lake, enhancing the "village" effect of the resort. The bungalows ranged in size from four to twenty rooms. Built between 1928 and 1931, each of the three best-appointed cabins—Point, Outlook and Viewpoint (the cabin where Sir Henry stayed when in Jasper)—had its own kitchen, dining room and servant's quarters. (Sadly, Outlook Cabin burned down in November 2000.) A golf clubhouse and greenhouses were added in 1929.

Boathouse on Lac Beauvert. The Lodge had canoes and rowboats available for guests.

First officials at Jasper Park Lodge

By the early 1930s, both Canadian railways were in trouble due to the Depression. After the Conservatives came to power, the CNR was attacked as a public "White elephant." Sir Henry Thornton was accused of wasting money on frivolous luxuries such as Jasper Park Lodge and its famous golf course. Overnight, Thornton became a symbol of a Liberal conspiracy against the taxpayer.

Despite the controversy, Jasper National Park continued to develop. In 1935, relief workers were hired to complete the Wonder Road, a gravel two-lane highway connecting Jasper to Lake Louise and Banff. Even during the leanest years, visitors came to Jasper Park Lodge. When King George VI and his wife Elizabeth stayed in Outlook Cabin in 1939, the reputation of the resort was assured. But once again, international events intervened. During World War II, the lodge was closed to the public and became a training base for the Lovat Scouts, a regiment of Scottish mountain troops.

Both the terrible Depression and the lost revenues during World War II were devastating for resort properties generally, but Jasper remained popular after 1945. Jasper Park Lodge was just what postwar visitors wanted: elegance amidst the grandeur of the Rockies. So the resort was packed with visitors in mid-July

(Right) Bing Crosby hamming it up. (Below) Room service meals by bicycle was a theatrical way to serve guests at their cabins, but the Lodge had to stop the delivery of free ice as guests were calling for ice simply so they could take a snapshot of the bicycle waiters when they arrived.

1952, when disaster struck the main lodge. That evening, flames broke out in the cloakroom and swept down the newly varnished dance floor. Len Hopkins and his band continued to play as people vacated the hall. The telephone wires were down and more valuable time was lost when lookouts who spotted the fire were first told that the flames came from a permitted burn at the Lodge. That night, as the fire at the main building burned out of control, the fire fighters and hotel staff worked to save the surrounding cabins, some by rolling around on the dry cabin roofs in wet blankets to douse the landing sparks.

Food was brought in from town during the night, and at 7:00 a.m. a simple, cafeteria-style breakfast was served to guests, staff and fire fighters—some 1,200 in all. By nightfall, new silverware and china had arrived from the Hotel Macdonald in Edmonton. The beauty salon, barber shop and valet service were back up and running, and Len Hopkins and his orchestra began playing for dancers in the staff recreation hall. The hotel ledgers had been destroyed, but management was delighted when virtually all the guests came forward and tallied up their charges as best they could, many remembering their incidental expenses to the penny. Few chose to leave on the special train brought in to evacuate the guests. By 1953, a new, fireproofed main lodge had been built in an architectural style reminiscent of Frank Lloyd Wright.

(Above) Pages carrying the trophy for the prestigious Totem Pole Tournament. Bing Crosby, who had fallen in love with Jasper while on a film shoot, returned in 1947 to win the award.

Jasper Park was part of "Hollywood of the North." As early as 1927, a feature film, *The Country Beyond*, had been filmed in the Park, with scenes in the Lodge. According to writer Cyndi Smith, 98 packhorses were assembled to serve the film crew. The Lodge, complete with trophy heads on the walls and wicker chairs, was also drawn to scale and then reproduced as a Hollywood set. In 1946, *Emperor Waltz* was made at the Columbia Icefield, starring a yodelling Bing Crosby. The story goes that the film's director, Billy Wilder, posted guards around the Lodge grounds—not to keep curious onlookers away, but to keep Bing, tempted by the golf and fishing, from wandering off the set.

Hollywood did not portray Jasper as itself. For example, the 1953 Universal Studios film *Far Country*, starring James Stewart, was set in Alaska during the gold rush, with the Columbia Icefield doubling as the Klondike. Probably the most famous film ever made in the Rockies was the 1953 production of *River of No Return*. Many scenes from the picture, which starred Robert Mitchum and Marilyn Monroe, were set in Jasper. Having movie stars at Jasper Park Lodge was good for business. Famous American families such as the Colgates, the Kennedys and the Rockefellers have also enjoyed its luxurious cabins, as have heads of state and other celebrities. The resort was exclusive—guests had to be registered at the front gate in order to be admitted to the grounds.

The complex went through several modernization phases. Between 1953 and 1972, old cabins were removed and replaced with fire-resistant cedar chalets with peaked roofs to match the newly built lodge. In 1988, Canadian Pacific Hotels absorbed the famous Canadian National Railways hotels, including Jasper Park Lodge, and began a continuous program of upgrading.

As Charlene Petrowsky, former Chief Concierge, points out, there are unique logistical problems to running such a sprawling place in such a remote location. Edmonton, the closest big city, is two hundred

miles away. Room service delivery of hot meals does not simply involve a trip up an elevator. The Lodge has 111 structures, so there are 111 roofs to keep in repair. The grounds crew has to tend 16 miles of walkways. The Lodge also has to pave its own roads, maintain its own fleet of vehicles, hire its own mechanic and operate its own gas station and car wash.

But it is worth it. Each cabin is situated to take full advantage of grand mountain views that radiate outward in every direction from the Athabasca Valley. Deer and elk graze on the green lawns. Coyotes, bears and even cougars occasionally wander past. The wind hisses through huge firs and ancient spruce. Lac Beauvert sparkles in the afternoon sun. Jasper National Park is now part of a UNESCO World Heritage Site. Henry Thornton would be content.

(Left) President of the CNR, Sir Henry Thornton was known as the "Big Man on the Horse." At Jasper Park Lodge, he sought to combine luxury with a rustic setting.

61

(Above) The Prince of Wales Hotel was designed to enhance the appreciation of the surrounding mountain peaks. (Opposite page) The hotel has a commanding view of Upper Waterton Lake. Seven-mile-long Upper Waterton Lake is dissected by the Canada/U.S. border. The tour boat International brought Americans from Goat Haunt, at the south end of the lake, to Waterton and the Prince of Wales Hotel.

PRINCE OF WALES HOTEL

Waterton Lakes National Park, Alberta

In 1927, when American patrons entered the new Prince of Wales Hotel in Alberta's Waterton Lakes National Park, their first question was: "Which way to the bar?" Still in the throes of Prohibition, the thirsty Americans were looking for a place to wet their whistles in Alberta, which had ceased to ban alcohol sales four years earlier. Due to last-minute plan changes, the bar was not ready, but bell captain Victor Harrison was prepared. He took the Americans' requests and had their bottles the next day when the supply truck returned from Lethbridge, ninety miles away.

The Prince of Wales Hotel was the brainchild of Louis Warren Hill Sr., head of the St. Paul, Minnesota-based Great Northern Railway. "Louie" Hill planned the hotel as an addition to the chain of hostelries he had built in Glacier National Park, Montana, just across the border from Waterton. When Hill first came to Waterton in September 1913, he was so impressed with the scenery that he vowed to build a grand hotel on the 250-foot-high knoll overlooking the lake. The advent of World War I, and the subsequent abandonment of a plan to build a dam across the narrows on which the hotel now sits, put a temporary halt to Hill's scheme. What swayed Hill to dust off the proposal was the end of Prohibition in Alberta in 1923. Hill figured building a hotel in Canada would lure thousands of thirsty Americans to Glacier, where they could cross the border on buses or saddle horses to drink legally. It was an inventive way to circumvent Prohibition while boosting passenger traffic on Hill's Chicago-to-Seattle railway.

Construction of the Prince of Wales Hotel began in July 1926 and lasted a year. It was an incredible feat, overcoming bad roads, terrible weather and the fickleness of Louis Hill who kept changing his mind about the look of the hotel. The first

PRINCE OF WALES HOTEL

Location: Waterton Lakes National Park, Alberta

1927: Opened July 25

Initial Owner: Great Northern Railway Hotel Company

Architect: Thomas McMahon

Style: Swiss chalet

Principal Materials: Douglas fir timbers

1933-35: Closed due to Depression

1942-45: Closed during WW II

Prominent Guests: Pierre Trudeau, Clint Eastwood, Steve McQueen

Named After: Britain's Edward, Prince of Wales, later to become King Edward VIII. The owners hoped that naming the hotel in his honour would entice him to stay there on his 1927 Canadian tour, but instead, he stayed at his private ranch north of Waterton.

obstacle faced by the Canadian contractors (Doug Oland and Jim Scott) was the thirty-mile distance between Waterton Park and the nearest rail terminus in Cardston. Great Northern could ship supplies as far as Cardston, but it was up to the builders to get the material to the construction site.

When the September rains came, the freight trucks churned the route into a "sea of mud," making it impassable for days at a time. "I had to revert to horses [and wagons] and the more I hauled the worse the roads got," Oland recalled later. Winter's freeze brought some relief, but in December Waterton was hit by one of the worst blizzards in its history, with winds gusting to over ninety miles per hour. "Planks and boards were seen flying over men's heads who, not even looking back to see if any more were coming, only put on a little more speed...," the *Lethbridge Herald* reported.

Surprisingly, the unfinished hotel withstood the onslaught, although it was blown slightly out of kilter and had to be winched back into alignment. A second storm, in the spring of 1927, again knocked the hotel out of plumb. Work had progressed so far that the contractors feared realigning the building would do more harm than good and decided to leave it that way. That may account for the hotel's tendency to sway in strong winds, which some say causes whitecaps in the toilets.

While dealing with Mother Nature's fury, Oland and Scott also had to contend with Hill's ever-changing vision. The original blueprints show a four-storey building with a low-sloped, hipped-gable roof, reflecting the style Great Northern used for its hotels and chalets in Glacier Park. But when Hill returned from a summer vacation in Europe, he ordered architect Thomas McMahon to make the hotel look like the French and Swiss chalets he had just seen. Various changes were made, including the addition of three storeys, and construction of a thirty-foot tower to top the whole thing off. Some months later, Hill decided to add a fifth floor in the east and west wings. This entailed tearing apart and rebuilding each of the twelve dormers, but it also increased the number of rooms to the present ninety, making the Prince of Wales one of the largest all-wood buildings in Western Canada.

Hill's tinkering caused the builders to miss their completion deadline by more than a month. But they were pleased with the result, particularly the open post-and-beam construction of the lobby, which was fitted and pegged together from huge Douglas fir planks without the aid of any powered equipment. "There are no nails in it anywhere," Oland used to boast to his daughter, Mary O'Brien. The hotel was opened to the public on July 25, 1927 to universal acclaim. The Wall Street Journal deemed its architecture "striking and unique." Others have called the whimsical, Swiss-inspired design a cross between a chalet and a Japanese pagoda. In any event, it was an oasis of luxury in the wilderness, proof that man could master nature in even the most primitive of places.

The Prince of Wales marked a new era in tourism in Waterton. The national park attracted international attention and the hotel became a destination resort—especially for Americans, to whom Great Northern directed its advertising. Railway calendars, brochures, menus, playing cards, matchbooks and other give-aways featured the images of local Native Americans (usually painted by Winold Reiss). Tourists wanting to see members of the Blackfoot Confederacy were urged to visit Waterton and Glacier where tribal elders were paid to put up their tepees and perform songs and dances. But the Prince of Wales' time in the lime-light was short. Two years after it opened, North America was jolted by the October 1929 stock market crash. Then Prohibition was lifted in the United States, dissolving the original purpose for building the hotel. Business was so slow during the Depression that the hotel was closed for three summers, beginning in 1933. When a Great Northern employee boasted in 1935 that he had

(Inset) The Prince of Wales' design was inspired by French and Swiss chalets. Louis Hill, the owner, changed his mind so often about the design that the contractors claimed that much of the structure had to be built four times over. (Below) Dignitaries and tourists on opening day, July 25, 1927.

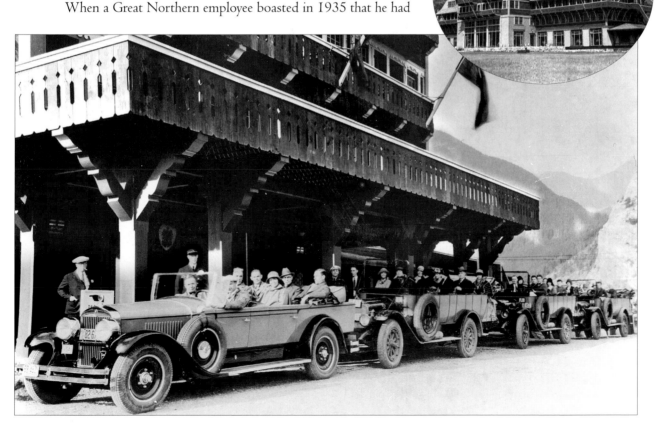

(*Right*) *Interior, 1927. Through the two-storey windows, the grandeur of Upper Waterton Lake could be viewed in comfort and style. Although the hotel was constructed to show off the Canadian Rockies to Americans, much of the view from the lobby windows is of the United States.*

saved the hotel from a forest fire that came close to devastating the Waterton townsite, the telegram from the president of the railway asked: "Why?" The insurance money must have looked very tempting.

Yet, in the midst of the worst economic crisis of the 20th century, a meeting at the hotel offered people a glimmer of hope. Spurred on by Canon Samuel Middleton of Cardston, Alberta and Harry Mitchell of Great Falls, Montana, a group of Rotarians from Montana, Alberta and Saskatchewan suggested that Waterton and Glacier parks be joined. They argued that the amalgamation of adjacent national parks on the longest undefended border in the world could set an example of peaceful relations between countries. Middleton and Mitchell's resolution to create the world's first international peace park was passed unanimously and became law when it was approved by Canada's Parliament and the United States Congress. Since then, Rotarians have been meeting every second year at the hotel to reaffirm their commitment to world peace and to celebrate the special place that is now hailed as Waterton-Glacier International Peace Park.

The Depression was not an entire loss for Great Northern Railway. The motor vessel *International*, a 250-seat tour boat the company had built in conjunction with the hotel, continued to operate and pulled in some of its best revenues ever. The boat's role changed with the end of Prohibition, however. Rather than carrying thirsty Americans from Goat Haunt, at the south end of the lake, to Waterton, it instead carried Canadians to Montana where they could skirt Alberta's "blue laws" that prevented drinking and dancing on Sundays.

People flocked to Waterton each weekend during the 1930s for what became known as "midnight frolics." The *International* would leave Waterton late Sunday evening for the special cruise. Members of Mart Kenney and His Western Gentlemen, a popular Vancouver dance band, provided the music. At Goathaunt Chalet, beyond the reach of Alberta's morality police, the partygoers could drink and kick up their heels, returning to Waterton just after midnight. Sometimes "we'd disembark and with the whole band playing, we'd lead the revellers up main street like the Pied Piper of Hamelin and directly into the hall," bandleader Mart Kenney said.

The Prince of Wales survived numerous ups and downs, including closure during World War II. It did so because of the dedication and professionalism of one man: its manager, Harley Boswell. Boswell was always ready to greet any guest with a warm smile and firm handshake. He had an uncanny ability to remember names. "After I left Waterton in 1932, I never returned till about 25 years," recalled bellhop Ainslie Pankhurst. "I walked in the hotel in the summer and Mr. Boswell was at the front desk. He said: 'How are you, Ainslie?' I nearly flipped. I was so surprised he would remember my name after all those years."

Boswell's easy manner belied his tough managerial style. He insisted that staff follow the rigid rules set down by the hotel company to ensure guests were pampered during their stay. "Never allow a guest to put on his coat in your presence without offering to assist" the staff services regulation manual read, adding that a guest was never "to pick up anything he may drop." Patrons staying a week or more could expect an invitation to dine with the Boswells; repeat guests found a bottle of their favourite beverage and flowers in their room. It was not uncommon for families to return twenty summers in a row.

By the 1970s, despite the best efforts of staff and management, the Prince of Wales Hotel had lost some of its lustre. Guests balked at paying premium prices for rooms that were small, unchanged from forty years before, and without TV or radio. Yet just two decades later, in 1995, partly because of the failure of its frugal owners to update the hotel, it was designated a national historic site by the Canadian government!

The Prince of Wales remains little changed from the day it opened. New furnishings in the lobby have not affected the grandeur of the space. The rooms have retained their essential simplicity and such original features as fir and cedar wainscoting. The current hotel owner, Glacier Park Inc. of Phoenix, Arizona, has plans to build more bedrooms and add convention facilities, bringing to fruition Louie Hill's original idea for a large-scale resort. But a recent government decision against the development means that the hotel is unlikely to be changed in any major way for years to come.

The Great Northern Railway opened the Prince of Wales in 1927 to boost passenger traffic on its rail lines. Americans (still in the throes of Prohibition) were easily enticed to vacation in Alberta where they could skirt Prohibition.

Bathers enjoying a Prince Edward Island beach. To escape the city heat, vacationers flocked to the sea. (Opposite page) The Digby Pines promoted its gentle sea breezes as being "acceptable to the weakest lungs."

To The

SEA

The Algonquin St. Andrews, N·B·

CHAMCOOK MTS.

ST. ANDREWS AND THE BAY, FROM THE ALGONQUIN.

The first Algonquin Hotel was constructed of wood and featured steep roofs, gables and a prominent observation tower. On a clear day, it is said one could see 75 miles down the coastline.

THE ALGONQUIN

St. Andrews, New Brunswick

At the beginning of each season, the "summer people" arrived in St. Andrews. They came by Canadian Pacific Railway from Montreal, Pullman coaches from New England, or by steamer from Saint John, Boston, or Portland, Maine. Some, like William Van Horne of the CPR, arrived in their own private rail cars. Many brought personal servants, their own automobiles, chauffeurs, and riding horses—and even furnishings for their suites. They were moving into the Algonquin Hotel or their summer homes for the season. They were coming to the sea.

Situated high on the hill that overlooked the town and Passamaquoddy Bay, the Algonquin had a marvellous sea view. From the long veranda, it was claimed, one could see over 75 miles of shoreline. A pamphlet before the first hotel's opening boasted that the establishment was to be provided with an elevator, steam heat, a steam laundry, a Western Union telegraph office, parlours and reception, card, smoking, writing and billiard rooms. The Algonquin was to be lit by gas. Room rates were $3 to $5 per day.

The first season, in 1889, began splendidly with eight hundred invitees to the hotel's opening. Soon after, Prime Minister John A. and Lady Macdonald came for a short stay, during which they attended the regular Saturday "hop" and enjoyed fireworks set off in their honour. At the end of July, Miss White of Montreal enchanted the guests with her "Scotch Selections" of songs. After one ball, the *Beacon* headlined, "Gay St. Andrews. The Old Town Shaken from Centre to Circumference. Another Brilliant Ball at the Algonquin." By early August, all the rooms were filled, and cots were brought in to accommodate the overflow. An advertisement claimed success: "The First Season's Verdict Regarding St. Andrews and The Algonquin confirms all that had been said and written. Nearly 1400 guests, representing the best class of Americans and Canadians, pronounced the location unsurpassed, and The Algonquin an ideal summer hotel."

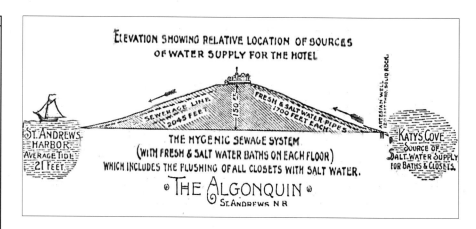

THE ALGONQUIN

Location: St. Andrews, New Brunswick

1889: Opened June 28

Initial Owner: St. Andrews Land Co.

Architects: Rand & Taylor, Boston

Style: Version of American Shingle

Principal Material: Wood

Number of storeys when opened: 4

1905: Reopened under CPR management

1908: Addition by W.S. Painter

1912-13: Casino building added

1914: Destroyed by fire April 11

1915: New hotel opened June 15

Architects: Firm of Barrott, Blackader and Webster, Montreal

Number of storeys: 6

Principal Materials: Reinforced concrete

Prominent Guests: Prime Minister John A. and Lady Macdonald, Governor General Frederick A. Stanley, Sir Thomas Shaughnessy, René Lévesque

Named After: The Algonquin peoples

Early Algonquin pamphlet promoting its hygienic sewage system in which salt water was pumped into the water closets and baths from Katy's Cove while sewage was carried over a third of a mile away to St. Andrews Harbour.

"An elysium for the hay-fever patient," touted the advertisements. From its opening in 1889, the Algonquin attracted hay fever sufferers from the Eastern seaboard in droves, with its promise of healthful ocean air from Passamaquoddy Bay on the Bay of Fundy. The hotel reproduced testimonials from physicians and patients, including Hon. Emory Speer, vice-president of the U.S. Hay Fever Association, and a major industry sprang up in St. Andrews around the summer people's itchy noses. In 1890, the town's hotels lengthened their season well into the autumn.

To compete with resorts in the southern U.S., the Algonquin also boasted, "NO Mosquitoes—A Malaria Free zone." And for those who came to alleviate "neurasthenia," a nervous condition that was associated with stress among the urban rich, it touted St. Andrews' "general air of restfulness," and its "balsam-laden atmosphere." Seawater bathing was considered therapeutic, and guests at the Algonquin had a choice of salt or freshwater baths. The baths had four taps, for hot and cold, salt and fresh water—but there was only one bath per floor! Water closets in the rooms were flushed by salt water, and in an age still discovering sanitation, the Algonquin boasted "drainage by perfect sewers…[falling] directly into the sea 2,000 feet distant."

Spring water from "Sampson's Spring" near the Cemetery Road, believed to alleviate rheumatism and dyspepsia, allegedly had already been sought out by Indians in the 17th and 18th centuries. Near the spring, seats and a portico were provided for use by hotel guests. Until 1910, when a pipeline was

(Above) Mrs. Shaughnessy (holding parasol), wife of CPR President Thomas Shaughnessy, at Katy's Cove beach. William Van Horne had an estate on a nearby island, and many CPR executives followed him to St. Andrews and had homes built by distinguished architects like the Maxwell brothers of Montreal.

installed, horse teams hauled the water from the spring to the dining room; from there, bellboys delivered the healing waters to the rooms.

Atlantic specialties were served in the dining room. A menu of 1890 included fish chowder, Consommé princess à la royale, Oysters à la crème, boiled salmon, egg sauce and potatoes julienne. In the dining room one knew one's place. The veranda section—Peacock Alley—was reserved for permanent residents or important visitors; others were led to tables inside the main room. There was a private dining room for children and nurses, and another for officers.

(Above) After one early ball, the St. Andrews Beacon *headline ran, "Gay St. Andrews. The Old Town Shaken from Centre to Circumference. Another Brilliant Ball at the Algonquin."*

In 1902, the Canadian Pacific Railway bought this popular hotel, despite a negative report to Sir Thomas Shaughnessy, president of the CPR, from the property assessor, Frederick Todd. In Todd's opinion, "The present hotel is exceedingly unattractive. It is out of proportion, painted a disagreeable color, and is located wrongly, while adjacent to it is a conspicuous water tank and a laundry shack." By 1904 Shaughnessy, who spent his summers in St. Andrews, nonetheless concluded that the CPR's hotel department should take over the management of the Algonquin, "at the risk of having my life made a burden…by the complaints and recommendations of patrons…."

Presumably, Todd would not have been one of those weeping on the afternoon of April 11, 1914. That day, the following telegram from the site was fired off to Shaughnessy:

> Received advice 1240 Pm that roof of painter wing algonquin Hotel standrews caught fire while tar being applied. Strong south west wind blowing and little hope of saving hotel as without water supply, it having been shut off for winter. PS There is no hope save Algonquin now, its in flames.

Fire fighters tried to douse the fire with buckets of water, but in half an hour the wooden hotel was destroyed. Only some recent concrete additions were partially saved.

Despite wartime constraints, a new building opened the very next year, in June 1915. This time, the hotel was constructed of relatively fireproof

The second Algonquin Hotel opened in June 1915, a year after the earlier wooden hotel burned to the ground. (Inset) A gentle breeze for Captain Rigby and guest on Passamaquoddy Bay. CPR publicists dubbed St. Andrews the "Newport of the North."

reinforced concrete. The exterior was very pleasing, a mock Tudor façade topped by a red slate roof. Kate Reed, who designed so many of the CPR hotel interiors, accentuated the summery feel with wicker furniture and brightly coloured chintz fabrics. A telephone system connected with each room, and the new hotel featured electric lights. On the evening of the opening, one observer remarked as the lights came on that the hotel rose from the hill like "a palace of the fairies."

Advertised by CPR publicists as "St. Andrews-by-the-Sea," the town became one of the most fashionable destinations in the Northeast. There was fishing in Passamaquoddy Bay and in nearby lakes and rivers, as well as boat excursions and yachting. Golf fever was raging, and the Algonquin extended its course by purchasing the lands of the "Poor House Farm." Horseback riding, drives along the coast, and walks through the shady streets of the old Loyalist town filled many a summer day. According to Willa Walker in *No Hay Fever and the Railway*, dirt roads around town were sprayed with water to keep down the red dust and protect the ladies' and gentlemen's clothes. At the hotel, tennis was popular, as were games of croquet or bowls on the lawn.

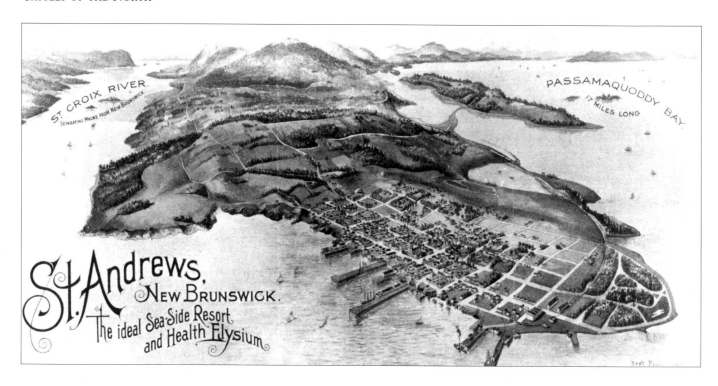

In 1907, nearby Katy's Cove was dredged out and dammed to create a permanent salt water bathing place. It was fashionable to swim in the mornings. The beach would be packed with umbrellas, tea would be served, and for the hour between 10 and 11 o'clock, guests were serenaded by the hotel orchestra. Town residents were only allowed on the beach in the afternoons, and staff had a beach of their own.

Townspeople were not allowed into the hotel at all. A long-time employee, Lila Haughn, recalls the unwritten, unspoken rule: "We knew it wasn't our place. The hotel was for guests and summer residents only." Along with other local girls, she remembers standing near the entrance to the Casino to watch costumed guests arrive at the masquerade dances before she and her friends were shooed away. She claims there are still people in town who have never stepped inside, not even for lunch.

The other thing not allowed in the hotel—in all of New Brunswick in fact—was alcohol. Even after Prohibition was lifted in the province in 1927, and indeed until 1962, liquor

(Above) Algonquin Hotel from the south, 1924 (Inset) The casino was built in 1913 facing the hotel. (Opposite page top) An early promotional pamphlet. (Opposite page bottom) The Algonquin has attracted golfers to its course along beautiful Passamaquoddy Bay for over a century.

could not be sold in public places. In that era, the Algonquin circumvented the law by operating a discreet, dimly lit bar in the basement which sold milkshakes and soft drinks, but where guests could bring their bottles of choice.

Codes have since relaxed. Staff members are allowed to speak without first being spoken to and can use the front door. In fact, everyone is now welcome. Wooden screened doors lead out to the veranda, still a favoured spot for enjoying the pleasant sea air and the beautiful lawn and garden. St. Andrews continues to exude a serene charm and the Algonquin, from atop the hill, watches over it all.

"Moon-drenched evenings on the balcony of the Digby Pines," ran the wording under this photograph in a CPR brochure. (Opposite page) The Pines at Digby. The hotel was closed during World War I, when there were rumours of German submarines in the Bay of Fundy.

DIGBY PINES

Digby, Nova Scotia

The Pines has been attracting vacationers to the town of Digby since Henry Churchill opened his first small summer resort there at the turn of the twentieth century. An early brochure sought to entice vacationers by promoting the sublime view of the Annapolis Basin from the veranda: "a palpitating, shimmering sea of blue, mirroring Nova Scotia skies, and a background of indigo peaks faintly wreathed with a veil of cloud gauze." To appeal to hay fever sufferers, another brochure assured prospective guests that "The sea breezes coming over the wooded lands which intervene between the Ocean and the Basin are gently tempered by the passage, deprived of all harshness and are acceptable to the weakest lungs."

Many guests came to go boating, deep sea fishing, or casting for speckled trout and salmon on the Annapolis River or inland lakes. For landlubbers there was golf and tennis, horseback riding, motoring and mountain climbing, or just enjoying the "salubrious forest" from the perspective of a hammock. Guests were invited to explore Digby, advertised as "a pretty town of 2,000 inhabitants, many of whom are of old English origin and social worth." Four evenings a week, the hotel orchestra played for dances in the pavilion.

For a period during World War I, the hotel was used as an army officers' quarters. Near the end of the war, the Dominion Atlantic Railway, a subsidiary of Canadian Pacific, purchased and renovated it, but that building was demolished as early as 1928. The following year, a new, one hundred-room, fireproof hotel opened in its place. It was very popular with American tourists who came by rail: New Yorkers on the "New Yorker" and people from Boston on the "Bluenoser." Canadian guests from places like Toronto, Montreal, and Halifax arrived on the Dominion Atlantic rail lines. A special boat from New York came in once a week with three to four hundred passengers. Former manager, Ken Smith, recalls Babe Ruth coming in 1936 and playing golf. In one funny incident, Ruth wanted to go for a swim in the evening after the pool was closed. Undaunted, he climbed over the windscreen protecting the pool and jumped in. But he could not get out, and had to call for help.

Canadian Pacific Hotels owned the property from 1931 to 1965, when it was bought by the Nova Scotia government. At this beautiful spot, the breezes are still salubrious, the view still divine.

Perched atop the cliffs of Middle Head Peninsula on the northeast shore of Cape Breton Island, Keltic Lodge offers a breathtaking panorama of the coast.

(Left) Alexander Graham Bell, who had a summer retreat on Cape Breton, often camped at Ingonish Beach. While visiting Bell in the late 1890s, Henry Clay and Julia Corson first caught sight of the dramatic promontory, Middle Head. It was here they were to build their own summer idyll, which later became Keltic Lodge.

(Right inset) In 1925, work began on the Cabot Trail, a scenic highway loop along Cape Breton's coasts designed to attract tourists to the area. Previous to the highway's completion, at one of the biggest obstacles, Cape Smokey, early motorists commonly tied a spruce tree to the back bumper to slow their car down during the descent. Reports speak of a heap of dead trees at the base of the mountain.

KELTIC LODGE

Ingonish, Nova Scotia

O n Cape Breton's picturesque northern coast, near Ingonish, Keltic Lodge presides over Middle Head, a spectacular narrow two-mile-long promontory stretching out into the Atlantic. Ingonish was an isolated fishing and farming community back in the late 1890s, when American industrialist Henry Clay Corson and his wife Julia first chose Middle Head as the perfect place to build a private summer estate, a curative retreat from the stress, heat and smog of the city.

The region changed with the 1932 opening of the Cabot Trail, a scenic highway loop around Cape Breton's rugged coast. Provincial officials had realized the potential value of the magnificent scenery to tourism. As part of the creation of Cape Breton Highlands National Park, land was appropriated from local residents, including Julia Corson. (According to local lore, she was not given a fair deal, so Henry Corson continues to haunt the site.) In 1940, the Province of Nova Scotia and Canadian National converted the Corson home into a modest resort named Keltic Lodge. The construction suffered numerous delays, many due to bad weather encountered by the coastal supply ship. The lodge did manage to open in July 1940—only one month behind schedule—but apparently the head chef, pastry chef and laundress did not arrive until August. The same year, an impressive golf course created by world-renowned links architect Stanley Thompson, opened nearby.

In the 1940s, roads were still rough and few local residents had cars. Mabel MacDougall, who worked in the Lodge's kitchen in 1941, recalls returning home just once all summer—even though she lived only ten miles away! The Lodge closed from 1942 through until the end of the war, but after the war, as road improvements were made and tourists streamed into the Ingonish area, a new and larger building was needed. In 1950, the Province hired architect Welsford West who designed a white wooden structure with a red roof that remains a prominent landmark overlooking the cliff on Middle Head. Today, Keltic Lodge offers a breathtaking panoramic view of the Atlantic coastline, a scenic hiking trail to the end of Middle Head, excellent golfing, and proximity to Ingonish beach and the stunning landscape of Cape Breton Highlands National Park.

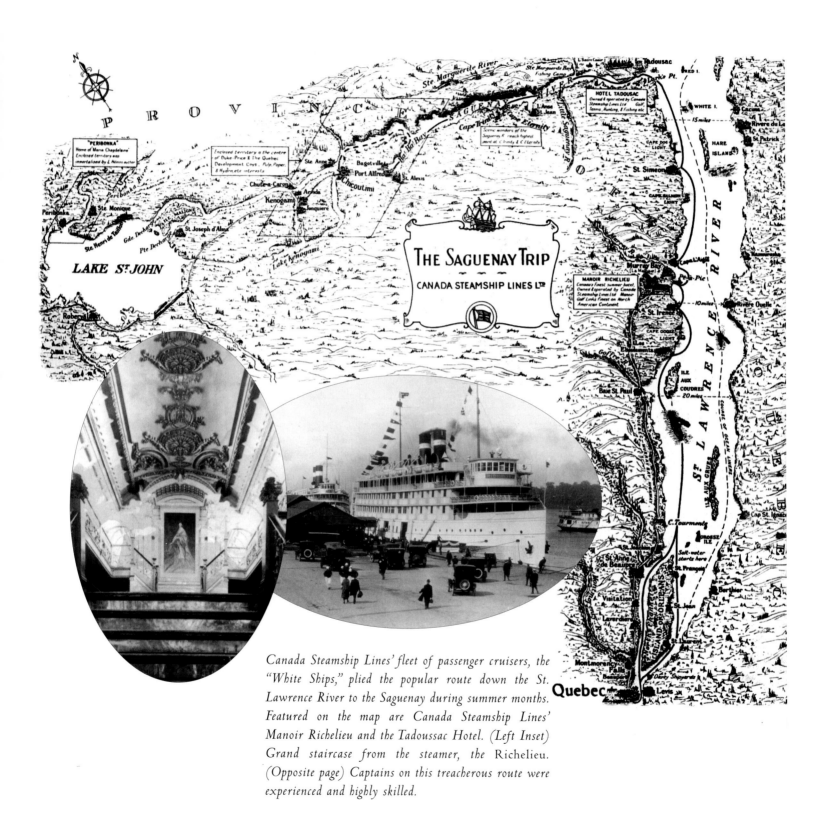

THE SAGUENAY TRIP

CANADA STEAMSHIP LINES LTD

Canada Steamship Lines' fleet of passenger cruisers, the "White Ships," plied the popular route down the St. Lawrence River to the Saguenay during summer months. Featured on the map are Canada Steamship Lines' Manoir Richelieu and the Tadoussac Hotel. (Left Inset) Grand staircase from the steamer, the Richelieu. (Opposite page) Captains on this treacherous route were experienced and highly skilled.

Down The

ST. LAWRENCE

(Above) Manoir Richelieu, and Canadian Steamship Lines' passenger ship St. Lawrence at the Pointe-au-Pic wharf. Les bateaux blancs, *"the White Ships," made regular scenic cruises down the St. Lawrence River and up the Saguenay River during the summer months. (Opposite page) The first Manoir Richelieu opened in June 1899. Steamers carried construction supplies—the wood, and cedar shingles for the roof—to the wharf, then horses hauled them up to the site. (Above inset) After the first hotel burned down in September 1928, construction of this second Manoir was so intensive that the magnificent structure was ready to welcome guests for the following summer season.*

MANOIR RICHELIEU

Pointe-au-Pic, Charlevoix, Quebec

In the 1890s, when Louis J. Forget, president of the Richelieu & Ontario Navigation Company, commissioned Montreal architect Edward Maxwell to design a 250-room hotel at Pointe-au-Pic, he was carrying on a century-old tradition of elegant hospitality in the area known as Murray Bay. This region along the north shore of the St. Lawrence River began developing after 1789 when the first British governor of Quebec, General James Murray, granted half of the seigniory of La Malbaie to John Nairne, an officer of the 78th Fraser Highlanders. Nairne loved inviting guests to his estate to enjoy the beautiful surroundings and to fish in the nearby rivers. When steamships began plying the St. Lawrence, they brought well-to-do tourists to the wharf at Pointe-au-Pic, and hotels and summer homes began to appear on the hillside.

None, however, compared to Maxwell's magnificent wood-and-cedar-shingle hotel that opened on June 15, 1899. The architecturally imposing structure was set dramatically on a cliff overlooking the St. Lawrence and given a name worthy of its seigniorial roots: Manoir Richelieu, after Cardinal Richelieu, the powerful prime minister of King Louis XIII of France. In the lounges, wood panelling, exposed ceiling beams and wicker furniture created a country-house ambience while large Belgian carpets, bronze-coloured woodwork and stone fireplaces added intimacy and refinement. The Manoir's beautifully decorated guest rooms had ensuite bathrooms with both fresh and salt water.

The Manoir helped make Pointe-au-Pic the most fashionable place in Quebec to spend one's summer holidays. Tourists came from Ottawa, Toronto, New York, Boston, Philadelphia, Montreal and Quebec City. To cater to its select clientele, the hotel had Herbert Strong put in a golf course. Strong, who had already designed the Inwood near Chicago, the Engineers on Long Island and the

MANOIR RICHELIEU

Location: Pointe-au-Pic, Quebec

1899: Opened June 15

Initial Owner: Richelieu & Ontario Navigation Company

Architect: Edward Maxwell

Style: Château in shingle style

Principal Materials: Wood and cedar shingles

1928: Fire September 12

1929: Second hotel opened June 15

Owner: Canada Steamship Lines

Architect: John S. Archibald

Style: Norman château

Principal Materials: Rough concrete

1998-99: Renovation and enlargement of hotel and casino

Prominent Guests: U.S. President William Taft, Fred Astaire, Bob Hope

Named After:

Cardinal Richelieu (1585-1642) Minister of King Louis XIII of France

Lakeview in Toronto, was the ideal person to do justice to the awesome panorama of the St. Lawrence and the Laurentians. Work began on June 18, 1924. A year to the day later, William Howard Taft, the former U.S. president and a resident of Pointe-au-Pic, presided over the opening ceremonies.

Twenty-nine years after it opened, the wooden Manoir burned down. The exact reason for the fire in the night of September 12, 1928, was never established. The very next day, however, T.R. Enderby, general manager of Canada Steamship Lines (CSL—the company that now owned the Manoir), informed reporters from the *Montreal Gazette* that a new hotel would be built on the site. The architect commissioned to design it, John S. Archibald, rather than merely replacing the old building, produced drawings for a magnificent Norman château.

The new building was to be ready to receive guests by the next summer season, so there was no time to delay. In October a thousand workers, divided into two shifts and equipped with pickaxes and shovels, began excavating the site to a depth of twenty feet. They then built a wooden cocoon around a frame, so that work could continue through the harsh winter. On the giant concrete foundation, they erected concrete walls that were brushed with steel to give a rough, stone-like finish. Concrete was used both inside and out to render the hotel thoroughly fireproof—a major consideration for the steamship company! Between October and the following June, workers were given only one day's holiday— Christmas. But, amazingly, the task was completed.

The new Manoir opened on June 15, 1929. High on a cliff overlooking the St. Lawrence, its steep copper roofs boldly silhouetted against the sky, the château made a majestic impression. Nor were guests entering through the high portico disappointed—the sumptuous interior matched the dramatic exterior. The Manoir

soon earned a reputation as the most luxurious resort hotel in eastern Canada. This was largely due to one man. Between 1929 and 1949, CSL president William Hugh Coverdale assembled a three-thousand piece collection of engravings, paintings, carpets, wrought iron, antique maps and art, complemented by Quebec crafts, that was displayed throughout the hotel. Tapestries and historical paintings hung in the hotel's vast lobby, including *Captain John Nairne landing at Murray Bay* and *Gaultier de Comporté, seigneur de la Malbaie* by Charles W. Jefferys; and a portrait of General James Murray by Adam Sheriff Scott. There were also 435 Audubon prints from The Birds of America. Since 1970, with the exception of five pieces still at the Manoir, this valuable art collection has been conserved at the National Archives of Canada.

The Manoir attracted wealthy Canadians and Americans who wanted both luxury and outdoor pleasures. Well-heeled, youthful and athletic guests, who often reserved suites for the entire summer, followed an extravagant routine. At daybreak, they were served breakfast in their suites or on the huge outdoor terraces, following which there would be time for a little exercise. The Manoir had its own riding trails and riding masters to accompany parents and children. On their return from riding, tennis or lawn bowling, what better than a refreshing swim in the enormous saltwater pool? At noon, one could enjoy a pre-lunch drink on the adjacent casino terrace while watching the antics of the swimmers and listening to the

(Left) Beautiful interiors at the Manoir Richelieu featured paintings from the Coverdale collection, c.1930. Prominent in this photograph is Christopher Columbus at the Court of Ferdinand and Isabella by Wenceslas de Brozik. (Above) Enjoying the Manoir terrace and the view out to the St. Lawrence River.

hotel orchestra. Elegantly dressed guests then had their luncheon on the Manoir terrace, with its view of the rugged Charlevoix landscape and the St. Lawrence—a vista immortalized by Canadian painters such as A.Y. Jackson, Clarence Gagnon, Marc-Aurèle Fortin and Jean-Paul Lemieux.

Many who had first come as visitors to the Manoir later built lovely country houses in the area. But the hotel pool remained a meeting place for all the summer people of Pointe-au-Pic—even more so after a sandy beach called the Lido was added next to the pool. Summer visitors also came to Le Casino, overlooking the pool, for dances and moving pictures.

Golf and tennis were popular in the afternoon. The Manoir Richelieu and the Murray Bay golf clubs competed in tournaments throughout the summer. Golfers coveted the hotel trophy—the Manoir Richelieu Golf Club Shield—and the award festivities were truly memorable. Other afternoon entertainment included dog shows that gave the summer people a chance to see the Manoir guests parade their pedigree pets, children's costume parties, and fashion shows that featured models parading in the sweltering sun to show off luxurious furs created by the best Canadian designers, or children sporting locally crafted clothing and knitwear. Many of these activities were organized to raise funds for such charities as the Red Cross.

After tea in the Pink Lounge, the ladies would don evening attire—breathtaking gowns created by Parisian couturiers and New York designers, splendid jewellery, daring hairdos. At seven o'clock they would gather in the salons to chat about a trip in the countryside to scout out crafts and the famous Murray Bay woollen blankets, or to reminisce about fishing trips into the backcountry where the Manoir kept fishing cottages, clubs and boats with guides.

When the new hotel opened, a widespread advertising campaign promoted winter sports at the Manoir: "You will revel in the luxurious hospitality of the Manoir Richelieu after a long day in the open. Indoors there is supreme comfort, wonderful meals and jolly companionship. At the door lies the greatest snow country in Eastern Canada!" A complete weekend at the Manoir, including the Pullman train fare, was offered for $38.85 a day. The winter season began with the Christmas holidays, when the decorative lights and mantle of snow gave the hotel a magical look. Guests could enjoy ski outings in the hills, rushing down the newly built bobsleigh run, dogsled rides, skijoring in the valleys, figure skating, hockey and curling. The event of the season was a ski marathon between Montreal and the Manoir. Unfortunately the winter experience was unsuccessful and was soon discontinued.

With the growth of passenger air travel after World War II, people began seeking out more exotic holiday destinations. By the mid-1960s, Canada Steamship Lines had abandoned its passenger cruises along the St. Lawrence. A few years later, the Manoir was sold to Warnock Hersey International. Over the next thirty years, the Manoir was re-sold numerous times, with each owner hoping to boost tourism in Charlevoix and keep the grand hotel from deteriorating further. However, only in 1998 was a solution finally found. In that year, a consortium composed of Canadian Pacific Hotels, Loto-Québec and the Fonds des travailleurs du Québec decided to renovate and expand the Manoir and casino at a cost of $140 million, with the aim of returning the hotel to the grandeur of its early years.

Throughout the renovation, the architects were mindful of incorporating the volumes, mass, materials and spaces that had made the former hotel a cohesive whole, while the designer sought to recreate the charm of Hugh Coverdale's Manoir by devoting special attention to finishes and detailing when choosing furniture, fabrics and art. When the hotel reopened in June 1999, on the hotel's hundredth birthday, original paintings, French mirrors, old maps and charts, period engravings and historical watercolours once more graced the walls. Today, old photographs offer compelling glimpses of the preceding century; an important piece from Coverdale's collection—de Brozik's painting of *Christopher Columbus at the Court of Ferdinand and Isabella*—graces the ballroom; and the impressive lounges have been restored to their original uses. The men's lounge or cigar room, with its clubby look, is a replica of the old Murray Room; and the former Pink Lounge or ladies' tea room has been redone in light, sunny tones.

The Manoir Richelieu now has an enlarged casino, a new spa with two heated saltwater swimming pools, and a large convention centre. But the real draw remains its magnificent presence on the cliff that towers above Pointe-au-Pic, offering an exceptional panorama of Charlevoix's rolling hills and of the timeless St. Lawrence.

(Left) Bellmen at the Manoir. (Above) Spectators and those lounging at the pool enjoyed live music. (Inset) Former U.S. President, William H. Taft, (at right) presided over the opening ceremonies of the golf course in June 1925. To the left is William Hugh Coverdale, president of Canada Steamship Lines. The Manoir was filled with treasures from Coverdale's important collection of historical art collected between 1929-49.

Vacationers gathered on the veranda of the Tadoussac Hotel, c.1900 (Opposite page) Close to the hotel, early guests enjoyed playing lawn tennis, quoits or lacrosse. Many, however, were drawn to Tadoussac for the excellent salmon and trout fishing.

TADOUSSAC HOTEL

Tadoussac, Quebec

Mysterious, unfathomed Saguenay, your stupendous capes would prove but the crests of gigantic mountains were your black waters drained to their unknown depths. Before the Roman Empire, before the dawn of history, you flowed in silent splendour through the oldest ranges in the world, bearing the secret of the north.

—*Romantic Appreciation by Henry P. Toler printed in "Up the Saguenay, Canada's Historic Waterway," Canada Steamship Lines booklet, c.1950s*

Located near the confluence of the St. Lawrence and Saguenay Rivers, the historic village of Tadoussac has been a gathering place, trading centre, and early port for centuries. And since the mid-1800s, tourists have been drawn to the area's beauty. Tadoussac was a stop on the early cruises that left Montreal and headed down the St. Lawrence, then up the legendary Saguenay, a fjord banked by soul-stirring cliffs. To capitalize on this growing tourism, a group of businessmen from Montreal and Quebec City built the Tadoussac Hotel in the mid-1860s. Bought by the steamship line, the Richelieu and Ontario Navigation Company (R & O), the hotel was enlarged in the 1880s.

Generations of English-speaking vacationers from the United States, Montreal, and Toronto would stay at the hotel for weeks in the summer, if not for the entire season. Many reserved the same room year after year—in fact, the hotel sent the floor plans to guests in order of seniority, so they could choose their preferred accommodation. Many also had their particular table and their preferred waitress for the summer.

*(Above) Cruise ship under the powerful cliffs along the Saguenay River.
(Below) The Tadoussac Hotel as depicted in an 1885 hotel guide.*

In an 1885 advertisement, manager James Fennell confidently stated that "Tadousac [sic] being so widely known for its superb trout fishing, yachting and boating, requires no puffing." In the early years, those who did not engage in these activities might have tried lawn tennis, quoits or lacrosse. In later years, they shifted to golf, tennis and lounging by the hotel pool—or taking afternoon tea to orchestral accompaniment. But the activity that everyone enjoyed centered around the scheduled arrival of the R & O, later Canada Steamship Lines' (CSL's), river boats. The "White Ships" cued their entrance to the bay by emitting three long, deep blasts, and everyone would head to the wharf to meet the boats. With the steamers came communication with the outside world—new visitors, mail, supplies and provisions.

The hotel became the fortunate recipient of many pieces of old pine furniture, paintings and Quebec crafts, part of CSL president W.H. Coverdale's important collection of Canadian art and artefacts. Despite these precious holdings, the building was not maintained and was torn down in 1941. Yet even with supplies scarce during World War II, CSL managed to build another hotel to be ready for the following year's season. (It did not hurt that the company owned the Davie Shipyard, and could thus procure the piping and other necessary materials.)

Soon after the war, the leisurely summer lifestyle gave way to overnight traffic. Cars appeared, slowly at first, as it was a a 12-hour drive from Quebec City, and the first ferry across the Saguenay could carry only one car at a time. One of the White Ships, the *Quebec*, burned at the Tadoussac wharf in 1950; the last three CSL river boats were withdrawn from service in the mid-1960s. The end of these pleasure cruises concluded over 150 years of passenger navigation on this route and as a result the Tadoussac Hotel suffered many lean years. Today, buses of tourists roll into town daily, as Tadoussac is a popular jumping-off point for whale watching excursions.

(Above) Tadoussac Hotel after additions, c.1900. (Inset) When the bateaux blancs— the White Ships—entered the bay at Tadoussac, calèche drivers would head to the wharf to greet new arrivals and to carry up their luggage.

(Above) Group planning their back-country route on the Seigniory Club estate, now part of the Château Montebello's wilderness property known as Kenauk. The antidote to a hectic life was a return to simplicity and nature, a holiday in the wilds. (Opposite page) Officers of the steamer, Sagamo, 1910. As many Muskoka resorts were located on islands, steamboats were needed to reach them.

To The

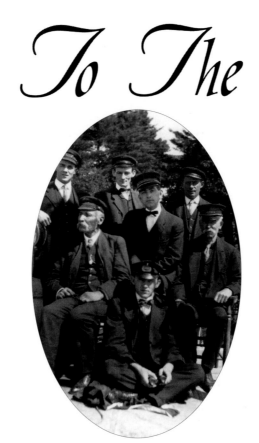

LAKES & WOODS

Bell staff on patio steps outside dining room. Sometimes pages at the hotels were as young as 12 years old. (Right) The Château's low, horizontal lines harmonize beautifully with the landscape. Bedroom wings like this one offer views of the Ottawa River and the gentle western edge of the Laurentian mountains.

Château Montebello

Montebello, Quebec

Few hotels in Canada have such a distinguished lineage as the Château Montebello. It was built in 1930 on the grounds of the seigniory granted in 1674 by the King of France to Bishop Laval, first Bishop of Quebec. The estate then passed into the hands of the illustrious Papineau family, whose manor still graces this beautiful property, overlooking the Ottawa River and hugged in by the gentle western edge of the Laurentian mountains. After abolition of the seigneurial system in 1854, Louis-Joseph Papineau, the famous reformer, chose the name Monte-Bello for his manor house. Today, Le Château Montebello is an immense log hotel in the woods near the Papineau manor, surrounded by a preserve of over one hundred square miles of the former seigniory.

This elaborate log building began as the dream of a Swiss-American entrepreneur, H.M. Saddlemire. In the late 1920s, Saddlemire wanted a private club, a wilderness retreat for the business and political elite of America and Canada. The project was called Lucerne-in-Quebec, and later, the Seigniory Club. Despite the shattering stock market crash of October 1929, construction went ahead in early 1930. How was this possible? A man accustomed to getting things done, Saddlemire was able to bring on as directors of the club people who had millions of dollars at their fingertips—three bank presidents; Louis-Alexandre Taschereau, premier of Quebec; E.W. Beatty, president of the CPR; and others connected to both the banks and the CPR.

Not only did construction proceed during the early months of the Depression, it did so with feverish speed and on an immense scale. Miraculously, only four months elapsed between groundbreaking in early March, and the grand opening on July 1, 1930.

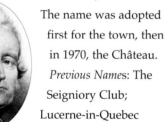

(Above) The dining room, 1930. (Inset right) The hotel's construction schedule was so tight that plans were rushed to the site as the building was going up (in some cases, the plans actually arrived after all the logs had been installed). Instead of starting at the centre, work began at the southwest wing, in order that kitchen equipment could be installed and in operation in the short time frame.

This prodigious feat was accomplished by using a Scandinavian log-building technique new to Canada and bringing in an army of over three thousand labourers, who were kept to a tight schedule. The first task was to clear and drain the site, lay gravel and build boardwalks and elevated runways for the logs. Workers also constructed a spur from the CPR line to the site, along which logs and other supplies were delivered with clockwork precision. A temporary construction village was erected for the hordes of labourers who worked on the site—just "a big swamp," according to Victor Nymark, the Finnish master builder, in which you were "jumping from one stump to another."

The first log was set in April. Many French-Canadian craftsmen were borrowed from neighbouring logging camps, but there were also workers of Scandinavian origin who were familiar with the precise construction techniques. They soon cut, grooved and scribed ten thousand western red cedar logs which, placed end to end, would have stretched most of the forty miles to Ottawa!

Green logs were used in the construction, employing a method that allowed them to settle after construction without affecting the solidity of the structure.

The men worked ten-hour days, and, near the end, twelve-hour shifts, seven days a week; they earned fifty cents an hour. Since work continued through Sunday, someone had the bright idea of shipping the local curate off to Rome for a two-month holiday—all expenses paid—so that he would not give trouble. The schedule was so tight that plans were being rushed to the site as building progressed (in some cases, apparently, the plans actually arrived after all the logs had been put up!).

The newspapers followed the construction closely and their enthusiasm drew curiosity seekers from Ottawa, Montreal and beyond. Three log buildings were going up simultaneously: the château, an immense garage, and Cedar Hall which was to be used as staff quarters. But what most were coming to see was the centrepiece of the château's dramatic, hexagonal rotunda—a massive, six-sided fireplace that rose 66 feet to the roof. The tapered fireplace led the eye up to the soaring rafters made of 60-foot logs. Galleries wrapped around the room on the second and third levels. Guest rooms fanned out from this central core in four wings, offering views of the

(Above) West entrance, July 14, 1930. In this photograph, taken a few weeks after the opening, the rail spur used to haul the logs to the building site can still be seen.

Enjoying Montebello's beautiful grounds

sparkling Ottawa River and the peaceful forest. No simple log cabin this!

The week before opening saw a flurry of landscaping, cleaning up and painting. Temporary buildings disappeared almost overnight. One observer recalled, "Just prior to the opening there was confusion, and there was mud everywhere; furniture, china and cutlery were being delivered at the back entrance as the first guests came in the main door."

The log château opened with a costume ball. Guests had access to a temporary nine-hole golf course, and later, Seigniory Club directors had cabins built in the forest for the enjoyment of those who wanted to explore the property, to fish, hunt or canoe. They hired rangers and guides to care for the forest and visitors, and installed a fish hatchery to ensure the lakes were well stocked. Many

(Above) Shooting clay pigeons. (Above right) Basking at the Seigniory Club, 1940. (Below right) The woman in the photograph is Lady Willingdon, wife of Governor General Lord Willingdon. Sleigh riding continues to be a popular winter activity at Montebello.

The Six-hearthed Fireplace Chimney and Main Lounge, Log Lodge.

The centrepiece of the entire building is the monolithic 66-foot-high fireplace in the rotunda. The huge fieldstones were carted to the site by local farmers in 1930.

(Right) Curling in the east wing of the garage. (Below) Many business-men flew in to enjoy short retreats at the Seigniory Club.

members appreciated the protective buffer of lake and forest, but cared most for the golf course, carefully laid out by Stanley Thompson, one of the country's most admired golf course designers. Others preferred horseback riding, boating on the Ottawa River, lounging or playing tennis on the château grounds. Some swam in the pool, often doing the backstroke to admire the elaborate hand-painted wooden ceiling. In addition, Seigniory Club members were each granted land on which they could build a private home, provided that it fit in with the log-cabin or Swiss-chalet style of the main buildings.

Seigniory Club members enjoyed their woodland haven in all seasons, but in winter, Montebello glowed with a special warmth. Right outside the front door, one could skate or curl, walk in the woods, go snowshoeing, dog sledding, sleigh riding, cross-country and downhill skiing, or "skijoring" (skiing while being pulled behind a horse and rider). Not content with these varied winter pleasures, club directors brought in an expert from Austria to oversee construction of a mile-long bobsled run. They also built an Olympic-

sized ski jump, modelled after the one Lake Placid installed for the 1932 Olympics (not surprisingly, Montebello's was ready even before Lake Placid's!).

Despite the Club's focus on the outdoors and the casual comfort of its foyer, it never lowered its standards. When an Italian countess arrived at the dining room in riding boots,

(Left) Waiter at the bun warmer. (Below) Prime Minister Pierre Trudeau on the Montebello grounds. Trudeau hosted the G7 International Summit at Montebello in 1981.

covered in dust and still carrying her riding crop, the maitre d' told her a table would be waiting in half an hour. When she insisted on being served right away, the maitre d' firmly rebuffed her until she had dressed for dinner. In addition to the business elite, the Seigniory Club was frequented by prime ministers and governor generals. Foreign dignitaries who visited included Prince Akihito, the Japanese heir; Harry S. Truman; Prince Rainier and Princess Grace of Monaco. Crown Princess Juliana of the Netherlands had a whole floor of a wing to herself during World War II while a home was being prepared for her in Ottawa. During her stay, security was so high that most employees did not know who was occupying the floor. Entertainers like Bing Crosby and Perry Como, Bette Davis and Joan Crawford were drawn to the golf course or to the romantically elegant "cabin" in the woods.

After forty years as a private club, the château was purchased in 1970 by Canadian Pacific Hotels and opened to the public. The grounds closed temporarily in the summer of 1981 for a meeting of the G7 industrialized nations, hosted by Prime Minister Trudeau. The woods and river were closely patrolled while Ronald Reagan, François Mitterand, Margaret Thatcher and others held discussions and enjoyed the pleasant setting.

Today, one can canoe, fish, go horseback riding, cycle or hike any of the forty kilometres of trails in the immense estate around Montebello, now known as Kenauk. The domain also contains private chalets—some even on their own lake, one of seventy on the property. Guests can boat on the Ottawa River, or, staying closer to the château, golf, play tennis or swim. On the Montebello grounds, the newly restored Manoir Papineau which dates back to 1850 is a National Historic Site open to visitors.

(Above) Before it became a resort hotel, the Château Montebello was a private club known as the Seigniory Club. (Left) To ensure exclusivity in the early years, a police force patrolled the grounds, and visitors had to show their credentials at the front gate in order to be admitted.

Walking through the lobby doors at the end of a long day outdoors, the height of the soaring fireplace and rafters never fails to impress. Strains of jazz wafting from the piano set a calming tone. Sinking lower in one's chair while enjoying the blazing fire or staring at beams of light coming through the high windows, it is worth reflecting on the intensity of work involved in creating this, perhaps the most beautiful and elaborate log building on the continent.

(Above) Royal Muskoka's dining room (Inset) This key was one of the few items to survive the 1952 fire in which the Royal Muskoka burned to the ground.

(Above left) Photo opportunity on the verandas of the Royal Muskoka, early 1900s. Notice the two children on the top balcony who sneaked into the shot. (Above right) Veranda of the Royal Muskoka (Opposite page) Brochure image of the Royal Muskoka Hotel, 1902. The owners—the Muskoka Lakes Navigation and Hotel Company and the Grand Trunk Railway—sought to make a bold statement by hiring Lucius Boomer, architect of the Waldorf-Astoria in New York City, to design their resort.

ROYAL MUSKOKA HOTEL

Lake Rosseau, Muskoka, Ontario

When the Royal Muskoka opened in 1901 on Royal Muskoka Island in Lake Rosseau, it ushered in an age of elegance and sophistication on the Muskoka Lakes. Before its appearance, the emphasis of a northern vacation was on returning to the simplicity of the romantic wilds. Afterwards, nature and the outdoors served more as a backdrop, something to appreciate while reclining on the Royal's expansive veranda, sipping a Tom Collins and enjoying pleasant conversation. Dining in the enormous formal dining room and dressing in fancy gowns or jackets and white flannels to dance to a live orchestra were even more of a draw. The dances attracted people from all around, although guests from other resorts needed permission to attend from the Royal's manager. Noted bands would bring up to two thousand revellers to the island. On those occasions, the boats anchored offshore were a spectacular sight.

The Royal had barbers, stenographers, manicurists, and hair stylists to cater to every whim, and patrons could keep in touch with the world through the long distance telephone service. On one occasion, world events came right to the hotel's door. Prime Minister Sir Robert Borden and Lady Borden were vacationing at the Royal Muskoka in the summer of 1914 when war broke out. Borden hurriedly returned to Ottawa on August 2, 1914, to sign the declaration of war on behalf of Canada.

As with many of the grand resorts in the years following World War II, the Royal Muskoka lost its cachet. Its story ended on May 18, 1952 when the impressive wood hotel went up in flames.

(Above) Owner Charles Orlando Shaw wanted his extravagant resort to last. Having seen many Muskoka resorts go up in flames, Shaw insisted Bigwin Inn be made of poured concrete. The immense hotel opened on Bigwin Island, Lake of Bays, in 1920. (Inset) Chief John Bigwin, descendant of Chief Joseph Big Wind after whom the hotel was named. (Opposite page) Guests relaxing on the Venetian Terrace had a marvellous view.

(Above) Bigwin's most identifiable structure, the Indian Head Room, seated up to 750 at one sitting. Twelve-sided in design, this expansive room boasted a vaulted ceiling, three fireplaces and an orchestra gallery. Owner C.O. Shaw and his wife would oversee the performance of the waitresses from their table, noting any improvements that needed to be made.

BIGWIN INN

Lake of Bays, Muskoka, Ontario

Charles Orlando Shaw's vision for Bigwin Inn was magnificent, and he was a man who put plans into action. When Bigwin opened on Lake of Bays in June 1920, it was touted as the largest resort in the British Empire. Its main buildings covered a third of a mile and could accommodate over five hundred guests. Shaw had seen many of the earlier wooden Muskoka resorts meet fiery ends, so he commissioned architect John Wilson to design his buildings using fireproof poured concrete.

Bigwin was nicknamed "Bigwig" Inn because of the constant flow of the rich and famous, including actors Clark Gable and Carol Lombard, and families like the Rockefellers and the Wrigleys. Not surprisingly, Shaw demanded perfection of his staff. A stay at Bigwin was to be an event. In the Indian Head Room, 750 people could dine at one sitting. At the start of the meal, 95 waitresses came out of the kitchen with trays held aloft. On cue, the trays were lowered in unison to present the finest fare to Bigwin's guests. Shaw and his wife took their meals at these sittings, their roving eyes searching for any flaw in service.

After Shaw died, the hotel changed hands a number of times. Despite much neglect over the years, the buildings have survived and are still an impressive sight as one approaches Bigwin Island, especially the twelve-sided dance pavilion, and the immense twelve-sided dining room, the Indian Head Room. The Administration building has nine fireplaces—some large enough to burn six-foot logs. In the 1990s, part of the complex was developed into condominiums. The dining rooms are currently being converted to become a clubhouse for the Bigwin Island Golf Club.

(Opposite page) Minaki Lodge, near Kenora, Ontario. The long sweeping lines of the main building hug the land and the log walls blend in with their forest surroundings. Like at the CNR's other wilderness operation, Jasper Park Lodge, Minaki's designers aimed for rustic comfort. (Above left) Gift shop, Minaki Lodge. Note the newspaper headline, "REDS TEST SUPER ROCKETS."

(Above right) After a day of outdoor activity, guests returned to the lodge for hearty northern repasts. Menus included roast caribou, lake trout, potage au riz sauvage, and Reindeer Louis Riel.

(Left) The early dining room at Minaki was modelled on the one at Jasper Park Lodge. The similarity did not end there: both of their original lodge buildings burned to the ground.

MINAKI LODGE

Minaki, Ontario

This spectacular log and fieldstone resort on Sand Lake has had a troubled history. The Grand Trunk Pacific Railway opened a smaller Minaki Inn in 1914, but the outbreak of war forced it to close. In 1919, Canadian National Railways took over the property from the bankrupt GTP and conducted extensive renovations, but a day before the scheduled June 12, 1925 opening, fire destroyed the building. (A pile of oily rags stuffed under some wicker chairs ignited. Sadly, new fire hoses and a hydrant had not yet been connected.)

The reconstructed Minaki Lodge opened in 1927. Modelled on the CNR's successful Jasper Park Lodge, it had a main lodge surrounded by cabins. In the words of CNR advertisers, Minaki aimed to blend "the primitive and the elegance of civilization." Using the image of the romantic Indian to attract visitors to the elegant resort, a 1930s CNR brochure assured prospective guests that from the veranda one could hear "the throb of drums and tom-toms," and could watch "an old Ojibwa slip silently past in a canoe."

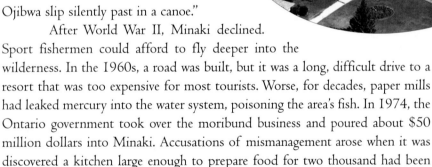

After World War II, Minaki declined. Sport fishermen could afford to fly deeper into the wilderness. In the 1960s, a road was built, but it was a long, difficult drive to a resort that was too expensive for most tourists. Worse, for decades, paper mills had leaked mercury into the water system, poisoning the area's fish. In 1974, the Ontario government took over the moribund business and poured about $50 million dollars into Minaki. Accusations of mismanagement arose when it was discovered a kitchen large enough to prepare food for two thousand had been built even though the dining room only seated two hundred!

Minaki Lodge finally reopened in 1983, managed for the Province by Radisson Hotels. Once again it failed and the Province then sold it to Four Seasons Hotels Limited in 1986 for $4 million. The resort has since changed hands several times. At one point it was owned by the Wabaseemoong First Nation, but Minaki is now closed and once again for sale.

Entrance loggia of the
Château Laurier, 1916

CITY
HOTELS

The Nova Scotian opened on the Halifax waterfront in 1930.

NOVA SCOTIAN HOTEL

Halifax, Nova Scotia

"The Nova Scotian Hotel will be a new front door for Halifax," declared the headlines when the city's second grand railway hotel opened in 1930. The immense Nova Scotian was one of several new hotels that the Canadian National Railways was building across the country in the late 1920s, just before the Depression hit. It was joined by a covered walkway to Halifax's Union Station (near the port terminal) so that arriving travellers could enter the Nova Scotian without having to step outdoors.

In general, the Nova Scotian featured amenities similar to those of its major competitor, the CPR's Lord Nelson Hotel, with which it vied for the patronage of Haligonians and visitors. But the hotel also had some distinct features. Its bedrooms were furnished in mahogany, and for men's convenience while grooming, bathrooms were fitted out with cigar rests, electric outlets and special receptacles for used razor blades. The hotel's massive kitchen prepared meals for both its own guests and the CNR passenger trains that pulled into Union Station. And, as part of the CNR chain, the Nova Scotian had CN radio broadcasting studios on the eighth floor overlooking the harbour. The studios were quite elaborate, in an Italian style that featured black marble, murals, pillars and metal filigree on the doors. The hotel also had a house orchestra,

Guests in the Rose Garden alongside Pier 20 in 1931

and its public rooms, including the grand ball-room, were fitted out with microphones to record local programs for the radio network. As well, loudspeakers were provided so that guests could enjoy broadcasts from other CN stations across the country, including Montreal, Toronto, Ottawa, Winnipeg, Jasper Park, Regina and Vancouver.

The Nova Scotian was a good place to watch the arrival and departure of ships from all parts of the world. For many of those who were arriving—including the over 1.5 million immigrants who passed through nearby Pier 21 between 1928 and 1971—the station and hotel were some of the first buildings encountered. The immigrants' landing in Halifax

marked the end of a long, exhausting sea journey and a hopeful beginning in Canada. Like Peter C. Newman, who arrived at age ten with his family in 1940, many stopped first to refresh themselves at the Nova Scotian's coffee shop before boarding the train to their final destination.

Periodically renovated and enlarged, the Nova Scotian ran into difficulties and was forced to close in 1993. It reopened in 1996 as part of the Westin hotel chain. Since then, extensive renovations have returned the Nova Scotian to its proud place on the Halifax waterfront.

(Above) The Nova Scotian, at the hub of rail and port activity. Note Union Station at the far right of the photograph. (Lower) Crowds coming to catch a glimpse of King George VI and Queen Elizabeth during their 1939 Royal Tour .

When the Lord Nelson opened in October 1928, traffic lights had to be installed at the corner of South Park Street and Spring Garden Road to control the steady stream of curious motorists.

THE LORD NELSON

Halifax, Nova Scotia

On October 28, 1928, fourteen years from the time the idea of a grand hotel for Halifax was first proposed, the Lord Nelson finally swung open its doors. Halifax had strong ties to the British Navy lasting several centuries, so it seemed logical for Canadian Pacific to name its new hotel after Britain's naval hero, Admiral Lord Horatio Nelson. The Admiral never visited Halifax, but the hotel is filled with his portraits, including two in the hotel lobby commissioned from a local artist, Sister Agnes Berchman. There are also model ships and paintings of the Battle of Trafalgar. Woven rugs with a depiction of Nelson's ship, HMS *Victory*, and bordered with an anchor pattern were made specifically for the hotel.

When it opened, Canadian Pacific's Lord Nelson, an elegant Georgian building situated in the city centre and facing the beautiful Public Gardens, was in a class by itself. But CP's rival, Canadian National, was already in mid-construction on the Nova Scotian Hotel, which opened one year later at the hub of Halifax's rail and port activity. Having a competitor made the Lord Nelson even more anxious to exude an aura of style and elegance. Betty Findlay, waitress at the Lord Nelson from 1947 to 1954, recalls that the dress code for men was jacket-and-tie, and that no gentleman would dare be caught improperly attired. According to another long-time employee, Pearl LeFrense, the hotel was known for its refined, white-gloved French table service. It was a place for special occasions—wedding receptions and university proms; a place where one came on a Sunday to take afternoon tea. In many ways, the Lord Nelson was woven into the social fabric of the city. And during World War II,

Admiral Lord Horatio Nelson (1758-1805), the famed British naval commander who fought crucial battles in the wars against Revolutionary and Napoleonic France.

THE LORD NELSON

Location: Corner of South Park Street and
Spring Garden Road, Halifax, N.S.

1928: Opened October 22

Initial Owner: CPR and local consortium

Architect: Kenneth Campbell with Whitney
Warren & Charles Wetmore

Style: Georgian

Principal Materials: Nova Scotia granite,
Bedford limestone, Bluenose brick

Number of rooms when opened: 200

Number of storeys when opened: 7

1966: 8th and 9th floor added

1967: Fire on 7th floor

1969: South Tower section added

1975: North Tower section added

1985: Fire causing $3.5 million in damages

Prominent Guests: Andrei Andreyevich
Gromyko, Ronald Reagan, Victor Borge,
Louis Armstrong, Count Basie

Named After: Admiral Lord Horatio
Nelson (1758-1805), the famed British
naval commander who fought crucial battles in the wars against Revolutionary and
Napoleonic France.

military and naval personnel stayed at this distinguished address.

One unusual guest was Admiral Emile
Henri Muselier who served General Charles de
Gaulle's Free French government-in-exile during
World War II. At a time when the Nazi-allied
Vichy government held power in France,
Muselier was given the task of seizing the Vichy-
controlled islands of St. Pierre and Miquelon.
He and his staff stayed at the Lord Nelson in
1941 while planning the operation. On the
morning of December 22, Muselier's fleet sailed
from Halifax to the islands through an Atlantic
storm. Without firing a shot, Muselier captured
St. Pierre and Miquelon, garnering overwhelm-
ing support from their five thousand residents.
According to historian Douglas Anglin,
Muselier's ousting of the islands' Vichy governor
inspired a wave of international reaction.
Though far from France, these tiny islands
played a significant role in the Free French quest
to liberate that country.

Mitchell Franklin, the Lord Nelson's
owner between 1961 and 1998, tells the story of
another unusual guest: Fidel Castro. According to
Franklin, when Castro's airplane had to make an
unscheduled landing in Halifax, he and his
entourage paid a surprise overnight visit to the
hotel. They took an entire floor and demanded
complete secrecy, an understandable request in the
1960s, with the Cold War at its height. Castro's
security measures apparently included punch-
ing holes in the walls and doors through
which his men could aim their guns if
the need arose. There was no shootout

*Admiral Emile Henri Muselier and his Free
French staff stayed at the Lord Nelson in
1941 while plotting to seize the Vichy-con-
trolled islands of St. Pierre and Miquelon.*

Bride and groom descending the lobby staircase, 1941

in the Lord Nelson that night; in fact, it is impossible to confirm Castro's stay at all. But Mitchell Franklin swears the famous man was there—and that he left without paying his bill.

In the mid-1980s, a serious fire and an economic recession left the hotel in a sad state. Deteriorating inside and out, it was totally drained of its charm. Things turned around when Centennial Hotels and Suites purchased the business in 1998 and spent $10 million to return the Lord Nelson to its past splendour. The rejuvenation project garnered a groundswell of support from Haligonians who proved very protective of "their" hotel. They did not want the historic spirit of the hotel to be tampered with. Even moving the grandfather clock from its usual spot in the lobby provoked an outcry from many who feared it had been sold.

During the renovation, the walls began to offer up fragments of the past. Old instructions for how to handle one's horse and buggy while at the hotel were found behind a wall, and some floors still had notices that told guests what to do in the wartime blackout.

The eyes of the world were on Halifax again in September 1998, when Swiss Air Flight 111 crashed off Nova Scotia. The Lord Nelson accommodated the families of the victims. During their stay, someone slipped a printed message into each guest room, assuring the bereaved that the people of Nova Scotia would never forget. "We are tied to you in sorrow and in friendship. We hope that one day you will feel strong enough to return to our province and that you will always feel that you are coming home."

The old Hotel Newfoundland was built on the site of the 17th-century British Fort William.
Excavating for the hotel in 1925, workers found flint-and-steel guns with powder horns from
the old Fort, and two tunnels that led to Signal Hill, the site of a 1672 struggle between the
French and British for control of St. John's. (Inset) Mid-demolition, 1983

HOTEL NEWFOUNDLAND

St. John's, Newfoundland

"As the tourist approaches St. John's and his stately ship steams in towards the harbor—overlooking which the Newfoundland Hotel stands—on every side a lofty ironbound coast presents itself to view; the grim, hoary rocks seem to frown defiance to the Atlantic." So enthused the *Newfoundland Quarterly* in December 1925, when the magnificent Hotel Newfoundland first rose over the city of St. John's. That the hotel had such a commanding presence is not surprising as it was constructed on the site of the 17th-century British stronghold, Fort William. Indeed, stone from this old fort was built right into the Hotel Newfoundland's retaining wall.

The Hotel Newfoundland opened on July 1, 1926. In the 1920s, Newfoundland was still a British colony and ties with the mother country were strong. Hotel Newfoundland employees were trained in the finer points of service aboard luxury British passenger liners. Everything had to be in place. Exquisite meals were prepared by chefs in starched uniforms and, in winter, bellhops in pillbox hats and immaculately clean white gloves used little brushes to dust snow from their patrons' shoulders as they entered the hotel.

But in the 1930s, Newfoundland was experiencing difficulties. The island's economy was bankrupt and its government unable to cope. In 1934, it was replaced by a Commission of Government, with a governor and commissioners appointed by Britain. Some of these new officials—including the Commissioner for Natural Resources, Sir John Hope Simpson—took up residence with their families in the Hotel Newfoundland. Government House and the Colonial Building were close by, and the day-to-day life of the British officials revolved around these three buildings. It was in the hotel that the Commission of Government was inaugurated; here its members took their afternoon tea and their wives played bridge.

HOTEL NEWFOUNDLAND

Location: Cavendish Square, St. John's, Newfoundland

1926: Opened July 1

Initial Owner: Newfoundland Hotel Facilities Ltd.

Architect: A.B. Sanford

Number of rooms when opened: 142

Principal Materials: Reinforced steel and brick

1931: Purchased by the government of Newfoundland

1949: CNR purchased for $1.00

1982: New Hotel Newfoundland built

1983: Old hotel demolished

1988: CP Hotels and partners purchased hotel

Prominent Guests: Prince Charles and Princess Diana, Queen Elizabeth II, Frank Sinatra, Robert Ripley

Name: Was originally planned as the Royal Newfoundland Hotel. For an unknown reason the term "Royal" was not first approved by Buckingham Palace, and it was dropped.

In 1931, rumour has it that Chicago mobster Legs Diamond arrived at the hotel with his gang. As the story goes, the bellhop who assisted him had no inkling that he was escorting a dangerous criminal to his room. What he did notice was the extreme weight of the luggage. "Open it up," instructed Legs when the bellhop commented about a particularly weighty suitcase. The contents, sawed-off shotguns, piqued the bellhop's curiosity. "Where were you, out on the barrens shooting birds?" Apparently, the two became friendly during the gangster's stay, and Legs even paid for the staff Christmas party, so impressed was he with the hotel's service. And apparently he was not stingy—the staff was still drinking champagne a week later. No one suspected Diamond's identity until long after his visit.

The Hotel Newfoundland played a role throughout the turbulent political era leading to the controversial 1949 referendum that brought Newfoundland into Confederation. Between 1937 and 1943, Joey Smallwood, who spearheaded the pro-Canada movement, had hosted the popular radio program, "Barrelman," that was broadcast from the Voice of Newfoundland (VONF) radio station housed on the top floor of the Hotel Newfoundland. (A barrelman was the sailor who climbed the mast to the barrel-shaped lookout, to watch for ice packs, whales or other danger.) Airing Monday to Friday at 6:45 p.m., Smallwood's program featured fifteen minutes of local history, geography, economics, tall tales, and people's personal stories. Smallwood's aim was to make "Newfoundland better known to Newfoundlanders" and to destroy what he saw as the colony's "inferiority complex." Because of the popularity of his show, Smallwood became one of the best-known men on the island.

As soon as Newfoundland joined Canada, Canadian National Railways gained control of the province's rail system and invested $80 million to integrate it into the national network. CNR also purchased the Hotel Newfoundland for one dollar. The hotel became the Railway's most easterly hotel and completed its luxury chain across the Canadian provinces.

The old Hotel Newfoundland dominated the St. John's skyline.

As time passed, the Hotel Newfoundland lost its appeal. By the 1980s, the CNR had decided to replace the old Hotel Newfoundland with a larger, more modern hotel that could accommodate the city's growing tourist and convention business. Upset at the idea of losing this landmark, many Newfoundlanders fought the plan. Mayor John Murphy proposed a tax break for the hotel and suggested it stay open only from May to mid-October in order to reduce heating costs. Captain Gunnar Tannis, an Air Canada pilot from Ontario who had flown into St. John's for twenty years, held a candlelight vigil two days before the demo-

lition date in a last-ditch effort to convince the public, the government and the CNR of the hotel's importance. But there was no miracle. Just before the 1983 demolition, many people took souvenirs from the old building. One regular visitor was presented with the door from his favourite room. The only significant item from the old hotel that has been integrated into the new, large, V-shaped Hotel Newfoundland is the brass Cutler mailbox.

Wait staff uniforms reflect the maritime character of St. John's. Seal flipper pie, partridge berries, baked apple, and calabogus (a rum-based drink) gave a local flavour to the menu.

Gathering on the front portico of The Charlottetown

THE CHARLOTTETOWN

Charlottetown, Prince Edward Island

Tourism had been important to Prince Edward Island's economy since the early 1900s, when travellers discovered the Island's pastoral charm and its splendid panoramas of red soil and green fields, sand and Gulf waters. Long evident, Charlottetown's woeful inability to host visitors in style became critical when the Victoria Hotel on Water Street burned to the ground in January 1929. At this point, a delegation from the city's Tourist Association and Board of Trade approached CNR president, Sir Henry Thornton, to request that the railway build a new hotel in their city. The CNR, meanwhile, had undertaken to provide luxury accommodations along its rail lines in every province of the country. To the delegation's delight, therefore, Thornton was able to promise a hotel—and one grander than any it had dared to hope for.

Canadian National Railways architect John Schofield and his assistant, G.F. Drummond, set out to design a building that would combine the modern conveniences of a big-city hotel with the homelike atmosphere one would expect to find in a city with the old world charm of Charlottetown. What emerged, in 1931, was an elegant five-storey, red brick Georgian building. Upon entering, one's first impression was of the intimate and handsome lobby, with its marble floor and barrel-vaulted ceiling. Leading off the lobby was the Georgian Room, a warm and intimate space in the delicate neo-classical Adam style, where one could dine and dance under sparkling crystal chandeliers.

THE CHARLOTTETOWN

Location: 75 Kent Street, Charlottetown, P.E.I.

1931: Opened April 14

Initial Owner: CNR

Architects: John Schofield and G.F. Drummond

Style: Georgian

Principal Materials: Steel structure, brick exterior

Number of rooms when opened: 110

Number of storeys when opened: 5

1964: CNR sold hotel to Island Development Company

1985: Bought by Rodd Hotels & Resorts

2000: Renamed Rodd Charlottetown

Prominent Guests: King George VI and Queen Elizabeth, Queen Elizabeth II and Prince Philip

Named After: The city, which was named after Queen Charlotte (1744-1818), wife of King George III. The hotel was known as the Canadian National until 1939.

(Above) Queen Elizabeth II and Prince Philip on their 1973 Royal Tour.

Elmer Gallant, who has played the clarinet and saxophone in the hotel band since 1939, remembers the World War II years when the Royal Air Force was stationed in Charlottetown. Officers and pilots staying at the hotel would throw wild parties after the dances. "We were always sure to play patriotic English songs at these dances," said Elmer, "because we knew the British pilots would invite us back to their rooms for drinks afterwards." The band members wore their white cuffs hanging out of their jackets to more easily record the room numbers of the night's parties. After the dance, they simply consulted their cuffs and worked their way from room to room.

Tudor Lounge, 1931. The Charlottetown's architects strove for a "homelike atmosphere." The coats of arms of the Canadian provinces are still found on the oak pilasters surrounding the room, now called the Provinces Lounge.

Small, intimate and a little quirky, the Charlottetown has not taken on the antiseptic, homogenous, brightly-lit feel of many of the larger grand hotels across the country. Currently owned by Rodd Hotels and Resorts, the Rodd Charlottetown retains many original elements. CN's initials are still woven into the outside grille work, and original fixtures in the bathrooms, like the luxurious extra-long bathtubs, are a delight. Throughout, one still feels the homelike comfort that Schofield and Drummond first intended.

(Inset) The CNR opened the Charlottetown Hotel beside Rochford Square in 1931.

"The site was an inspiration.... It was practically at the apex of the picturesque old city, and if ever there was the natural place and a natural reason for a picturesque building it was here...."
　　　　　　　　　　　　　　—Bruce Price

Le Château Frontenac

Quebec City, Quebec

High atop Cap Diamant, the Château Frontenac dominates the Quebec City skyline. As early as 1620, Samuel de Champlain noted the exceptional strategic value of this impressive site and ordered the first fort of Quebec, the Château St. Louis, to be built here. In 1690, it was destroyed by the attacking British, but the French governor, the Comte de Frontenac, quickly had it rebuilt in 1692. For over a hundred years, the fort stood proudly on this strikingly beautiful cliff, until it burned down in 1834. The luxury hotel that took its place was named in the Comte's honour. Although designed by an American architect, with interiors by English Canadians, it quickly became the visual symbol of Quebec City—the centre of French civilization in North America.

In 1892, Sir Donald Alexander Smith (Lord Strathcona), Sir William Van Horne, Sir Thomas Shaughnessy and a number of their business acquaintances from Montreal formed the Château Frontenac Company to finance its construction. They chose Bruce Price of New York to design it. Instead of the contemporary structure contemplated by these barons of Canadian high finance, the architect designed his masterpiece in the style of a French Renaissance château. In Price's words, as quoted in the June 1899 *Architectural Record*:

> The motif is…the early French château adapted to modern requirements, a style certainly in keeping with the tradition of the old French city….the materials I believe to be also in harmony with

The first Château Frontenac, by architect Bruce Price, was placed atop Cap Diamant, the site of earlier French forts.

CHÂTEAU FRONTENAC

Location: 1 rue des Carrières, Quebec, Qc.

1893: Opened December 18

Initial Owner: The Château Frontenac Co.

Architect: Bruce Price

Style: Château

Principal Materials: "Glenboig" brick

1898-99: Citadel Wing and Citadel Pavilion

Architect: Bruce Price

1909-10: Addition of Mont Carmel Wing

Architect: W.S. Painter

1915: Addition of Archway Wing

Architect: W.S. Painter

1920-24: Addition of St. Louis Wing, Service Wing, and Central Tower Block

Architects: Edward and W.S. Maxwell

1926: January 16 fire destroyed Price's Riverview Wing (rebuilt in only 127 days)

1993: Addition of Claude Pratte Wing

Prominent guests: King George V, King George VI and Queen Elizabeth, King and Queen of Siam, Mme. Chiang Kai-Shek, Princess Juliana of Holland, Alfred Hitchcock, Princess Grace of Monaco

Named After: Louis de Buade, comte de Frontenac, who guided the destiny of New France from 1672-82 and 1689-98. (His coat of arms is preserved on the outside wall of the Courtyard.)

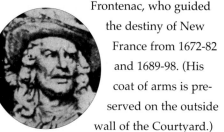

(Above) Bruce Price's drawing for the Château Frontenac (Inset) Sketch by W.S. Maxwell. Edward Maxwell had the enviable task of searching through European museums for designs to be copied for the Château's furnishings.

the surroundings: blue limestone, Glenboig brick, hard, coarse materials, giving broad effects, with plenty of light and colour. The hotel is placed in the center of a big landscape, and hence needs every advantage of bigness, both from the materials and from the simplicity of its designs.

On the Château Frontenac's opening day, December 18, 1893, the *Quebec Chronicle* gave its pleased verdict:

> Beyond the shadow of a doubt, the finest hotel site in the world is that now occupied by the Château Frontenac....The roofing throughout is of copper....The turrets and towers lend to the whole structure the appearance of a medieval castle perched upon a precipice....

Bruce Price not only oversaw the construction, but also the equally acclaimed interior design and decoration of the 170-room establishment. According to the *Quebec Chronicle* article, upon entering the vestibule, the visitor "is at once struck with the beauty of the mosaic flooring and the richness of the woodwork and mural decorations...the carved oaken mouldings…the grand staircase…the arms of Frontenac…." The writer was particularly impressed that both Frontenac and Charles Huault de Montmagny (an earlier governor of New France) were represented in complete armour. Price created four extravagant suites—the Canadian, the Chinese, the Dutch and the Royal. And at Van Horne's insistence, the hotel was equipped with the very latest amenities: central heating, hydraulic steam-powered elevators, and electric light.

From the start, the Château fulfilled Van Horne's promise to make it the "most talked about hotel on this continent." Before long, it was bought by Canadian Pacific. In the late 1890s, CP was promoting its round-the-world cruises heavily to Europeans, with Quebec City as the gateway to North America. With its commanding position on the cliff, the Château was thought to provide an appropriately impressive welcome to Canada. Contrary to expectations, in the early years CP's clientele was predominantly American and Canadian. Nevertheless, by 1898 the hotel was highly profitable. There were soon too few rooms, so Bruce Price was asked to design two additions: the Citadel Wing and the Citadel Pavilion. Continuously rising demand led to four subsequent additions: the Mont Carmel Wing by W.S. Painter in 1909–1910, an extension in 1915, and the Maxwell Tower and the Saint Louis Wing, by Montreal architects Edward and William Maxwell, in 1924.

The grand staircase to the Palm Court and ballroom, 1925.

(Above) View from the Château Frontenac roofs, n.d. The Château Frontenac was the first stop in Canada for British and European tourists on Canadian Pacific's "Around the World" tours. Disembarking at Quebec City, they would travel by train to the West Coast, where they would board CP's Empress liners for Asia. (Below) First erected in 1893, the Chateau Frontenac was repeatedly enlarged in order to meet demand. After the 1926 fire, Bruce Price's original wing was restored by Maxwell & Pitts.

The Maxwells' central tower added 16 new suites on the tower's top floors. To furnish the suites and the rest of the hotel, Edward Maxwell went to Europe on a buying expedition. The Historical Monuments Committee of France gave permission to a Parisian firm to remove rare furnishings from museums and make copies for the Château. Among Maxwell's purchases were a Louis XV bronze mirror frame, a Louis XIV dressing table, Louis XV chairs and sofas, beds and pedestal tables. In Italy he bought carved mirrors and chose marble for the fireplaces. From England he brought back Jacobean bedsteads, great wing chairs, grandfather clocks and rare prints; from Holland, pottery and wall hangings. Those who poured into the Château from Montreal, Toronto, Ottawa and the United States were transported to another place, another time. In a building reminiscent of the Continent's castles, they could imagine themselves surrounded by the opulence of court life.

The Château's elegant European style was an irresistible draw for residents of the city. Ladies

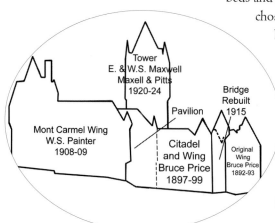

Tower
E. & W.S. Maxwell
Maxell & Pitts
1920-24

Bridge
Rebuilt
1915

Pavilion

Mont Carmel Wing
W.S. Painter
1908-09

Citadel
and Wing
Bruce Price
1897-99

Original
Wing
Bruce Price
1892-93

Fire in the early Riverview wing, January 16, 1926. Firefighting efforts were frustrated by high winds that blew the water back from the flames. The Riverview wing was quickly restored, using architect Bruce Price's original blueprints.

QUEBEC

CHATEAU FRONTENAC

CANADIAN PACIFIC

Canadian Pacific poster, 1924. The Château Frontenac, along with the Banff Springs and the Empress Hotels, established the château style for Canadian Pacific. The Château Frontenac has been designated a National Historic Site.

arrived in carriages for afternoon tea in the subdued atmosphere of the Palm Court. The room's soft reflected light enhanced the complexion, and classical music was provided by a trio dressed in period costume. Often members of the Club Musical des Dames came to listen to Bach or Chopin in one of the salons.

Many special occasions have been celebrated in the Château's romantic ballroom, which was inspired by the Hall of Mirrors at Versailles. Both young and old favoured the Jacques Cartier Room for dancing, and the Château's extravagant Christmas and Easter festivities were not to be missed. In fact, four generations of one Quebec family have come to the Château for Christmas dinner—without ever having broken the tradition. During the Winter Carnival, another tradition is to dine at the Château while viewing the annual boat races on the St. Lawrence below.

The Château has an allure that has reached far beyond the city limits. As one of the most famous hotels in the world, throughout the century of its existence, it has attracted hundreds of dignitaries and celebrities. Kings and queens of England, Russian princes and Indian maharajahs, and various World War I heroes have graced its salons. Among its visitors were French marshals Fayolle and Foch, and Baron Byng, who distinguished himself at Vimy Ridge. Then, on April 24, 1928, a most striking figure strode up to the lobby's front desk. It was Charles Lindberg, complete with parachute. He had flown from New York directly onto the Plains of Abraham to come to the assistance of the famous aviator Floyd Bennett who was in a hospital with pneumonia. Lindberg had brought Dr. Thomas Applegath to administer a special serum to his friend. (Unfortunately, the treatment failed to save Bennett's life.)

When Charles de Gaulle attended a government banquet in his honour in 1967, the French president ignored protocol to chat merrily with the wine steward— a fellow Maquisard named Henri d'Orange—who was wearing a decoration he had received while serving with the Free French Forces during World War II. Hollywood also came, notably Errol Flynn, and Elizabeth Taylor who, bellmen remember, arrived with four hundred pieces of luggage. In 1969, Princess Grace of Monaco presided over the Winter Carnival festivities, including the Queen's Ball, held in the Château, at which Pierre Elliott Trudeau danced with the local Winter Carnival Queen.

During World War II, the Château took a central role on the world stage. In 1943, at a point when the outcome of the war was still far from determined, Canadian Prime Minister William Lyon Mackenzie King agreed to host a war conference in Quebec City between British prime minister Winston Churchill and United States president Franklin Delano Roosevelt to ensure the success of the forthcoming military campaign. All international members of the projected conference decided that the only building that could accommodate a meeting of this magnitude was the Château Frontenac. The three heads of state were to stay in the Citadel for reasons of security, but the meetings themselves were to be held at the Château.

On July 31, 1943, General Manager Neale was informed that the Château had been requisitioned by the Canadian Government for a period of two weeks starting August 8. The premises were to be completely evacuated— and the reason for this was to remain absolutely secret. No easy assignment! The 849 guests and permanent residents of the hotel were asked to vacate their

Entrance courtyard of the Château Frontenac, c.1939

(Left) Official photograph taken at the Citadel during the Second Quebec Conference, 1944. In the front row from left to right are: Mackenzie King, Franklin Delano Roosevelt, and Winston Churchill. Converted into an armed camp, the Château Frontenac accommodated the advisory staff and was the site of war strategy meetings and evening receptions. (Below) Churchill and Roosevelt greet one another during the Second Quebec Conference, 1944. The ten-day event focused on planning for the capitulation of Germany and for the campaign in the Pacific.

accommodations by August 6. Some two to three thousand reservations were cancelled. Only three people were allowed to stay: the manager and his wife, and Lucien de Celles, because of his advanced age. Even former premier Maurice Duplessis, a resident of the hotel, was refused permission to remain. Outside, the Château was converted into an armed camp. Inside, Neale and his staff had the huge job of converting the third floor into 85 offices, installing a private switchboard system, diplomatically organizing all the bookings, and requisitioning enormous amounts of food under conditions of wartime rationing. The kitchen faced the task of serving over 35,000 meals during the conference—about 2,000 each day.

On Tuesday August 10, the whole world learned that a major conference that could alter the course of the war was taking place in Quebec City. Once the news broke, curiosity seekers descended on Quebec, many crowding around the arched entrance to the Château in hopes of spotting one of the heads of state. Some of the early planning for D-Day took place here. Conference participants spent their days strategizing and their evenings socializing at sumptuous receptions and banquets, most notably a state dinner for 510 hosted by Prime Minister Mackenzie King. Although staff members were renowned for

Pageant during Quebec City's tercentenary celebrations, 1908

their discretion, a few stories leaked out. One bellman is said to have found a pile of D-Day-related papers and plans under the conference table after one of the meetings—which he duly turned in to officials. The proceedings went very smoothly, and as Winston Churchill said in a radio address from the Conference:

> Certainly no more fitting and splendid setting could have been chosen for a meeting of those who guide the war policy of the two great western democracies at this cardinal moment in the Second World War than we have here in the Plains of Abraham, in the Château Frontenac and the ramparts of the Citadel of Quebec....

In fact, General Manager Neale and his army of staff at the Château did such a wonderful job as hosts that the following year, Churchill and Roosevelt decided to return to Quebec for the Second Quebec Conference.

A much smaller assemblage moved into the Château in 1952—the cast of Alfred Hitchcock's film, *I Confess.* Among the stars were Montgomery Cliff and Ann Baxter, who created quite a sensation when she smoked her big cigars. With his perfect French, Hitchcock acquired a wonderful reputation at the Château. Apparently, he had a deal whereby the Château gave him free accommodation for his crew on condition that the hotel's rooms appeared in the film. The dramatic

Bienvenue! **Winter Sports in Old Quebec**

(Above left) The toboggan slide has operated almost every winter since it was erected in 1894—the year following the Château's opening. (The current slide is less steep than the original.) (Above right) The Château Frontenac played a major role in promoting winter sports in Quebec, and was central to Quebec City's Winter Carnival from its beginnings. Many have learned to ski on the Plains of Abraham at the Château's Ski Hawks Club.

opening sequence of the film did indeed feature the Château from the river, and near the end there is a chase scene through its many rooms, with the Château's manager, Jessop, playing himself. Fittingly, the world premiere of *I Confess* was held at the Capitol Theatre in Quebec City in 1953.

Working at the Château is not like working anywhere else. For more than a century, wearing a Château uniform has been a source of pride. A powerful esprit de corps and a strong sense of loyalty have created a feeling of family. Many employees have spent most of their lives at the hotel. As late as 2000, Lionel Verret was working with room service—fifty-four years after he started as a busboy in 1946 earning $28.57 a week. Verret has had about thirty members of his extended family work for the Château. Others have links back to the Château's beginnings. Bellman Roger Martel's uncle, Henri Martel, rode in a horse and buggy as a young boy to help pick up coal from the ships down at the wharf.

Retiring as assistant to the head housekeeper after a 33-year career at the Château, Rose-Aimée L'Heureux has her own stories. When she began as a chambermaid, the maids had to live on the hotel premises and they had to be single—if you married, you lost your job. The young women were subject to a strict curfew and prohibited from receiving visitors in their rooms. For years, the old chambermaids' quarters remained empty, but in 2001, they were converted to elegant suites and rooms.

In 1993, Canadian Pacific decided to celebrate the hotel's centennial in grand style. In March, the management announced a 65-million dollar restoration and renovation program that included the construction of the Claude Pratte Wing adjoining Painter's Mont Carmel Wing, to accommodate a spa and spaces for conventions. Montreal architects, The Arcop Group, designed the new wing to echo Painter's work. Steep copper roofs with numerous dormers blend in with a corbelled turret at the centre of the street facade. The exterior masonry is of limestone identical in colour and texture to that used for the other wings, and grey stone is used for ornamentation. Indeed, each of the numerous additions to the Château over the years has managed to blend in, creating a harmonious and striking whole.

On a magical evening in February 1993, an extravagant centennial reception took place at the Château Frontenac. The facade was ablaze with lights. Inside there were flowers, lavish buffets, orchestral music, and five hundred guests decked out in all their finery. William Van Horne's hotel was showing off its splendid dining rooms, the panelling and warm hues of its halls, its chandeliers with their dancing reflections, its beautiful carpets, gilt ornamentation, mirrors, paintings and interior spaces. Today, the Château Frontenac retains its original spirit. It constitutes a living legend, one built on over a hundred years of memories and dreams.

(Inset) Cocktails on ice, 1945

St. Andrew's Society Ball, November 1878. The magnificent ball at the Windsor Hotel was presided over by Princess Louise and the Marquis of Lorne. Quadrilles, waltzes, polkas, cotillions and Scottish country dancing filled the dance program that night, and every subsequent St. Andrew's ball for many decades.

WINDSOR HOTEL

Montreal, Quebec

When actress Sarah Bernhardt wanted to stay in Montreal's two-year-old Windsor Hotel one snowy night in 1880, the manager spared her the long walk there from the local Academy of Music, where she had been performing, by sending a team of porters to fetch her—in a sleigh. Some years later, when Bernhardt returned to the hotel after having had a leg amputated following an accident on stage in Brazil, she was carried between her automobile and her room in a Louis XVI chair that was hoisted by a team of red-clad bellboys. Such personal attention was expected of the Windsor. It was, after all, Canada's first and biggest grand hotel. Built in 1878, before any Canadian Pacific hotel, it was promptly labelled "the best in all the Dominion."

It was also a prime example of the Victorian era's notion of palatial splendour—a richly embellished, nine-storey structure of sandstone and granite that sported a vast, gold-embossed lobby, six restaurants, two ballrooms, and a concert hall. The Great Rotunda had a black and white marble floor, and was surmounted by an impressive dome with "artistic frescoing upon the sides." On the circumference of the room were a barber's shop, a cigar shop, a room for reading and writing, another for billiards, a men's smoking room and a huge stained-glass window. On the mezzanine were Turkish and Egyptian salons and the Victorian Vice-Regal Suite. Above them, the hotel's 382 rooms could accommodate eight hundred guests. All had hot and cold water, push-button bells for summoning chambermaids and easy access to three public bathrooms strategically situated on each floor. A west-facing chamber cost four dollars a night; one that looked across Peel Street to Dominion Square was six dollars.

WINDSOR HOTEL

Location: Dominion Square (now Dorchester Square), Montreal, Quebec

1878: Opened January 28

Initial Owners: Windsor Hotel Company

Architect: William Boyington of Chicago

Style: Second Empire

Principal Materials: Sandstone, granite

Number of rooms when opened: 382

Number of storeys when opened: 9

1906: Fire destroyed over 100 rooms

1908: North Annex built by H.J. Hardenbergh and B.L. Gilbert

1924: Annex built by J.S. Archibald

1957: Fire May 31

1959: Original building demolished

1981: Closed

Prominent Guests: Mark Twain, Sarah Bernhardt, Princess Louise and the Marquis of Lorne, Sir John A. Macdonald, Winston Churchill, John F. Kennedy, Charles de Gaulle, Jean-Paul Sartre, Lillie Langtree, King George VI and Queen Elizabeth

Grand Promenade, 1878. Canada's first grand hotel claimed the title: "The Dominion's first, biggest, and best."

After Sarah Bernhardt came Mark Twain. When he decided to spend six months in Canada to lecture on his books, he rented an eighth-floor room at the Windsor. The hotel soon became a second home to numerous turn-of-the-century writers and actors. John Barrymore's "silver screen" wife Dolores Costello stayed there often, as did Rudyard Kipling, most notably in 1907 when he received an honorary doctorate from McGill University.

The university's official photographer in those days was considered one of Canada's very best. William Notman, a brusque Scottish immigrant who was also a businessman, had been one of the six investors who had formed the Windsor Hotel Company in 1875 to build an inn for visitors arriving at Windsor Station, just along the road. Work on the station began that year, but a particularly spiteful winter delayed a start on the hotel until the spring of 1876. Nonetheless, the Windsor was inaugurated on January 28, 1878, by Lady Dufferin, wife of Canada's governor general, at a giant banquet and ball she later described in her diary as "absolutely gorgeous." It was Montreal's largest social gathering to date, and crowds jammed the streets to watch the guests arrive. Queen Victoria's daughter, Princess Louise, was there with her husband, the Marquis of Lorne—Canada's next governor general. So

were Canada's first prime minister, Sir John A. Macdonald, and members of Montreal's most prestigious families.

On November 30, 1878, the Windsor's resplendent ballrooms were in action once again, this time for a St. Andrew's Society ball, which remained an annual event at the hotel for nearly one hundred years. Each year, more than fifty young debutantes "came out" at the ball, in their quest for society marriages. Another tradition was the ball marking Montreal's annual Winter Carnival. For the first of these, in 1883, citizens in blanket-coats and moccasins sledded down Peel Street to visit the Ice Palace in Dominion Square, then danced until 3:00 a.m. to the Band of the 65th Regiment.

While functions like these placed the hotel at the hub of Montreal's social life, much of its success hinged on its proximity to Windsor Station. Trains brought in visitors from all over North America. "In our chambers and our Rotunda," a hotel brochure claimed,

(Above) Windsor Hotel, 1916. Guests enjoyed the view of Montreal from the lookout tower above the sixth storey. There was also access to the dome 150 feet above ground. The 1908 North Annex can be seen to the right of the photograph. This portion of the former hotel still stands. The Shareholder, September 19, 1878 wrote, "[The Windsor] is built upon the healthy upper plateau of the city... The approach from the railway station is direct and easy, and the distance short."

"Canadian statesmen and men of affairs have planned much of the marvellous development of Montreal, and of the Dominion itself." But once at the Windsor, these often dour, black-suited financiers and pugnacious politicians came face to face with artists, writers, and actors, who gravitated to it naturally. For them, the hotel was itself a piece of theatre—ornate, diverse, and dramatic, with black figurines dominating the lobby and an abundance of atmospheric gas lighting throughout the public areas.

Actress Fanny Davenport, in Montreal to play Lady Macbeth, also stayed at the hotel, and actually dared to enjoy a cigarette in the lobby—in an era when women were not supposed to smoke at all, let alone in public. Not long afterwards, the demure, peach-skinned British actress Lillie Langtree, star of a play called *The Degenerates*, arrived. Crowds rushed to see her because she was rumoured to have had a steamy liaison with King Edward VII, when he was Prince of Wales.

In 1906, fire ravaged the Windsor, destroying more than one hundred rooms. Two years later, however, the North Annex, a functional, limestone-and-brick structure in an unpretentious Parisian architectural style was built northwards on Peel Street. The Windsor now filled an entire Peel Street block and offered 750 rooms, most with private bathrooms. The annex had two elevators, a vast, steam-powered heating system, a long, wide hallway known as Peacock Alley (because of the peacock design in its stained-glass window) and two more decorative ballrooms!

On November 22, 1917, over drinks and dinner in one of the hotel's restaurants, the owners of four hockey teams—the Montreal Canadiens, the Quebec Bulldogs, the Montreal Wanderers, and the Ottawa Senators—formed the National Hockey League "to perpetuate the game of hockey." By then, the Windsor was not only a nationally established meeting place but had enticed many thriving businesses, such as Henry Birks & Sons, Morgan's, and Ogilvy's, to leave the financial district and open premises nearby.

With so many amenities close at hand, executives at both the Canadian Pacific and the Grand Trunk railway companies established permanent homes in the hotel, as did several McGill professors. The writer Stephen Leacock kept a summer home in Ontario, but wintered at the

(Above) Grand dining room, Windsor Hotel, c.1885. The Windsor Hotel Guide of that year effused: "Here Almini, the famous decorative artist of Chicago… has painted a series of beautiful landscape views, which entirely circle the hall; they comprise scenes from Great Britain, the Continent, and tropical climes, and form subjects for prolonged study. It is beyond the power of description to literally portray the magnificent appearance of this princely hall."

(Left) R.J. Tooke's store, 1878

(Opposite page) Medical Hall branch, Windsor Hotel, c.1880. Having amenities conveniently located inside the hotel was a new luxury.

Montreal Mayor Camillien Houde with King George VI and Queen Elizabeth on their 1939 Royal Tour. A year later Houde was imprisoned for treasonous utterances.

Windsor for the last eight years of his life and was often seen in Peacock Alley, a somewhat dishevelled figure leaning heavily on a walking cane and clad in a shabby raincoat and battered hat. Some of Leacock's later writing was done at the Windsor and much of his correspondence was written on hotel stationery.

On May 18, 1939, King George VI and Queen Elizabeth stayed at the Windsor during their cross-Canada tour. What an occasion it was! "Those who waited many hours to cheer the Royals," the *Montreal Star* reported, "couldn't because they were crying." In the crush, one person died of a heart attack and numerous more collapsed from a mixture of fatigue and excitement. Police reported 64 lost children, all of whom had been reunited with their parents by evening's end. They also acceded to repeated requests by the Windsor's management to put Montreal's busiest illegal gambling den on adjacent Cyprus Street out of action for the night, so the king and queen wouldn't notice it. The job was swiftly accomplished by closing little Cyprus Street until the royal couple had left.

The royal visit culminated with a state banquet at the Windsor. The *Montreal Gazette* called it "the most brilliant scene of fashion ever witnessed" and devoted two pages to reporting what each of the women among the thousand guests wore. Montreal's rags-to-riches mayor, Camillien Houde, sat between Britain's king and queen. Houde, two months earlier, had publicly declared that he would support Benito Mussolini, Italy's fascist dictator, if he chose to aid Hitler in his war with Britain. That night, he glanced repeatedly at a list of topics his advisors said he should avoid in the royal presence. At one point, the King asked Houde what he was reading. When the mayor handed him his sheet of paper, the King howled with laughter. No one ever knew what had so amused King George at the Windsor Hotel that night. We do know that when Mayor Houde rose to address the monarchs, he was a bit nervous. "I thank you from the bottom of my heart for coming," he said, "and my wife thanks you from her bottom, too."

Not long after that, Houde was back at the Windsor, which had consolidated its place as a hangout for local politicians. This was shortly after Houde had been jailed, in August 1940, for telling French-Canadians to ignore Canada's war effort. The young *Gazette* editor, Charles Peters, had branded Houde "a traitor." To heal a bitter rift between Houde and the province's federalists, Peters offered to buy him lunch. Houde agreed, but insisted that they meet first in Peacock Alley and then eat in the middle of the hotel's main dining room, so that the many important people present that day could witness their truce.

Lit up for another royal tour. On October 29, 1951, Montrealers crowded Dominion Square to see Princess Elizabeth and Prince Philip at the Windsor Hotel.

The stately Windsor later appealed to such notables as Winston Churchill, the young Princess Elizabeth, John F. Kennedy and Charles de Gaulle. Many performers savoured it, as well. In 1942, four French actors performed the existentialist play *Huis clos (No Exit)* in a North Annex ballroom. The playwright, Jean-Paul Sartre, came from Paris to see the production himself, and even helped adjust the overhead lighting.

On May 31, 1957, another fire gutted a third of the hotel's rooms. Although the blaze was confined to the original building, the damage was so great that, in July 1959, the structure had to be demolished. All that remained of the Windsor Hotel was its 1908 North Annex, but the hotel still had two hundred rooms, two ballrooms, and the impressive Peacock Alley—enough to carry on.

In September 1969, Montreal's mayor, Jean Drapeau, opened a restaurant called Le Vaisseau d'Or in the cavernous basement. At this opulent eatery, which employed a thirty-piece orchestra that cost the mayor $3,000 a week, diners were offered a seven-course dinner, served by a battalion of impeccable waiters. Meals lasted up to four hours, and speaking during musical performances was—according to a menu note—"absolutely forbidden."

Predictably, most visitors to Le Vaisseau d'Or dined there only once or twice, so its future among Montreal eateries was doubtful. The venue also attracted negative notice when, one night in 1970, a sewer backed up, flooding the hotel's basement. Although most of the black sludge was shovelled away, Jean Drapeau's restaurant retained a musty smell until it served its last meal in January 1971.

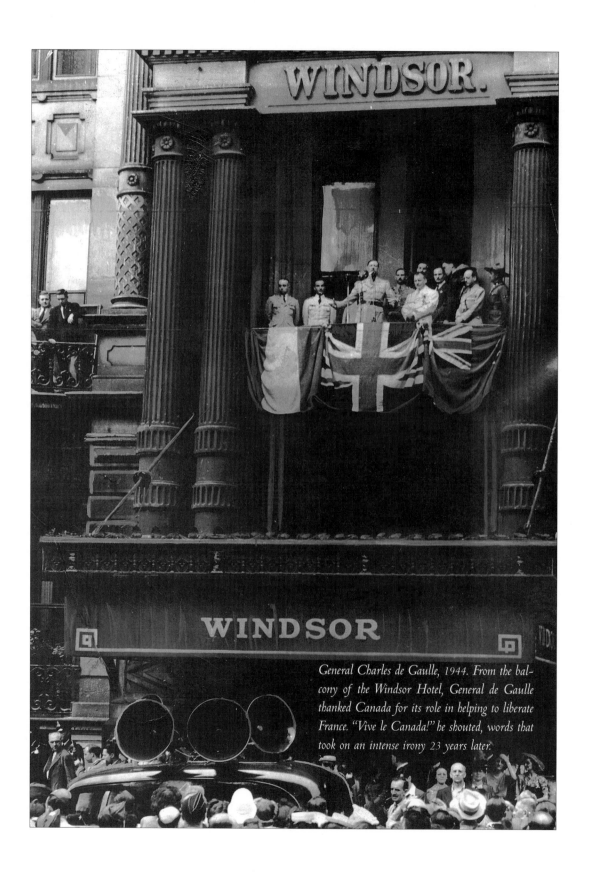

General Charles de Gaulle, 1944. From the balcony of the Windsor Hotel, General de Gaulle thanked Canada for its role in helping to liberate France. "Vive le Canada!" he shouted, words that took on an intense irony 23 years later.

Hard times had now descended upon the Windsor. A glut of newer hotels lured younger customers to their discotheques and beer parlours. The hotel was fraying at the edges and found it hard to compete. Only loyalty kept it alive. In 1975, John Barrymore's wife Dolores, now a widow, travelled from her California avocado farm to celebrate her seventieth birthday at the Windsor in the company of fifty friends, who threw a party for her. They remembered that the hotel had been her second home twelve times during the 1920s and 1930s. "I got to really love this place," Dolores Costello said. That night's banquet—served by lithe, light-footed waiters in mauve jackets—was one of the closing acts of a distinctly theatrical hotel. Sadly, in 1981, the curtain descended on it for the last time.

Six years later, as modern skyscrapers started to dwarf it, the Windsor began a second life as an office block. Efforts have been made to honour its former glory. White marble staircases reaching from the basement to the top floor have been carefully preserved, as have the beautiful maple banisters, the ornate Peacock Alley, and two pristine ballrooms, now used for banquets, wedding receptions, conferences and an occasional dance.

In 1995, the Windsor Hotel briefly reappeared on the national stage. Jean-clad men and women spent three days positioning television cameras, desks, lighting, and scenery under the ornamental ceiling and big chandelier in one of the ballrooms to create a bustling, and suitably central, studio from which the Canadian Broadcasting Corporation could beam its world-wide coverage of that year's Quebec Referendum. Since then, life has been quiet at the Windsor. Each day all too many younger Montrealers pass by, unaware of the treasure in their midst.

One who has not forgotten is dentist Dr. Hershel Bernstein. He was married there, saw Quebec Premier Jean Lesage and his grandchildren wandering the hotel's corridors during Sunday brunch, heard string quartets in its ballrooms, attended formal dinners in its restaurants and now fervently laments its passing. "The Windsor not only gave Montreal its downtown centre," Bernstein recollects, it also "emerged as a truly world-class place when Canada needed one most, as it affirmed itself well beyond its shores. It has been very sorely missed."

Sleighs outside the Windsor, 1878. In addition to the hotel's main entrance on Peel, a ladies' entrance opened onto Dorchester (now René Lévesque Boulevard).

Place Viger Hotel and Station by architect Bruce Price, c.1915. The striking limestone and brick facade has an arcade of twenty-one arches and the building is crowned by a massive tower, turrets and gables. The idea of a combined station/hotel was borrowed from England. (Right) The Viger Hotel's dramatic staircase of Corona marble, c.1900.

PLACE VIGER HOTEL

Montreal, Quebec

In the 1890s, the CPR decided to build a new railway station and hotel in Montreal, the commercial and financial engine of Canada. The idea of a combined station and grand hotel, prevalent in Victorian England, was new to Canada. The chosen architect, Bruce Price, was to use the same château style he had employed with dramatic effect when designing the Château Frontenac in Quebec City earlier that decade. The Montreal design, however, was less bold and the location more serene—facing the Viger Gardens rather than towering above the city's heights.

The CPR opened the Place Viger on rue Saint-Antoine in August 1898. A brochure stressed the "historic associations which cling to this spot." As the palatial CPR cars carried them into the mammoth station, or while they dined on "delicacies from the most distant parts of the earth," guests were urged to reflect on the site's past— as a windmill, "the first industrial building in Montreal," or as La citadelle, "filled with memories which will be immortal as long as courage and stout-heartedness are honored."

More likely, guests focussed simply on the enjoyment of strolling through the Viger Gardens, past mature trees, walkways, ornamental fountains and a bandstand where the regimental bands of the British garrison played on occasion; or of attending the Saturday night "Dinner Dance and Special Orchestra." Close to the financial district, maritime businesses, the Courthouse, City Hall, and Notre-Dame Cathedral, the Place Viger attracted judges, clergy, politicians and the business elite and enjoyed great social prestige—until the 1929 stock market crash.

As the centre of Montreal shifted north-west, the Hotel fell into disrepair. In 1935 it closed its doors, although the station remained open. In 1951, the station also closed and the building was bought by the City of Montreal. The once-gracious interiors were transformed into dreary office spaces. Even the beautiful gardens were destroyed during excavations for the underground Ville Marie Expressway in the early 1970s. What was once a striking complex at the centre of Montreal life is now sadly neglected.

The Ritz-Carlton had such cachet that many Montreal companies, like Murray Hill Taxis Ltd., wanted to promote themselves in association with the hotel. (Opposite page) The main staircase, designed to complement the sweep of a ballgown.

THE RITZ-CARLTON

Montreal, Quebec

Every summer for twenty-seven years, a Manhattan attorney named Harry Minden took his wife Beryl to spend at least two long weekends basking in the "mulled splendour" of their favourite hotel. The Mindens could easily have afforded to stay anywhere, but ever since sampling Montreal's Ritz-Carlton while attending a wedding there, they pronounced it a "bastion of elegance, refinement, and sensibility," and always hurried back. "It's hard to imagine," Minden said just before he died in 1997, "walls that tell more stories, or a better place to stay."

Many agree. The Ritz, "The Grande Dame of Sherbrooke Street"—which was hurriedly opened on New Year's Eve, 1912 so as to avoid seeking business in a year that contained "13"—is widely recognized as an impeccably preserved example of a gracious hostelry in the old-world, European tradition. Through good years and bad, its immaculate doormen have doffed their hats to a veritable kaleidoscope of celebrities who came from afar.

Many were heads of state: Britain's Stanley Baldwin and Anthony Eden, Israel's Golda Meir, France's Charles de Gaulle and the Shah of Iran. Once, Prince Philip dropped into the Café de Paris, the main dining room. "I like this place," he told a manager, "I'd say you are running one of the really few good hotels left." Few, however, were more convinced of this than Quebec's long-serving premier, Maurice Duplessis. Waiters often helped Duplessis break one of his very own laws by allowing him to drink alcohol there on Sundays without ordering a meal! They discreetly hid him from public view with a screen kept handy for that very purpose.

THE RITZ-CARLTON

Location: 1228 Sherbrooke Street West, Montreal, Quebec

1912: Opened December 31

Initial Owners: The Ritz-Carlton Hotel Co.

Architects: Whitney Warren & Charles Wetmore (in collaboration with Fred Garfield Robb)

Style: Beaux-Arts

Principal Materials: Limestone with terra cotta trimmings

Number of rooms when opened: 261

Number of storeys when opened: 10

1957: Addition by Gratton D. Thompson

Prominent Guests: Mary Pickford and Douglas Fairbanks, Richard Burton and Elizabeth Taylor, Gina Lollobrigida

Named After: César Ritz, who had opened the acclaimed Ritz Hotel in Paris in 1898. He endorsed the Montreal hotel but insisted on numerous stipulations for its layout and management. The Carlton component of the name was derived from London's prestigious Carlton Hotel.

The Ritz-Carlton had touring cars to shuttle American guests and their luggage to the river boats berthed at Lachine.

Indeed, beneath the Ritz's formal facade an informal, sometimes eccentric character prevailed. One executive chef, Pierre Demers, winner of eight Culinary Olympic gold medals, often allowed guests—including the Mindens—to watch him prepare their dinners in the Ritz's cavernous, white-tiled kitchen and, for many years, the staff maintained a shed for guests' pets near the hotel's back door. This was once known to accommodate six dogs, four cats, a hamster—and a parakeet that had been making a nuisance of itself on the mezzanine.

Actress Elizabeth Taylor, a hard-to-please connoisseur of fine hotels, loved the Ritz-Carlton, too. She married Richard Burton there in 1964, recruiting the room service manager to witness the ceremony. Not long after that, the management fitted the Royal Suite with saucepans so that actress Sophia Loren, who was filming in Montreal, could cook her own pasta. "Believe me," she told the housekeeper, "this is no ordinary hotel."

It never was "ordinary." House detectives have babysat and porters have escorted guests to railway stations. One story goes that a long-serving doorman

(Left) The Ritz-Carlton—
a symbol of early 20th century elegance on Sherbrooke
Street. Architects Warren &
Wetmore of New York were
considered specialists in the
Beaux-Arts style.

known only as Jamieson was placing a woman's luggage on the overhead rack of her New York-bound train when it suddenly started off. He disembarked at the next station and returned to the hotel by taxi. "Where in heaven's name have you been?" the head porter asked him. "You've been gone more than an hour!" "Doing my job," Jamieson replied, and nothing more was ever said about the incident.

The Ritz was the dream of a group of investors who lamented that their city lacked a hotel to cater to the caviar-and-champagne tastes that they shared with the city's European visitors. So, in 1910, they decided to build one. They first bought a plot of land near McGill University from tobacco magnate Sir William Macdonald, but the idea drew a flood of protest against the "proposed desecration of scholastic sanctity." The matter was resolved with the diplomacy and aplomb that has always been a Ritz-Carlton trait—the investors, who included Sir Herbert Holt and Sir Charles Gordon, promptly sold back the land for the price they had

(Left) The elegant Dutch Garden, later called the Ritz Garden. (Inset) Feeding the ducks at the Ritz Garden pond. Predictably, many of the birds died of indigestion!

paid for it, before settling quietly on the hotel's present site at Sherbrooke and Drum-mond Streets.

At first, the men planned to name their venture after London's prestigious Carlton Hotel. Then, one of them, Charles Hosmer, founder of Canadian Pacific Telegrams, mentioned César Ritz, a former Swiss shepherd who in 1898 had opened a hotel in Paris that had quickly been acclaimed as one of the very best. Hosmer convinced his colleagues that his friend Ritz's name would guarantee instant good fortune.

César Ritz agreed to endorse the Montreal venture, but in exchange for a $25,000 fee and a barrage of conditions. All rooms, he said, needed bathrooms and telephones, and there had to be a kitchen on each floor so that room-service meals—"unspoiled by strong sauces"—could be served course by course, and hot. Ritz also stipulated a round-the-clock valet to clean shoes, and a head porter to trace lost luggage, order theatre tickets and cabs, and give directions. He was just as adamant that the Ritz-Carlton lobby should be small enough to be intimate, yet have a wide, curving staircase from the mezzanine to the lobby so that, on special occasions, women could make dramatic entrances that showed their gowns to full effect.

One such occasion was the 1912 opening, when the $3-million hotel attracted one of the decade's biggest social gatherings. Crowds gathered to admire a building that had been designed by architects Warren & Wetmore of New York City and Fred Garfield of Montreal. "Externally," reported *The Montreal Gazette*, "the general appearance is a masterpiece of refinement and dignity." So was the interior. On that opening night, nearly four hundred socialites crowded under the ballroom chandeliers for a banquet, their gaiety silenced only at midnight by the roll of drums announcing "God Save the King" and "O,

(Right) Posing outside the Ritz-Carlton. (Inset) Canada's fur business was based in Montreal, and furriers were regular advertisers in the hotel's pamphlet for guests.

Canada." The next morning—January 1, 1913—the Ritz-Carlton opened to the public.

The new hotel soon attracted a slew of patrons, many of whom stayed around for years. Men like black-bearded Sir Frederick Williams-Taylor, president of the Bank of Montreal, and shipping magnate Sir Montagu Allan, donor of amateur hockey's Allan Cup, lunched in the Oak Room, dined in the Oval Room, and sipped "Le five o'clock tea" in the Palm Court. In those days, about two-thirds of the guests who slept there did so permanently—for example Sir Frederick Williams-Taylor and Hugh MacKay, a director of Montreal Light, Heat & Power. Indeed, many residents moved in with their paintings and furniture, and treated the hotel as a private club where they could entertain in style.

One early resident was a woman who sailed from Liverpool, England, to spend a month's vacation in the hotel. "How long will Madame be staying?" the desk clerk asked her. "I'll let you know," she said, and was still there some twenty-three years later.

Another permanent guest was Alphonse Jongers, a Basque portrait painter who took rooms 901 and 902 and became better known for his amorous pursuits than his pictures. Jongers—and the woman from Liverpool—lived good lives at the Ritz-Carlton, and both died there, in their beds.

All who entered, meanwhile, admired the elevator boys' smart blue uniforms, the cloakroom attendants' satin knee-breeches, the doormen's brown bearskin hats, and the punctilio of the first manager, a Prussian named Rudolf Bischoff who resigned on the outbreak of World War I because, he confessed, he was embarrassed by being "an alien."

After that, other managers came and went, but each left his mark. Bischoff's immediate successor was a rotund Englishman named Frank Quick—"Humpty Dumpty," guests called him—who was "borrowed" from the Canadian Pacific Railway Hotel Company during World War I to help the Ritz survive in tough times. He complained that

The Ritz-Carlton was chosen as the site for the first transcontinental telephone call. It was made from the Ritz's ballroom to Vancouver on February 14, 1916, by Bell Telephone's president, C. F. Sise.

prospective employees were hard to find because too many of them were serving Canada overseas, but he nonetheless prepared the hotel for better days by teaching women workers how to curtsy, and the men how to bow.

In 1924, Quick was replaced by Emile Charles des Baillets, a gaunt, fearsome-looking Swiss who stood six-feet-three inches tall and sported a huge, shovel-shaped beard that earned him the nickname "Rasputin." His disciplined stewardship saw the hotel become so internationally revered that the Prince of Wales made the first of five visits to the Royal Suite. Romania's Queen Marie later stayed there, too. Just before Prince Takamatsu, the Emperor of Japan's brother, arrived to spend his honeymoon in the suite, the housekeeper scurried down to Morgan's Department Store to borrow a complete set of Oriental furnishings to make the hotel's first Asian visitor welcome.

Also in the 1920s, crowds waited outside the hotel to glimpse other celebrated guests, including Mary Pickford and Douglas Fairbanks, "sweethearts of the silent movies," who performed the un-Ritz-like act of climbing from a window onto the hotel's glass parapet to acknowledge the crowd. "And while all this nonsense was going on outside," a horrified doorman complained, "dear Madame Amelita Galli-Curci, one of the greatest opera sopranos of our age, no less, was standing in the lobby completely unnoticed! Can you imagine it?"

(Left) Elevator attendants, 1940s. (Below) One of the Ritz-Carlton's directors, Elwood Hosmer, was known as "The Grey Ghost of the Ritz," as he was ever-present in the Palm Court, engrossed in crossword puzzles.

In the late 1920s, the Ritz fell on hard times. Many guests, unable to pay their bills when their incomes dwindled in the stock market crash, moved out. The Ritz was forced to close more than half its rooms and cover furniture in dust sheets. Among those directors who dug deeply into their own pockets to keep the hotel afloat was Elwood Hosmer, a scrawny man known as "The Grey Ghost of the Ritz," who had inherited his father's shares in the business, but not, by any stretch of the imagination, his same desire for success. Elwood was usually to be found engrossed in crossword puzzles in the Palm Court, drinking gin, smoking cigars and deterring others from entering. During Saturday lunch, a three-hour ritual for those who could still afford it, his loud, complaining voice echoed up to the mezzanine: "How long are these wretched women staying? Will someone please get them out of here?"

Dignity had to triumph, though, even in the worst of times. Thus the lean, gaunt des Baillets was often seen ridding the sidewalk outside the Ritz of prostitutes—"Shoo! Get away! You are not welcome here!" And about this time a bankrupt businessman leapt to his death from an eighth-floor bathroom window, not, however, before presenting the cashier with a box of fine chocolates.

Des Baillets left the Ritz in 1940, when hotel prices were frozen on account of World War II. Another Swiss, Albert Frossard, took over and battled hard to maintain standards despite falling profits. He reluctantly relaxed the custom of asking guests to "dress" for dinner so that ordinary people could also enjoy the establishment. Fortunately, many did.

In the late 1950s, a new manager, French-born Jean Contat, impressed on the staff the importance of remembering guests' names and preferences for specific meals and rooms. He ordered the housekeeper to buy a complete set of softer bed sheets for

(Above) General Manager Jean Contat began his career as a waiter at the Ritz, both in London and Paris.

a woman who complained the ones the hotel normally used were too "hard," and insisted that the cloakroom staff memorize which hats and coats belonged to which guests or visitors.

Not long after that, a night manager spotted the young and boisterous Rolling Stones entering the Café de Paris without ties and asked them—politely, of course—to return to their rooms to "dress properly." Since then, the rule that ties must be worn at dinner has been relaxed, but to this day regular Café de Paris diners still prefer to see men in jackets.

Notable additions to the hotel under Contat were a new sixty-room wing abutting Mountain Street, and the Ritz Garden, where patrons could lunch and dine in summer. It fell to Contat's wife, Yvonne, to stock the garden's pond with twenty-four ducklings she bought from a local farmer, but there were unforeseen difficulties. The first batch of birds turned out to be a non-swimming variety —one by one, they keeled over and drowned.

Like his predecessors, Contat had fastidious eyes that were easily offended. One day he was dismayed to see a bespectacled man standing in the lobby in a frayed jacket and maroon carpet slippers. "I do not want to see that kind of person around here again!" he hissed at the front desk manager "Order him out—at once!" "We can't, Mr. Contat," the manager replied. "The man you speak of is our very esteemed Mr. Howard Hughes." The eccentric billionaire had rented half the eighth floor at the Ritz to house a retinue that comprised six bodyguards, three private detectives, eight financial advisors, two valets, three butlers, a barber and a chemist whose job it was to make sure the Ritz did not poison his food.

In the mid-1960s, during widespread renovations, the hotel's 247 guest rooms and suites, plus its 12 banquet and conference rooms, were refurbished in the grandiose style of Louis XIV. Appropriately, the work was done by the same French designer who had sumptuously redecorated the Hôtel de Paris in Monte Carlo and the homes of the Aga Khan and the Baron de Rothschild. Renovations, which ended by costing some $10 million and continued well into the 1970s, carefully preserved much of the hotel's original interior: big fireplaces and high, embossed ceilings and an abundance of gleaming brass. In 1980, the black-gold lobby and the Ritz Garden were temporarily transformed to resemble New York City's luxurious Russian Tea Room as part of the setting for the movie, *Dreamworld.*

Times have changed at the Ritz-Carlton, but thanks to more recent managers, dignity and good taste continue to prevail. The hotel's furniture, much of it antique, has never been profaned by varnish, and every afternoon the steward's staff hand-polishes more than three hundred pieces of silverware, including a huge, egg-shaped roast beef trolley that dates back to the hotel's beginnings. Not only that, manager Carel Folkersma and the current owner, Sheik Abdullaziz Abdallash Al-Sulaman of Saudi Arabia, recently ordered the Palm Court restored to the way it was when, to the dismay of the front lobby staff, Elwood Hosmer had made it his home away from home.

Such detail and care have won the Ritz-Carlton a reputation it protects with zeal. Maintaining it, staffers have always recalled, meant doing the littlest things for the biggest people without even thinking about them—walking Zsa Zsa Gabor's dog, cooking three double-size sirloins for the gargantuan Soviet weightlifter, Vasily Alekseyev, and moving the grand piano from the Café de Paris into pianist Arthur Rubinstein's suite so he could practice there before a concert.

One day, Queen Elizabeth unexpectedly dropped by to relax before a gala, and had to be ushered into room 310 because entertainer Liberace was enjoying a bubble bath in the Royal Suite. But it mattered not. "Wherever you end up at the Ritz," a visiting journalist once wrote, "service is always such a leisurely, loving, handcrafted thing that is always so extravagant of steps and time." Those far-sighted investors who envisioned a world-class hotel in the tradition of the very, very best, would be eminently proud of it today.

(Above) Prime Minister Louis St. Laurent welcomes a debutante to Le bal des petits souliers, a ball which raised money to buy shoes for under-privileged children. For years, the ball launched Montreal's social season.

(Left) Montreal rabbis inaugurate the Ritz-Carlton's kosher kitchen in November 1971. The kitchen was designed to cater both occasional meals and banquets.

The Mount Royal rotunda looking south, 1923. In the 1980s, the hotel was completely transformed into Les Cours Mont-Royal, a complex of boutiques, restaurants, offices, residential condominiums and a cinema. All the hotel rooms disappeared, including a ballroom that could hold 2,000 people. What remains is a fragment of the coffered ceiling pictured here.

MOUNT ROYAL HOTEL

Montreal, Quebec

If you were a tycoon or a prime minister arriving in Montreal in the 1940s or 1950s in your private railway car, you would surely stay at the venerable Windsor Hotel, just up the street from Windsor Station. If you were a British aristocrat, arriving in an ocean liner, you would probably head straight for the Ritz-Carlton. But if you were a show business personality, flying in from New York on a DC4 Skycruiser, you'd check in at the much livelier Mount Royal, a hotel where the music was more rumba than waltz.

As the newest of Montreal's leading hotels, the Mount Royal was very much aviation-centred. Trans-Canada Air Lines had its ticket office in the lobby and the Colonial Airlines terminal was a stone's throw away on Peel Street. During the war, the hotel's busiest bar, the Piccadilly Lounge—known far and wide as "the Pic"—was the unofficial headquarters of pilots of the Royal Air Force Ferry Command. Here, between flights to Europe, where they delivered new bombers from the factories to the war fronts, these daring young men would sip their rye and ginger ale while competing for the attention of attractive young women.

Even back in the days when pilots were called aviators, airmen favoured the Mount Royal. The most famous was General Italo Balbo, who arrived in 1933. Up until then, only a few solitary adventurers had survived attempts to fly across the Atlantic from east to west. But here was General Balbo, from Rome, swooping down onto the St. Lawrence River with his "air armada" of 24 Italian military seaplanes. Cheered by an enormous

The Mount Royal Hotel, 1923. When it opened in 1922, it was billed as "the biggest hotel in the British Empire." When Toronto's Royal York succeeded to this title in 1929, the Mount Royal immediately changed its slogan to "the finest hotel in the British Empire."

MOUNT ROYAL HOTEL

Location: 1455 Peel St., Montreal, Quebec

1922: Opened December 20

Initial Owner: United Hotel Company of America

Architects: George Ross and R.H. Macdonald

Style: Beaux-Arts

Principal Materials: Stone base, brick

Number of rooms when opened: 1046

1984: Closed

Prominent Guests: William Lyon Mackenzie King, Camillien Houde, David Lloyd George, Prince of Wales (later King Edward VIII), Frank Sinatra

Named After: The mountain which is located in the city

crowd and escorted by Montreal Fascists in their black shirts, Balbo swept into the Mount Royal Hotel, where two whole floors had been reserved for his crew. After a few minutes in his suite, the phone rang and the hotel operator asked if he would take a call from Rome. Of course he would. It was Mussolini, calling to congratulate him.

The Mount Royal opened on December 20, 1922. Among the twelve hundred distinguished guests at the opening ceremonies were Prime Minister Mackenzie King, Baron Shaughnessy, Sir Arthur Currie, Sir Frederick Williams Taylor, Sir Henry Thornton and Sir Lomer Gouin—in those days, Canadians could still bear British titles. During the opening ceremonies Frank Dudley, president of United Hotels of America and owner of the new hotel, handed the golden key to the front door to Vernon Cardy, its first manager. Cardy was only thirty years old, but he already had considerable hotel experience, including a stint at the Ritz-Carlton, where, as a youth doing menial tasks, he had earned a dollar a day plus meals.

The hotel Cardy now presided over had 1,046 rooms, including luxury suites such as the Queen Anne and the Louis XIV. The decor was opulent. Visitors on opening day marvelled at the elegant bars, restaurants and ballrooms, one of which could accommodate two thousand. The hotel's kitchens could serve 2,500 at the same time; its lobby was said to be the largest room in Canada. Someone calculated that the bedsheets, laid end to end, would stretch 111 miles. There were abundant meeting rooms, shops and an indoor golf school. The presence of a medical clinic led the *Montreal Star* to observe that in this hotel "one might be born, pass an eventful life and shuffle off the mortal coil right on the premises."

In the booming 1920s, Montreal was incontestably the richest city in Canada, and the Mount Royal was close to the city's heart—the busy Peel and St. Catherine intersection, often called the crossroads of Canada. Nearby were the big department stores, movie palaces, fancy restaurants and nightclubs, a good selection of the city's many illegal gambling dens, and some "blind pigs," bars where one could drink after the 2:00 a.m. closing time. When the bar in the Mount Royal closed, patrons had only to stagger across Peel Street to where the all-night Cadillac Restaurant would serve booze in teacups. Amenities like these made Montreal a mecca for visitors from the United States, where prohibition was in force, or for those fleeing the puritan provinces of Canada.

(Above) Corner at end of Main Dining Room, 1923. (Left) Dining room

The new Mount Royal was billed as "the biggest hotel in the British Empire." When Toronto's Royal York succeeded to this title in 1929, the Mount Royal immediately changed its slogan to "the finest hotel in the British Empire." The hotel's appeal soon became evident. In 1923, Montrealers were surprised to find David Lloyd George, the British prime minister, checking in at the lively Mount Royal rather than the more sedate Windsor or Ritz. A later guest was Lord Renfrew, this being the name used by the Prince of Wales when travelling incognito. The young prince danced late into the night in the Piazza Room, where he pronounced Joseph C. Smith's orchestra to be the best dance band he had ever encountered.

The Piazza Room, where the prince danced in 1923, would later become the Normandie Roof, after the French Line's *Normandie*, the most luxurious of transatlantic ocean liners. The Normandie Roof, atop the hotel, soon became one of the continent's best-known supper clubs. There, Montreal's smart set would assemble to dine, dance and be entertained. Flashbulbs would pop as a photographer circulated through the room. Out-of-towners often bought these snapshots as cherished souvenirs of their sojourn in sophisticated Montreal. If a gentleman gave the photographer five dollars not to take a picture, you could be sure that his female companion was not his wife.

Even during the hard days of the Depression, the Normandie Roof had enough moneyed patrons for it to import American big bands (Paul Whiteman, the King of Jazz, played there, as did Rudy Vallee and his Connecticut Yankees), comedians like Billy de Wolfe and dancers like Gower and Champion. Later, when Jack Denny's Orchestra held sway, its music was broadcast on the radio across Canada on Saturday nights.

(Above) The Mount Royal's ornate entranceway. Note the display case filled with fine china.

Downstairs, in the elegant Palm Court, *le tout Montréal* would turn out for the English afternoon tea—served in cups of delicate china, with little cucumber sandwiches and dainty pastries. By contrast, during the war, the basement became the site of the rowdy Music Box, where servicemen gathered to drink, insult each other and fight over girls. The pitched battles became so destructive that the Music Box eventually had to be closed.

Another institution in the basement, the Montreal Men's Press Club, was only marginally better behaved. On its thirtieth anniversary, in 1978, its founding president could look back: "The club's history is blemished by a few (quite a few) raucous arguments, fisticuffs and suspensions, though it is a happy circumstance that not a single murder has occurred." In those hard-drinking, sexist years before women could join the club, this big room in the basement, with its long-running poker game, was the principal resort of Montreal's newspaper and public relations men, both English and French.

No detail was too small to escape the attention of the Mount Royal's manager. Each morning, guests would be impressed by the sight of the bellboys, lined up like soldiers in the lobby while Vernon Cardy inspected their uniforms, hair and fingernails. In securing the services of the suave Victor, as maitre d' for the Normandie Roof, Cardy assured himself he had engaged the best in the business. And Cardy had a keen eye for public relations. There was one guest who never paid his bill, but Cardy left instructions that the man was never to be bothered about that detail. The guest was Camillien Houde, the flamboyant mayor of Montreal, whose presence was seen as a major drawing card. The mayor lived in the hotel for several years—until his arrest by the RCMP in 1940 for having advised Montrealers not to register for possible war service, as required by Ottawa. For this treasonous act he was obliged to give up the exquisite soufflés of the Mount Royal's chefs for the pork-and-beans of an internment camp.

Cardy eventually assembled a group of shareholders to wrest control of the hotel from its original founders. Thus began the Cardy Hotels chain, which encompassed seven major Canadian hotels by 1939. In 1950 Cardy sold the Mount Royal to the Sheraton Corporation.

For the Sheraton-Mount Royal, the prosperous 1950s were, in the words of a French writer, *"les années de gloire pour la grande dame de la rue Peel."* The Normandie Roof moved downstairs and became the Normandie Room, which now featured singing stars from Paris like Charles Trenet, Gilbert Bécaud and Patachou. In 1959, Montrealers' new appetite for exotic food was recognized when the hotel's main dining room became the Polynesian Kon-Tiki. There, for the first time, patrons encountered cocktails adorned with little paper umbrellas. The hotel mounted fashion shows twice a week and distinguished guests kept coming to stay, among them Frank Sinatra, Bing Crosby, Jerry Lewis and Andy Williams.

But the next few decades saw the slow decline of the Mount Royal, as a new generation of big hotels arose in downtown Montreal. By the early 1980s, room occupancy seldom exceeded thirty percent. The hotel was losing money and eventually it was compelled to close.

On November 29, 1984, there were long lineups outside the doors of the Mount Royal. Everything inside was for sale, including the giant chandelier bought 62 years earlier from a casino on the French Riviera. You could get the original 1922 pine panelling from the Salle Dorée for $11,000. Seventy-eight thousand dollars bought the entire contents of the Kon-Tiki, including six carved Polynesian outrigger canoes. But ordinary people who just wanted a souvenir of this Montreal landmark could buy two water glasses for a dollar or, for $1.50, take home a towel marked "Mount Royal Hotel."

(Above) Coming out party for Anna and Ruth Cowans at the Normandie Roof, c.1920s. The Normandie Roof was where Montreal's smart set would assemble to dine, dance and be entertained. (Below) Normandie Roof, New Year's 1939.

*John Lennon and Yoko Ono during their week-long bed-in at the Queen Elizabeth Hotel in May 1969.
From their 17th-floor suite, they preached world peace and recorded the song, "Give Peace a Chance."*

QUEEN ELIZABETH HOTEL

Montreal, Quebec

Montrealers could not remember festivities more lavish, a social whirl more dizzying. During three days in April 1958, there were lunches, dinners, cocktail parties, flag raisings, speeches and a charity ball where high society danced to the music of Guy Lombardo and his orchestra. Special trains and planes brought distinguished guests to attend the ceremonies and the frolics. The occasion: the opening of the new Queen Elizabeth Hotel—an event that was emblematic of the city's growth and optimism in the 1950s.

Journalists covering the opening of the Queen Elizabeth were given a sixty-page press kit that extolled the comforts of this enormous new hotel. Built by Canadian National Railways and managed by the Hilton chain, the "Queen E" was 21 storeys high and had 1,216 guest rooms. This made it the biggest hotel in the Commonwealth and the biggest new hotel in the world. It was also the first major hotel especially designed to accommodate conventions.

Because the Queen E was linked to the Hilton Hotels' international convention circuit, it could expect to host major conventions that had never before considered coming to Montreal. Thousands of conventioneers, from dozens of countries, would boost business in the downtown area, which was being rapidly transformed by a building boom. From the start, the Queen E displayed great versatility. It operated all the bars and restaurants in mammoth 42-storey Place Ville Marie across the street, and in the underground city beneath it. Steaks were offered at the Stampede, seafood at the Bluenose, French cuisine at Le Carignan and a variety of menus at other restaurants in the complex.

Built in angular 1950s modern, the Queen E boldly stood apart from the older, more ornate hotels. But it did honour the city's history in its showplace restaurant, the Beaver Club. The original Beaver Club, defunct for a century and a half, had

QUEEN ELIZABETH HOTEL

LE REINE ELIZABETH

Location: 900 boulevard René Lévesque, Montreal, Quebec

1958: Opened in April

Initial Owner: CNR, managed by Hilton Hotels

Architect: G. F. Drummond

Style: Modern

Principal Materials: Concrete

Number of rooms when opened: 1216

Number of storeys when opened: 21

Prominent Guests: Mikhaïl Gorbachev, the Dalai Lama, Perry Como, Liberace, Zsa Zsa Gabor

Named After: Queen Elizabeth II, Britain's reigning monarch since 1952.

Other proposed name: Château Maisonneuve

been founded in 1785 by pioneer Montreal fur traders. To be a member one had to have spent a winter in the hazardous, unmapped Canadian Northwest. Back in Montreal, the fur traders used to consume enormous quantities of alcohol at lavish banquets, often ending up on the floor, paddling imaginary canoes in time to their boatmen's songs. The new Beaver Club of the late 1950s paid homage to this bibulous tradition by introducing the giant "birdbath martini" which contained three ounces of gin. The hotel's manager, Donald Mumford, who brought the idea from New York, was a man with an eye for the smallest detail. So as not to drown the icy gin with vermouth, he made his bartenders perfect a method of lightly spraying on the vermouth with a perfume bottle atomizer.

From the beginning, the hotel staff was almost completely bilingual, and all visitors were greeted with the word *bonjour* and addressed with a few words of French, whether they understood the language or not. Menus, hotel signs and the guest magazine were printed in both languages—something that was far from universal in the Montreal of the 1950s. The hotel was anxious to lay to rest a controversy that had enveloped it while it was being built. When it was announced that the new hotel would be called the Queen Elizabeth, there was a tremendous outcry from Quebec nationalists who felt that Montreal's biggest hotel should have a French name. But Donald Gordon, president of the federally owned CNR, was determined to give it the Queen's name. He was unmoved when the Ligue d'action nationale presented him with a petition containing two hundred thousand signatures, demanding that the hotel be called Le Château Maisonneuve. Even five hundred shouting students hanging his effigy from a lamppost outside his office failed to change his mind.

The Queen E has had to deal with some unusual situations. In 1969, when Montreal was the scene of week-long Grey Cup festivities, a group of Western football fans arrived at the hotel on horseback. The management solved the problem by setting up temporary stables in the underground parking garage. The following year, during the October Crisis, when two dignitaries were kidnapped and others were threatened, the Queen Elizabeth Hotel became an armed bastion when Quebec's Premier Robert Bourassa and his assistants moved in.

But no guests of the Queen Elizabeth ever attracted more attention than did John Lennon and Yoko Ono, who came on May 26, 1969 and stayed for a week in a suite on the 17th floor. On arrival, the newly married Beatle and his wife asked that all the furniture be removed from the bedroom. Only a large mattress was to be installed, and this would be the site of their "bed-in," an event that attracted world-wide attention. From the mattress, John and Yoko, clad in pyjamas, received journalists, TV crews and visitors from far and near, and preached a doctrine of world peace, a highly relevant message during the Vietnam War. And on the last night of their stay, the suite became a makeshift studio where they recorded "Give Peace a Chance," a song that would sell in the millions. Since then, the Queen E's suite 1742 has become a shrine for Beatles fans. Pilgrims come from afar to look in for a few minutes; some have been known to kiss the floor.

(Above) Queen Elizabeth II is shown the dramatic modern developments taking place in Montreal's downtown core in the late 1950s. The biggest new hotel in the world, the Queen Elizabeth was a reflection of the city's growth and optimism. (Left) A Beaver Club dinner, c.1960s. The Beaver Club at the Queen Elizabeth held its annual dinner until 1996.

Promotional drawing of the Château Laurier at the heart of an industri-ous Ottawa, c. 1912. Depicting (left to right): the Parliament Buildings, Post Office, Château Laurier and Central Union Passenger Station. The image also dramatizes the hotel's picturesque location along the Rideau Canal, with the Ottawa River and Gatineau hills in the distance. (Right) Oak panelling was added to the lobby in the 1929 renovations. The bust of Sir Wilfrid Laurier was the work of French sculptor Paul Chevre. Chevre also created the commanding statue of Samuel de Champlain located on Dufferin Terrace outside the Château Frontenac in Quebec City.

CHÂTEAU LAURIER

Ottawa, Ontario

The Château Laurier, the flagship hotel, first for the Grand Trunk Railway, then for Canadian National Railways, was planned as a showpiece for the country. Located along Wellington Street from Parliament Hill, it has witnessed many events of national import. On a sombre February day in 1919, Prime Minister Wilfrid Laurier's funeral cortège filed solemnly past his namesake hotel. When the Parliament Buildings burned in 1916, the Canadian government held a midnight cabinet meeting at the Château, and set up temporary office quarters there. Many parliamentarians have lived at the Laurier, such as Pierre Trudeau before he became prime minister. Through the years, the hotel has hosted innumerable political events. Because the Laurier was across the road from Central Union Passenger Station, it was the place where troops massed before heading off to war and where parades and spontaneous celebrations took place upon their return.

The opening in 1912 was to have been an extravagant affair, but fate intervened to make it anything but. In fact, the celebrations, planned for April, were cancelled altogether. This is because the man most responsible for spearheading the creation of Ottawa's elaborate hotel and rail station, Grand Trunk president Charles Melville Hays, was returning from Europe for the official celebrations on the *Titanic* and failed to survive the disaster. During the memorial service for Hays held in Montreal, the entire Grand Trunk system of railway and steamship lines throughout Canada, the U.S. and Britain halted for five minutes of respectful silence at 11:30 a.m.

CHÂTEAU LAURIER

Location: Wellington Street & Mackenzie Avenue, Ottawa, Ontario

1908-12: Constructed

1912: Opened June 1

Initial Owner: Grand Trunk Railway (later CNR)

Architects: Bradford Lee Gilbert of New York, replaced by Ross and MacFarlane of Montreal

Style: Château and late Gothic exterior detailing

Principal materials: Stanstead granite base, buff Indiana limestone walls

1919: Canadian National Railways took over management

1927-1929: East wing added

Architects: John S. Archibald and John Schofield

1988: Sold to Canadian Pacific Hotels

Prominent Guests: King and Queen of Siam, Emperor Haile Selassie of Ethiopia, Mme. Chiang Kai-shek, Winston Churchill, C.D. Howe, Field Marshall Sir Bernard Montgomery, Charles de Gaulle, Marlene Dietrich, Yousuf Karsh

Named After: Sir Wilfrid Laurier (1841–1919), 7th Prime Minister of Canada, 1896–1911, who supported the sale of lands for the Château Laurier

(Above left) Charles Melville Hays, president of the Grand Trunk Railway, was the counterpart of the CPR's William Van Horne. He envisioned a railway that would span the country, with grand hotels lining the route. (Above right) Hays met his end on the Titanic. He was returning to Canada to open the Grand Trunk's first landmark hotel, the Château Laurier.

Following the tragedy, the Grand Trunk delayed inauguration of the Château Laurier for six weeks. The doors of the hotel and the train station were finally opened—without ceremony—at 7:00 a.m. on June 1. First to sign the guest registry was Wilfrid Laurier, who had furthered the GTR's grandiose plans by persuading his government to authorize the sale of the prestigious site on Major's Hill Park. Laurier, however, may still have felt aggrieved by the previous day's events. He had been given a viewing of a marble bust of himself created by renowned French sculptor, Paul Chevre, that was destined for the centre of the hotel's lobby. But the story goes that prior to the presentation, workmen had dropped the statue, chipping the nose. Greatly displeased, the fastidious prime minister had left in a fit of pique. (The nose was quickly repaired.)

There had been much opposition to locating the GTR hotel in park lands. One newspaper columnist fretted that in public view would be "long, white, woollen underwear (male) dancing drunkenly in the wind, or stiffening in

Funeral procession of Sir Wilfrid Laurier on February 22, 1919. The Château Laurier was draped in black bunting to mourn his passing.

30 degrees below zero weather" and "black stockings that writhed against billowing petticoats of every variety and colour." Even more contentious than the site had been the contract for the building design. In 1907, Hays commissioned New Yorker Bradford Lee Gilbert to design the hotel and station, but a year later, Gilbert was dismissed. (According to one version of events, at the last minute Hays ordered the design plans changed in an effort to economize but the architect refused to be his scapegoat in the ensuing controversy.) The approved design by the Montreal firm of Ross and MacFarlane that took over from Gilbert proved remarkably similar to his. For the exterior, however, the new design successfully combined features of the 16th-century French château with the elegant, vertical lines of the neo-Gothic Parliament Buildings adjacent to the new hotel. Late Gothic turrets and three-pointed gabled dormers in the copper roof created a picturesque silhouette on the Ottawa skyline. The style was so well received that it was repeated in other Grand Trunk hotels, the Fort Garry and the Macdonald.

(Inset) When victory in Europe was declared on May 7, 1945, the city swarmed Confederation Square.

(Above left) "Morning light," Château Laurier, showing the 1929 addition along Mackenzie Avenue. (Above right) Sleighs lining Wellington Street near the Château Laurier, 1914. The Gothic-detailed château style of the Laurier inspired the design of other federal buildings in Ottawa. It soon evolved into a distinctive "national" style of architecture that was used in Canada until after World War II. The steep roofs (effective in shedding snow), the thick, insulating walls and the small windows were deemed well suited to a severe northern climate.

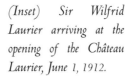

(Inset) Sir Wilfrid Laurier arriving at the opening of the Château Laurier, June 1, 1912.

The Laurier proved immensely popular through the 1920s. In 1929, a new east wing along Mackenzie Avenue opened with 240 more rooms. The wing, which changed the shape of the hotel from an L to a U, easily blended in with the old building—except for the new copper roof. It is said that in an effort to speed the oxidation process, workers were encouraged to urinate into buckets and then pour the contents down the roof.

It was not only the Château Laurier's striking exterior that drew attention. The interior was dignified and elegant. Ottawans took to the new oval dining room in the style of Robert Adam (now the Adam Room) and to the Empire-style ballroom. Designers added oak panelling to the lobby to give it a baronial solidity. Above, on the lobby's stone walls, were displayed the heads of moose, elk, buffalo, caribou and mountain sheep. A moulded plaster ceiling, with a design of grapes and vines signifying prosperity, completed the impressive space.

Bunting to celebrate the anniversary of Canada's Confederation on July 1, 1927. The Château hosted a celebratory dinner and concert at which the Château Laurier Orchestra played music composed for the event by Governor General Lord Willingdon.

(Top) The ironing room (Above) Yousuf Karsh's portrait of John Helders, Headwaiter of the Grill Room. Karsh opened a studio on the 6th floor of the Château Laurier in 1973 and kept it for almost 20 years.

Despite the auspicious symbols on the lobby ceiling, the Château Laurier was forced to close three floors for lack of business when the Depression hit. In an effort to attract tourists and revenue, the City of Ottawa stepped up promotion of its annual winter carnival. The Château Laurier, flanked along its Rideau Canal side with a giant ice slide, was the focal point of the week-long carnival. Special trains brought several thousand people to the city for the world championship snowshoe races. Participants came from as far away as Alaska for the dog derby race that began and ended in front of the Château. In Joan Rankin's *Meet Me at the Château*, R.H. Ayre recalled the 1930 Carnival Ball held at the hotel after the races. A Mrs. Richer, the "woman musher," was Queen of the Ball. Derby winners, St. Godard and his lead dog "Toby," were greeted with applause while the Château Laurier Orchestra played "See the Conquering Hero Come." Governor General Willingdon presented the victor with the Gold Challenge Cup, filled with warm milk for Toby, and a cheque for one thousand dollars. Carnival participants were so exuberant inside the Château that the annual trophy was presented outside thereafter!

The early 1930s also saw the opening of the Château's Hydro and Electro-Therapeutic department. Modelled on the great European spas like Carlsbad, Vichy and Marienbad, its centrepiece was an extravagant 18-metre (60-ft.) Art Deco swimming pool with pale pink Tennessee marble walls and pillars of dark green marble from Arizona. A gallery with a hand-wrought brass railing surrounded the pool, and a Greek fountain graced the far end. Guests could leave the Ottawa winter far behind by plunging into the pool's exotic "emerald green" waters, and afterwards, lounging on luxurious "Palm Beach," a row of chaises longues warmed by "sunlight" emitted from overhead brass lamps. According to the hotel brochure, the lamps "though strong enough to give one the full benefit of sun ray treatment and sunburn, are not in any way injurious to the sight...."

Advertised as the most complete and up-to-date in North America, the health facility offered an astonishing range of services. It included a Turkish Bath with steam room, hot room and scrub room, all finished in mosaic. "Colonic and Plombière Therapy" was available "under the skilful supervision of the head of the department, who obtained his training at Plombière, France." So was hydrotherapy

(for chronic rheumatism), electric therapy (for certain nervous afflictions), a Schnee Bath with electrified water (for arthritis) and a room with a "super-alpine-model ultra-violet ray lamp" (for rickets, polio or kidney and bladder trouble). For relief of high blood pressure, patients lay on a "Nagleschmidt couch," a special electrified table. Even warts and other growths were treated at this therapeutic department, which lasted until after World War II. (In recent years, it has been renovated as a fitness facility.)

Standing close to the Parliament Buildings and the train station, the Château was an important hub during World War II. Military and industrial leaders entered the hotel by a tunnel from Union Station for closed-door discussions on production and armaments. Winston Churchill stayed at the Laurier

The Ballroom, 1933. With its Louis XVI-style decoration, it opened in 1929.

181

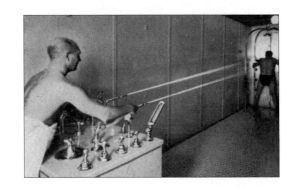

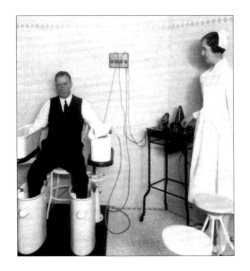

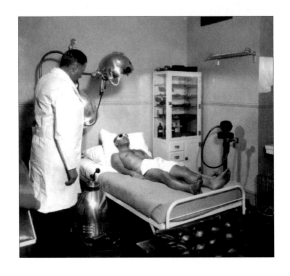

(Top left) Brochures assured patrons that amidst a setting of palms, they could "obtain their quota of tan from the ultra-violet rays overhead," and that the lamps "were not injurious to ...[their] sight."

(Top right) Exercise Room. Notice the man in the background riding a "horse." Presumably, the man in the foreground is toning his midriff.

(Middle left) "The Angel's Stairway," a private golden stair-case between the women's change room and the pool.

(Middle right) "Scotch douche." In a long room with walls and ceiling lined with aluminum, patients received an "electrified water douche." Their spines were sprayed with high-pressure jet streams of alternately hot and cold water.

(Below left) The electrified water of a Schnee Bath was used for treating arthritis.

(Below right) One room was equipped with a "super-alpine-model ultra-violet ray lamp" for people with rickets or polio.

in 1940 while in Ottawa to address Parliament, and again in 1941. Jack Benny and Shirley Temple came to promote War Bonds. Down in the Grill Room, servicemen did their best to forget their cares while dancing to the music of Len Hopkins. Meanwhile, back in the kitchen, hotel chefs struggled to provide memorable meals despite wartime food rationing. It was from the Canadian Broadcasting Corporation's radio studios on the seventh floor of the Laurier that Lorne Greene, "the voice of doom," reported to an anxious nation on the progress of the war. From there, in May 1945, Prime Minister Mackenzie King broadcast the news of victory in Europe, while jubilant Ottawans gathered outside in Confederation Square to celebrate.

Eileen and Grania have had Ultra Violet Ray treatment each winter and have never been sick.

Ottawa was "the stage across which the actors of Canada's destiny have moved through succeeding generations to shape the story of a nation," or so read a Château Laurier brochure. The hotel was, "the place where politics and pleasure, finance and fashion meet...the hub of the Capital's wheel of affairs, a great and worthy centre of Canadian life." It has been dubbed the third chamber of Parliament, and some have quipped that the Commons and the Senate merely approve the bills that have been agreed upon in the Château. The locus of such backroom politics was the lower-level Grill Room, later called the Canadian Grill. Open between 1929 and 1991, it was modelled after an English tap room, with oak plank walls, a low-beamed ceiling, leather banquette seats and deep alcoves that facilitated private discussions. The Grill was a favoured haunt of MPs, senators and business people. Prime Minister Louis St. Laurent was a frequent guest, and Pierre Trudeau and Senator Keith Davey, among others, had their favourite alcoves.

The Château also provided a home away from home for out-of-town parliamentarians and ambassadors. In 1930, Prime Minister R.B. Bennett was offered an opulent suite of rooms at a most favourable rate because of the prestige of having the Prime Minister in residence—an arrangement that did not endear him to Canadians sinking under the weight of the deepening Depression. Pierre Trudeau resided at the Château between 1965 and 1968 while a Member of Parliament and before becoming Prime Minister. Portrait photographer Yousuf Karsh lived in suite 358 with his wife and kept a studio on the sixth floor for almost twenty years. Karsh's first Canadian exhibition was in the Laurier's drawing room.

No one was more aware of the Château's role as a national showpiece than William Aylett, the hotel's manager from

(Above) Extract from brochure (Below) For half an hour every morning and afternoon, manager William Aylett stood steps behind the bust of Wilfrid Laurier in the Château Laurier's lobby to greet guests. Wanting to maintain an elegant appearance, he was in the habit of changing his expensive suits three times a day.

During their 1939 Royal Tour, King George VI and Queen Elizabeth unveiled the War Memorial in Confederation Square on May 21.

the late 1930s to the 1950s. Aylett was a meticulous gentleman who set rigorous standards. An imposing 6'4" tall, he stood in the lobby to greet guests for half an hour every morning and afternoon. In an article in *Maclean's*, Mackenzie Porter relates that in 1954, when Field Marshall Montgomery arrived in Halifax at the start of his Canadian tour, Aylett:

> telephoned the manager of the Nova Scotian to ascertain Montgomery's likes and dislikes. Then he distributed to his staff a bulletin informing them that Montgomery loved roast lamb, mutton chops and cheese; loathed fish; scorned bouillon but enjoyed cream soup; would eat eggs only in an omelette; and wanted his own batman to bring him his early morning tea. Montgomery, not easy to please, was pleased at the Château.

Every effort was made to dazzle hard-to-impress guests. Many of the staff were European-trained, like Master Chef Carlos Scarabelli, who was born in Milan and had experience at the Savoy and Claridges in London, and the Ritz-Carlton in New York. Generations of staff members recall this demand for excellence. Former waiter Danny Lupino remembered maitre d' John Adam:

Mr. Adam was a real disciplinarian. He walked around wearing a tuxedo, with his bow tie tucked under the corners of his collar. He stood beside the checker's desk where the waiters went by with their trays. If the platters weren't red hot, if the Welsh rarebit wasn't bubbling in the chafing dish, if you forgot the parsley with the fish or the watercress for the roast beef, he would order you to go back and do it properly.

A former pantryman, Emile Labranche, recalls that the head waiter, Mr. Siegrist, demanded perfection. Once in 1938, "Siegrist looked at me and said, 'you need a shave.' Although I had already shaved at 11:15 a.m. in order to go on duty at noon, I had to go to the locker room to shave again."

Not surprisingly, staff members have received some idiosyncratic requests over the years, such as Rudolph Nureyev's plea for an extra-large bed on which to practise his dancing. During the 1973 Commonwealth Conference, housekeeping staff had to sew two mattresses together to accommodate the frame of four-hundred-pound King Taufa'ahau Tupou IV of Tonga. And Mme. Chiang Kai-shek, on a tour of Canada to secure aid for China in its fight against Japan in 1943, wanted to use her own satin bed sheets.

Staff had regular access to some of the most important figures in the country. In a 1948 article in the *Montreal Standard*, Robert McKeown tells the story of head barber Paul E. Tasse, who was barber to Prime Minister Mackenzie King, many of his Cabinet members, ambassadors and diplomats, not to mention King George during the 1939 Royal Tour. Sitting in Tasse's chair, a man from England complained that he had not been able to secure a meeting with R.B. Bennett for an entire month and was going to give up and return home. An hour later, Tasse called to say he had lined up an appointment with Bennett. Stories like this are rare, but not because they do not happen. Staff members, protective of their guests, are reluctant to repeat tales—and are accustomed to the extraordinary.

Through the years, the world has walked through the Laurier's lobby doors. The red carpet is regularly rolled out at the Mackenzie Avenue entrance for important dignitaries, but staff, who have seen it all, take these special occasions in stride. Nothing unusual. Just another day.

State dinner in the Château Laurier ballroom for King George VI and Queen Elizabeth hosted by Prime Minister Mackenzie King, May 20, 1939. To the right is Governor General Lord Tweedsmuir. (Below) The Tudor Suite. The Château Laurier had gracious suites like this one, but it also had dormitory accommodation (as did many hotels) for those who could not afford a room.

Although dwarfed by Toronto's downtown towers, the Royal York continues to holds its own. (Inset) When it was built in 1929, the Royal York was the tallest building in the British Empire and dominated Toronto's skyline.

THE ROYAL YORK

Toronto, Ontario

Toronto's Royal York has been dwarfed for several decades by the skyline it once dominated. Opened on June 11, 1929, it was, for a time, one of the largest hotels in the world and the tallest building in the British Empire—claims to which Toronto held with considerable pride. Its massive kitchens and laundries, its roof gardens and cafes, its maintenance shops and dining rooms and dance floors and amenities, to say nothing of its population of 1,300 employees inspired journalists of the day to call the massive hotel "a city within a city."

Until well after World War II, the hotel towered over the city's lesser structures. But eventually that changed. In the last thirty years of the 20th century, at first slowly and then in a boom of construction, Toronto shot skyward. Now, the Royal York's height seems modest—even quaintly old-fashioned—when compared to the spectacular new bank towers and office buildings surrounding it.

And yet, there is a kind of persistence to the Royal York. If you stand on Toronto Island, and look northward across the harbour to the city itself, the Royal York still retains a commanding presence. Amid the flashy and grandiose display of the SkyDome and the Air Canada Centre and despite the impressive skyward reach of neighbouring buildings, an observer's gaze keeps returning to the massive limestone structure. It is solid, certainly—even palatial—and its steep roof makes it instantly recognizable as one of the grand château hotels with which Canadian Pacific marked the links of its railway system and asserted its corporate status across the country.

THE ROYAL YORK

Location: 100 Front Street W., Toronto, Ont.

1929: Opened June 11

Initial Owner: CPR

Architects: George Ross and R.H. Macdonald

Style: Modern Classical (château roof)

Principal Materials: Indiana limestone, granite

Number of rooms when opened: 1100

Number of storeys when opened: 28

1956-59: East wing added by Ross, Townsend, Patterson and Fish

Prominent Guests: Winston Churchill, Mikhaïl Gorbachev, Frank Sinatra, Gloria Swanson, Ella Fitzgerald

Named: To associate the hotel with the history of Toronto. When Governor John Graves Simcoe arrived in the area in 1793, he named the tiny settlement the Royal Town of York.

THE ROYAL·YORK·HOTEL
T O R O N T O
OPENING DATE   JUNE 15th 1929

THE
LARGEST HOTEL
IN THE
BRITISH EMPIRE

CANADIAN PACIFIC

But the Royal York's gravitas comes not only from a matter of tonnage. It is an institution that has stood at the centre of Toronto's social life for so long—and that has, over the years, hosted visitors such as Queen Elizabeth, Winston Churchill, Mikhaïl Gorbachev, Frank Sinatra, Gloria Swanson, and Charles de Gaulle (among dozens of other celebrities and hundreds of thousands of less well-known guests). It can

(Left) In their design for the Royal York, architects Ross and Macdonald placed the copper château roof characteristic of the other important Canadian railway hotels atop a skyscraper. The Royal York was built between 1927 and 1929 on the site of the old Queen's Hotel. (Above) The Royal York opened at the very moment when the affluence of the jazz age was about to be rudely transformed into the hardships of the Dirty Thirties.

(Above) Door staff of the new hotel, 1929. The hotel opened with 1,300 employees. (Right) Royal York entrance, 1930s. Facing Union Station, the Royal York was the first impression of Toronto for many newcomers. The hotel is connected to the station by a tunnel.

afford to remain quietly dignified and architecturally confident that it will not be overlooked.

The Royal York was not always quite so soft-spoken. When it opened, at the end of the Roaring Twenties, there were no signs of the approaching depression, although the crash of 1929 was only a few months away. Prosperity, it seemed, would never end, and the Royal York burst upon the scene with the boisterous "modern-day" pizzazz and ebullient optimism that we still associate with booming economies and soaring stock prices. "Over seventy thousand pieces of table cutlery and flatware will grace the tables of the Royal York," claimed an ad for McGlashan, Clarke silverware. "The very latest marvels of vertical transportation serve the guests of the Royal York," boasted the Otis-Fensom Elevator Company. "Radio Reception in Every Room!" was the unheard-of promise to hotel guests made by the Northern-Electric Company. "Hoover-cleaning will safeguard the fine carpetings of the new Royal York," ran an advertisement that showed a Hoover 108 de luxe in front of the hotel's immediately recognizable facade.

(Above right) Switchboard operators monitored guests' telephone conversations. If discussions contained any impropriety, management was immediately notified. (Above left) This publicity shot shows a modern telephone. (Left) The Royal York's reading library had a collection of over 12,000 books specially chosen by Dr. George Locke, the City of Toronto's chief librarian.

Newspapers of the day fell over themselves to communicate to their readers the splendour of the soaring tower, the vast lobbies, the abundant displays of flowers, the crystal chandeliers, the bustling bellhops and maids, the enormous kitchens, the elaborate switchboard. In the press rooms of Toronto papers, the exclamation marks must have been wearing a little thin by the time the hotel finally opened. Everything was exclamatory. The hotel had cost $16 million! It had employed three thousand workers throughout the year of its construction! The opening of the Royal York was a gala event, for which "the cream of Toronto society" turned out! Toronto was so bug-eyed that even sentences without exclamation marks sounded as if they had them hidden behind the commas. "Tons of caviar and tons of bread, delicacies hitherto associated with continental cosmopolitanism, and equipment unrivalled on the American continent, all met the eye of inspection." Even the infirmary—complete with an emergency operating theatre—promised that any guest whose plans had unluckily been altered by ill-health would be "Sick But Comfortable!"

But the exclamation marks died away and things settled down—rather abruptly, as it turned out. The luxurious, sophisticated, live-for-the-moment lifestyle to which an institution as grand as the Royal York was dedicated seemed frivolous as the Depression wore on. Radio reception in every room suddenly became less important than a meal on every table. Amazingly, the hotel did not close its doors—although there were times

The expansive lobby featured a hand-painted, coffered ceiling. Much has happened here: during the Depression, an eccentric millionaire threw dollar bills over the mezzanine railing; and on one terrible September night in 1949, the lobby was turned into a field hospital for victims of the Noronic fire on the Toronto waterfront. During the "Royal York Revelation" refurbishment in 1972, the original travertine columns were clad in wood, a situation that was reversed in the extensive and costly renovations undertaken between 1988 and 1994. In 2001, a spectacular new marble mosaic tile floor was laid in the lobby. The marble was imported from Italy and Jerusalem and cut into tiny tiles in Montreal. Each piece was placed individually.

(Right) Kitchen serving the English Grill Room and Coffee Shop, 1929. The Royal York's main kitchen is a city block long. (Below) Man standing by coffee urns. When it opened, the hotel featured four different kitchens, a bakery and a pastry room.

when the hard-pressed staff was being paid with little more than tips. It was not uncommon in those uncertain days for businessmen who were often quasi-permanent residents of the hotel to suffer terrible reversals of fortune on the stock market and to sneak out without paying their substantial bills—only to return several months later to settle their account, and be welcomed back by an extremely forgiving staff. Even the eccentric millionaire who seemed to enjoy demonstrating how untouched by the Depression he was by occasionally flinging dollar bills from the hotel's main mezzanine into the lobby, was accepted as simply one of the guests.

That the Royal York survived the transition from abundance to stringency shows how quickly the hotel had become a fixture of Toronto life. This may have had to do with its location. The Queen's Hotel—elegant enough, with its private garden; prominent enough, as headquarters for Toronto's business

and political elite; modern enough, with its innovative hot-air furnace; but too small for Toronto's growing ambitions—had stood on the site before construction began on the Royal York. Toronto's establishment had merely to wait out the year-long interruption of the new hotel's construction and could then return to the palm courts and restaurants at a familiar address. Also, the Royal York stood across the street from Union Station, and so quite naturally took on for visitors the role of gateway to the city. The Royal York was, quite literally, the first glimpse of Toronto afforded to most

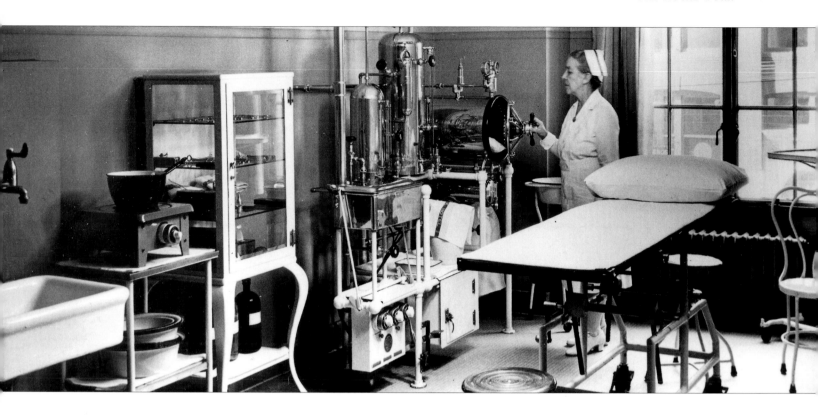

travellers. And an impressive glimpse it was—one to which, to be perfectly frank, the rest of the city did not always measure up.

Indeed, the role of the Royal York has often been to bolster Toronto's image of itself. The fact that Toronto was the site of the British Empire's tallest building and one of the world's most substantial hotels was a source of great civic pride, but it also seemed to surprise the modest citizenry. Really? Torontonians seemed to say. Us? The Royal York's impressive size and its dedication to a kind of hotel life that would later be described by the hackneyed term "world-class" seemed to keep reminding Toronto that it actually was a big metropolis, that it actually was important. After all, the city had a hotel that had ghosts, as all great hotels do. A gentleman in a smoking jacket made periodic appearances on the eighth floor; a woman in a Victorian evening dress was seen wandering the hallways, looking for her room or, if her period costume is authentic, perhaps looking for the old Queen's Hotel. There was the occasional murder—an unfortunate reality for even the very best hotels. And, of course, there have been the kinds of goings-on at that have required the Royal York's bellboys and doormen and desk staff to remain discreet about who was where and with whom. In 1934, in the middle of the night, a sleepy desk clerk was startled when beer magnate John Labatt stumbled into the lobby after surviving a three-day-long kidnapping ordeal. Every now and then, house detectives and

(Above) The Royal York's hospital on the mezzanine floor was complete with an operating theatre. Advertising from the hotel's opening in 1929 called the Royal York "a city within a city block," equipped as it was with its own printing shop, power plant, telephone system, carpentry and upholsterer's shop, and silver replating shop.

193

(Left) Rex Battle and His Royal York Orchestra in the main dining room (later known as the Imperial Room), 1929. (Middle) Engineers in the Royal York radio station. Imperial Room shows were broadcast live on radio across Canada. (Bottom) Advertisement for Connie Towers, appearing in the Imperial Room with Moxie Whitney and his Orchestra.

Toronto police broke up high-stakes poker games in Royal York rooms—tipped off, no doubt, by the clouds of expensive cigar smoke that escaped into the carpeted hallways when gentleman players came and went in the wee small hours. All of which gave the hotel a certain worldly sparkle to which Toronto was not accustomed.

When Toronto's self-confidence sagged, its citizens only needed to drop by the Royal York to be impressed by debutante balls, or by Ella Fitzgerald, backed by the Moxie Whitney band in the Imperial Room, or by the gargoyles, or the roof garden hall, or by the stories of Frank Daly, a doorman who, for many Torontonians, was as much a celebrity as those who he so regularly escorted to and from their limousines. If Toronto felt unsure of itself, it needed only to be reminded of how Alice Cilcus, who joined the hotel in 1941, knew how to point out discreetly to low-flying gentlemen in otherwise immaculate white-tie that they were only "partially dressed"; or of how she managed to operate an elevator without breaching protocol by turning her back on her pretty young passenger—Princess Elizabeth.

The Royal York was grand and sophisticated when Toronto aspired to these adjectives. But there were times when the city wanted something more solid and familiar—most particularly, in the war years. Then, the Royal York somehow managed to shed its image of

newness and became a place that seemed to have always been there. It's hard to believe, but the Royal York was only ten years old when World War II began. But even in so short a time, if a soldier returning home on leave wrote to his girl, "Meet me under the clock," no one needed to be told which clock. During the war, the gold clock in the lobby of the Royal York—built by the Self Winding Clock Company of New York—seemed often, as one wag remarked, to be made of mistletoe, so enthusiastic were the welcome-home greetings offered by girlfriends to returning servicemen.

Debutantes attending a ball at the Royal York, November 9, 1950.

   This wartime spirit continued after the armistice at the Royal York, just as the big band music that had been so popular during the war continued to draw well-dressed couples to the Imperial Room. On September 7, 1949, when the cruise ship *Noronic* caught fire in Toronto Harbour, one hundred people died. Survivors were brought to the Royal York, where the staff turned the lobby into a field hospital and guests gave up their rooms to the injured.

   A new east wing, with seventeen floors and four hundred rooms, was added to the hotel in the late 1950s—a $10 million expansion.

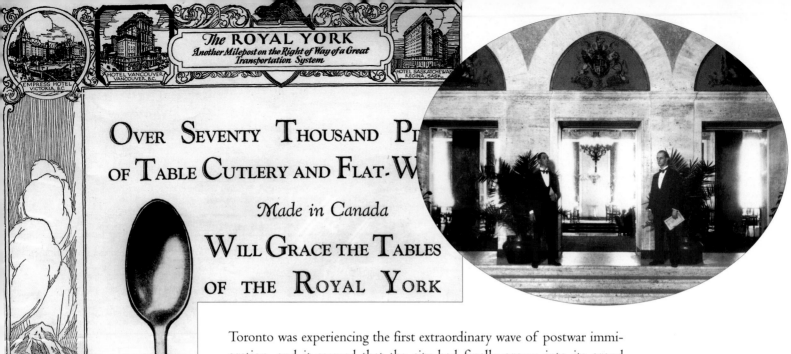

The ROYAL YORK
Another Milepost on the Right of Way of a Great
Transportation System

OVER SEVENTY THOUSAND P[IECES]
OF TABLE CUTLERY AND FLAT-W[ARE]

Made in Canada

WILL GRACE THE TABLES
OF THE ROYAL YORK

*Exclusive
Design
for the
Royal York*

Toronto was experiencing the first extraordinary wave of postwar immigration, and it seemed that the city had finally grown into its grand hotel. Throughout the 1950s and 1960s, the Royal York remained at the centre of civic affairs. Guests arrived for the Royal Winter Fair, Shriners' conventions, the St. Andrew's Ball, the Police Ball, and, of course, for the Grey Cup. The Canadian Football League's championship was always a mixed blessing for the Royal York whenever the game was held in Toronto. The rooms were full, of course—sometimes, as the exuberant parties raged into the wee hours, altogether too full. Spirits were so high that once a horse and cowboy—Western conference fans both—made a memorable entrance into the lobby.

If the hotel ever seemed to lose its way, it was, perhaps, in the 1970s and early 1980s. An uptown shift had taken place. The Four Seasons and the Windsor Arms had become the focal points for a renewed Yorkville and for such new cultural kids on the block as the Toronto Film Festival. In the age of air travel, proximity to Union Station was no longer the advantage it once had been. In 1972, this realignment of Toronto's centre of gravity coincided with what would prove to be an unfortunate renovation, one that seemed wilfully to diminish the grandeur of the original lobby, staircases and hallways. For reasons best known to designers of the seventies, the original travertine pillars were covered and the marble floors were smothered with broadloom. Adding insult to injury, the Imperial Room—an establishment that, only a few years before, had haughtily denied entry to women dressed in fashionable silk cocktail pants—announced that, to "keep up with the times," topless entertainment would be provided. Toronto was appropriately aghast, and, thankfully, it didn't take very long for the hotel to realize that there are times not worth keeping up with. By the early

1990s, a $100-million "face-lift" corrected many of the design mistakes that had been made over the years. An ad of the day announced a return to elegance and refinement. It showed a young couple in evening dress dancing in the Imperial Room to music that their parents and grandparents had probably danced to in their day. Plus ça change....

The Royal York has always had an important place in the heart of Toronto. Its staff were characters of the city as much as of the hotel—bellhop Johnny Ferguson, doorman Frank Daly, chef Marcel Didier, general manager Gordon Cardy and the Imperial Room's maitre d', Louis Jennetta, famous for his memory for names, but almost as famous for one celebrated blooper. (He greeted an Imperial Room guest he had not seen for some years with a confident "Good Evening Mr. Shave. Nice to see you again." The man's name was Razor.)

As the city shifted, it seemed somehow very un-Toronto that the Royal York be left on the periphery of things, and sure enough, Toronto found its way back. Not only Union Station, but a renewed and vibrant neighbourhood at Front and Church Streets, ambitious plans for a vast office and residential district in the railway lands, and the influx of visitors coming to the SkyDome, the Air Canada Centre and the Convention Centre—all these changes have put the Royal York right back where it always had been. Quietly, confidently, traditionally, elegantly, it holds its own in Toronto's new skyline. Today's Royal York is once more in the swing of things.

(Opposite page) Silverware advertisement in Maclean's Magazine, *May 15, 1929. (Inset) The entrance to the main dining room (later called the Imperial Room), 1930s. (Below) Celebrating in the Royal York ballroom.*

The Toronto Press Club Dinner at the King Edward, May 3, 1910

KING EDWARD HOTEL

Toronto, Ontario

It is no accident that the King Edward Hotel sits close to the traditional heart of Toronto's downtown.

A century ago the City of Toronto was facing many of the same problems it faces today, among them, the problem of unbridled growth and its attendant sprawl (minuscule, of course, in comparison to the sprawl we know today). But then, as now, establishing and maintaining a vibrant and focused downtown core was an important objective. The word "density" had not acquired the meaning that city planners give it today; nonetheless, density was the issue. In the last years of the 19th century, Toronto's business class began to worry that the city was spreading itself too thinly to fulfill its ambitions.

The construction of the new (what Torontonians now call the old) City Hall at Bay and Queen Streets—grand as the structure was and as proud as Torontonians were of it—was a worrisome development for an established business-man such as George Gooderham. Gooderham interpreted this as a sign that Toronto was shifting to the west, away from its traditional core, and he feared that if this trend were to continue, his own business—the prestigious Gooderham and Worts distillery, located on the eastern side of Toronto's old commercial centre—would end up on the periphery. Gooderham's fears were to prove prophetic over the long term, but not for his lack of trying to reverse the trend. He believed that what Toronto required was a centre of gravity—a place that would cater to the city's social and business elite and thereby hold the city's commercial centre in orbit.

Businessman George Gooderham hoped the King Eddie would anchor Toronto's social and business elite to the east end of Toronto.

199

KING EDWARD HOTEL

Location: 37 King Street East, Toronto, Ontario

1903: Opened May 11

Initial Owner: Toronto Hotel Company, chairman George Gooderham

Architect: E.J. Lennox

Style: Edwardian Classicism

Principal Materials: Terracotta stone and buff brick

1922: 18-storey tower added, hotel sold to United Hotels Company of America

1975: Designated a historic site

1979: Purchased by Trans National Inc., managed by Trusthouse Forte

1979-81: Closed for 18-month renovation

1985: Purchased by Trusthouse Forte

1998: Owned and managed by Le Royal Meridien King Edward Hotel

Prominent Guests: Rudyard Kipling, Anna Pavlova, Mark Twain, Theodore Roosevelt, Queen Sophia of Spain, Shirley Temple, Elvis, the Beatles, John Lennon & Yoko Ono, Richard Burton and Elizabeth Taylor

Named After: King Edward VII, British monarch from 1901–10

(Above) The American Dining Room. An early hotel brochure described it as being "hung with red silk, and superbly decorated." (Opposite page) When it opened on May 11, 1903, headlines announced the King Edward as Toronto's "new palace hotel."

To this end, George Gooderham—not a man to do anything by halves—spent $6 million to build the King Edward Hotel on King Street, between Yonge and Church. The architect, aptly enough, was E.J. Lennox, the man who had designed the City Hall that had inspired Gooderham's worries in the first place. With great fanfare, the King Edward Hotel opened on May 11, 1903—26 years before what would become its rival, the Royal York, was built. With its vaulted glass dome, marble mosaics, murals, Persian carpets, travertine pillars and palm court, the King Edward Hotel was positively European in its elegant hauteur. Toronto had never seen anything quite so grand. But as far as Gooderham was concerned, its grandness was less important than its location.

As one perceptive journalist of the day commented, the name "King Edward" must refer to "the company she kept," for the gender of the King Street hotel, if not entirely feminine, certainly acknowledged its feminine side more openly than did most Toronto hotels of the day. Hotels, for the most part, were for men—for travellers, for businessmen, for smoky, whisky-pouring, deal-making

The King Edward Hotel
Opened May 11, 1903

delegations of politicians. Moreover, Toronto's commerce was still, in those days, closely linked to the resources of the north, so the city's inns and hotels were accustomed to a not-always absolutely chic clientele. Bush pilots and mining prospectors from the Cobalt gold-rush (and, on occasion, their mules) were frequent guests. The women who did frequent the city's hotels were often not the sort a gentleman would bring home to mother.

The King Edward, however, appeared to understand that in order to gain acceptance as the social headquarters of Toronto's establishment, it would have to appeal to wives, to mothers, to daughters, as much as to the gentlemen who accompanied them. Clearly, its lavish and tasteful decor was aimed at impressing women who simply wanted a place to have tea or, rather less simply, wanted a reception room for a daughter's wedding or a ballroom for a coming-out dance. The velvet draperies, the marble floors, the paintings, the cut flowers, the Irish linens, the blankets from Scotland, the Wedgwood china, the antique statuary, the stained glass domed ceiling and (kept, pointedly enough, in the foyer of the ladies room) the jewel box of Diane de Poitiers, mistress of Henry II of France—all these appointments elicited the admiration of women guests unaccustomed to feeling perfectly at home in a Toronto hotel.

They were made to feel all the more at home by a designated Ladies Entrance. By the mid-20th century, in Toronto, the term "Ladies Entrance"

Canadian National Horse Show Association luncheon, King Edward Hotel, April 1911

would refer to the doorway to the nominally less seedy side of a hotel's "beverage room." But when the King Edward opened, and throughout the hotel's first few decades, the Ladies Entrance was the very height of graciousness and discretion. Ladies travelling on their own could enter the hotel and be ushered to their rooms—on a separate floor—without having to rub shoulders with the men who were staying there. The most churlishly brazen and ill-mannered womanizer and the most beautifully innocent young woman could be staying at the same hotel and never lay eyes on one another. And even the most nervous traveller—male or female— could sleep soundly, knowing that they were staying in "The only Fire-proof Hotel in Toronto." As the guest book boasted: "One could build a bonfire in any apartment and it would remain isolated."

The King Edward's graceful bow to its lady guests was much appreciated, and, sure enough, its appeal to the distaff side of the city's elite ensured that within a remarkably brief period of time, it had become the centre of Toronto's social calendar. The King Edward became the favoured haunt of "old money"—which, like the hotel itself, tended not to be quite as old as it liked to appear. Concerts and parties and private receptions were held in the King Edward. Tea dances were featured in the palm court. Ladies, in need of some rest, or some shopping, or both, found that it was quite acceptable and altogether pleasant to venture southward from Forest Hill or Rosedale to avail themselves of the tea room and the resident manicurist, and then— an unheard-of proposition a generation before—to stay overnight in one of the splendidly appointed rooms. Debutantes were presented in the Crystal Ballroom, and the cream of Toronto's WASP establishment could be seen eating roast beef and Yorkshire pudding on Sundays—after church, of course.

Almost as quickly, discerning travellers—the kind who stayed away from hotels near train stations, or airports, or surrounded by lines of tourist buses—found

their way to the King Edward. The hotel prided itself on providing first-class service to its guests—a boast exemplified by the experience of an Australian visitor. In 1928, a travelling businessman hurriedly consigned a bottle of whisky to the care of the King Eddie's checkroom as he rushed off to an appointment. He ended up forgetting his bottle, but 16 years later, while visiting Toronto again, he remembered it, and, miraculously found the checkroom ticket-stub in his wallet. More miraculously, the bottle was still there, untouched, waiting for its owner to claim it.

The hotel's history and its status in the city are closely associated with the illustrious names that appear in its guest book—the likes of Anna Pavlova, Rudyard Kipling, Mark Twain, Edward, Prince of Wales, Lady Astor, Theodore Roosevelt and Caruso all stayed at the King Edward. There was a night in 1904 when J. Pierpont Morgan and the Archbishop of Canterbury were guests on the same floor. In 1906, Premier Li Hung Chang of China arrived with a retinue of one hundred. The last Premier of Imperial China was not impressed with Toronto's modern transportation system. He insisted on being carried through the city's streets in his four-man litter, as passersby stared in disbelief.

The hotel's most talked-about guests, however, visited at the end of the King Edward's first glory days. The hotel was more or less coasting on its reputation by the 1960s, when Elizabeth Taylor and Richard Burton took up residence in the vice-regal suite. Burton was starring in *Camelot* at the O'Keefe Centre, and he and Taylor stayed for more than two months—a residency that was marked by their tempestuous relationship, and by the fact that this famous couple was not yet married. Toronto was a little more easily shocked in those days than it is now, and the hotel staff had to put up with pickets

The Rotunda's walls featured decorative murals depicting scenes from Canadian history. They were covered by wood panelling in the 1979-81 renovation. Covered by carpet on the Mezzanine are remnants of the original mosaic floor. One of the most wonderful secrets of the King Eddie is the abandoned Crystal Ballroom on its top floor. Few passersby even remember the jewel that lies behind those floor-to-ceiling windows. (Inset) The Buffet. As the King Edward is located in the financial district for the mining industry, promoters, speculators, and even a few prospectors and their burros made their deals at this hotel during the Cobalt mining rush.

Elizabeth Taylor and Richard Burton took a suite at the King Edward during Burton's run of the production Camelot *at the O'Keefe Centre in 1964. The fact that the couple (referred to as "Dicknliz") was unmarried caused quite a stir. A* Toronto Star *article described picketers carrying signs such as "Sin, Evilry, and Damnation," and "Corrupt Not Our Daughters."*

protesting Burton and Taylor's lax morality. In one famous photograph, a smiling Richard Burton dashes past a placard that says, "Sinners." A description, he said, with a wicked Welsh chuckle, which pretty much summed things up.

But if anyone thought the Burton-Taylor stay was a bit of a circus, their concept of three-ring media chaos was redefined when the Beatles stayed at the King Edward. Elizabeth Taylor's ill-trained dogs seemed the height of propriety compared to the obsessed fans of the Fab Four. No one—not the most experienced doorman, the most jaded bellhop, the most proficient maid—had ever seen anything like this. The hotel was besieged by hordes of screaming girls and an army of reporters and photographers. Fearing for the safety of the band, the enterprising hotel security staff brought two dark stretch limousines to the front of the hotel at the hour the Beatles would have to leave for their sold-out concerts at Maple Leaf Gardens. It was a ruse—like something out of a Beatles film, actually. The band left unnoticed from the rear of the hotel, in a paddy wagon.

Elizabeth Taylor and Richard Burton, the Beatles and, later, (post-Beatles) John Lennon and Yoko Ono remain the hotel's most celebrated guests. But the King Edward was in decline by the time they arrived. Faced with increased competition in a rapidly changing city, what was by then the King Edward Sheraton seemed to lose its way. As would be the case at the Royal York almost a decade later, the King Edward, in a series of misguided "renovations," appeared intentionally to cut itself off from the strengths of its past. Unbelievably, the stained glass dome was covered over—painted beige (!) on the inside, covered with tar on the exterior. The elegant cafes and restaurants were turned into dreary bars. A more sophisticated Toronto elite turned their backs on the hotel where their parents and grandparents had dined in such splendour. The King Edward, once the last word in Toronto elegance, was desperately close to becoming a dive. Looking back on those days now, it seems obvious that the hotel had shifted its gender considerably. It had become a much darker, more sombre and more masculine establishment. It was no longer a place for debutante balls and tea dances. Indeed, in the late 1960s and early 1970s, the best thing anyone had to say about the King Edward was that it was the residence of the popular Canadian writer and columnist, Gregory Clark. In his last years, when Greg Clark was confined to a wheelchair, the hotel still had room in its heart for him. When some of his old sporting friends brought him fish they had caught, the hotel's kitchen would always be happy to cook it up.

But then, in the early 1980s, having just barely been missed by the wrecker's ball, the King Edward was given the chance to return to its former glory. Purchased by Trans-National Inc. and operated by Trusthouse Forte—the firm that also managed the Pierre in New York, the George V in Paris and other great hotels—the King Edward closed for the better part of two years, underwent an extremely expensive facelift and, in 1981, re-opened to a Toronto that was no less agog than it had been in 1903 when the King Edward first arrived on the scene. Reports of the final price tag varied widely in the papers: $36 million was the highest guess, $6 million the lowest. Reporters noted that the royal suite—replacing the suite where Liz and Dick had paid the princely sum of $65 a night for accommodation—could be yours for a mere $1,875 a night. But the appeal of the new/old King Edward Hotel was probably best summed up by the distinguished writer and master of Massey College, John Fraser, who could remember being taken to Sunday luncheon at the Victoria Room as a young boy. The Room's intricate moulding, decorative plaster, hand-carved fixtures, tinted glass and plush banquettes made quite an impression. "Two old ladies, or so they seemed to me, were playing piano and violin music amid a forest of palm fronds. I thought it was a fabulous place, but recalling the memory today, the hotel seemed like an ancient relic sliding toward decrepitude." Then, in May 1981, Fraser had a sneak preview of the refurbished hotel. He wrote, "As I staggered around rolled-up carpets, unplaced furniture and a hundred workers deployed in a wild array of last-minute projects, I glimpsed for the first time what the King Edward's founder, George Gooderham, was trying to say to everyone: if you've got the loot this is the place to spend it; if you've got a dream, this is the place to live it."

(Top) Paul McCartney running through the crowd of fans outside the King Edward, September 8, 1964. (Middle) A crowd of 3,500 fans waited outside the hotel for the Beatles to make an appearance. The band was in town to give a concert at Maple Leaf Gardens. (Bottom) Fans tried to sneak into the hotel to see their idols by any means possible; two girls were even reportedly found in the closet of their room despite 30 Toronto police and house detectives assigned to the job.

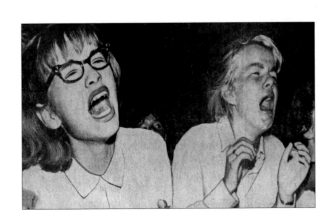

The Royal Alexandra's second dining room, originally known as the Oak Grill and later the Selkirk Room. The room survived the hotel's demolition—it was reassembled on Vancouver Island in the 1990s, after having been stored for over twenty years by the Winnipeg antique dealer and appraiser, Sal Aysan. (Opposite page) The Royal Alexandra, c.1906, was the first grand hotel on the Prairies, and the CPR's first not built in the château style of its earlier railway hotels. Winnipeggers worried about the quality of the neighbourhood and the "sea of mud" one had to wade through to reach the Royal Alexandra's entrance.

THE ROYAL ALEXANDRA

Winnipeg, Manitoba

The completion of the Canadian Pacific Railway in 1885 ushered in a period of major growth on the Prairies. The CPR's active emigration campaigns in Britain enticed waves of immigrants to the region. Winnipeg, near the Prairies' eastern edge, became the gateway to the West. At the turn of the twentieth century, it served as the regional financial centre, and impressive brick office buildings began lining its commercial heart at Portage and Main.

Such an important city needed a grand hotel, and the CPR's decision to build one was another sign that Winnipeg had "made it." Yet, in 1899, instead of considering a hotel location in the centre of town, the CPR proposed a site adjacent to its station in the north end. The north end, objected Winnipeggers, was out of the question. One local official wrote to Thomas Shaughnessy, vice-president of the CPR: "I have heard it discussed by all classes of people and I have not heard one single voice in favour of putting it in the vicinity of the station." He expressed concern that a hotel there could attract neither social functions nor regular boarders. And he was worried about the bar "attracting some of the custom of the neighbourhood which would be of a character that would be decidedly objectionable to the better class patrons of the house." But the CPR forged ahead, building the Royal Alexandra adjacent to the station, with a passageway connecting the two structures.

The CPR at first envisaged a combined railway station and hotel similar in design to the château-style Place Viger Hotel and Station in Montreal (see p. 153). But the CPR changed its plans to reflect the contemporary style in American luxury hotel design. Described by contemporaries as a "quiet, magnificent beauty," the

THE ROYAL ALEXANDRA

Location: NE corner of Main St. & Higgins Ave., Winnipeg, Manitoba

1906: Opened July 19

Initial Owner: CPR

Architects: Edward and W.S. Maxwell

Style: Simple block with Classical details

Principal Materials: Tyndall stone and brick

1910: Addition of two storeys

1967: Closed December 31

1971: Demolished (now a park)

Prominent guests: Edward, Prince of Wales (later King Edward VIII), King George VI & Queen Elizabeth, Queen Elizabeth II, Bob Hope

Named After: Queen Alexandra of Denmark (1844-1925), wife of King Edward VII, reigning British monarch the year the Royal Alexandra opened.

Harold Green's Royal Alexandrians, c.1935

Royal Alexandra eventually emerged as a simple block structure with classical details and a flat roof. For the interior, designer Kate Reed ably captured the elegance of the Edwardian age, creating a space that was welcoming to female and male travellers alike. Silk lined the walls of the Louis XVI-style Vice-Regal Suite. The adjoining Gold Drawing Room, filled with walnut furniture upholstered in gold silk brocade, provided an elegant venue for private receptions or afternoon teas. The impressive Alexandra Room, the main dining room, featured eight massive murals by Frederick Challener depicting Indian lore, with titles like "Indian Sun Dance," "Upper Fort Garry," "Sacred Pipe Stem Dance" and "Buffalo Hunt." In contrast, above the entrance door, there were cast bas-relief copies of Renaissance sculpture.

The neighbourhood had not improved by the time the Royal Alexandra opened in 1906. A *Free Press* article on December 6 of that year commented, "The only drawback to the hotel at this present time is its inharmonious surroundings. None of the buildings of the vicinity are in keeping with it, and the unsightly row of shacks immediately across the street spoils the picture." The surrounding streets were in such bad condition that it was "necessary to wade through a sea of mud to reach the hotel during the stormy weather."

In the 1920s, the Royal Alexandra hosted numerous actors who were appearing on stage at the nearby Pantages and Orpheum theatres. According to

Jocelyn Square, who lived there as a child, many of the stock players resided at the hotel and the management gave them a room for rehearsals. Until post-World War II, the hotel was where Winnipeggers of means partied, dined and danced, and enjoyed good times. Then, airplanes and cars began to pose a major challenge to the railway hotels, which also faced competition from new hotels. The biggest reason for the Royal Alexandra's decline, however, was the one Winnipeggers had been trying to tell Canadian Pacific about since before the hotel was built. It was in the wrong part of town. Unlike other cities such as Vancouver, Winnipeg had failed to develop around the CPR station and hotel. By the early 1960s, the Royal Alexandra was losing money, and the CPR decided to put it up for sale. In 1966 there were rumours of possible purchasers, but these did not materialize and on December 31, 1967, the hotel closed down. In 1969, Swedish interests aired plans to convert it into a residence for the elderly, and in 1970, the hotel re-opened briefly as the centre for Manitoba's centennial celebrations, but early in 1971, Canadian Pacific announced its intention to demolish the Royal Alexandra.

Winnipeggers protested and petitioned—but to no avail. Before the wreckers began demolition, some items were salvaged, including the ballroom's crystal chandelier, which was sent to the Royal York in Toronto. The demolition left a desolate lot that was converted into a public park. It was to have been temporary—but the park remains, unattractive and forlorn, to this day, while the railway station sits unanchored on Higgins Avenue. A back street lost to time.

(Above left) Gold Drawing Room, often used for private receptions or afternoon teas, c.1908. The Royal Alexandra was decorated by Kate Reed, who also designed the interiors of the Château Frontenac, the Place Viger and the Empress. (Above right) Grainmen convention, 1929

Workers sheathing the roof of the Fort Garry Hotel in copper, 1912. By this time, people were accustomed to associating the peaked copper roofs with first-class Canadian hotel accommodation. (Inset) Despite the châteauesque qualities, the Fort Garry perhaps more closely resembled the Plaza in New York City. Like early 20th-century office towers, it had an impressive base, a simple wall treatment and an elaborate roof. (Opposite page) Door handle with Manitoba crest and FG initials.

THE FORT GARRY

Winnipeg, Manitoba

As the Grand Trunk Pacific Railway pushed its line west in the years before World War I, GTP president Charles Melville Hays wanted luxury hotels along its route. In addition to the Château Laurier that was underway in Ottawa, the company began to construct the Fort Garry in Winnipeg in 1911, followed by the Macdonald Hotel in Edmonton two years later. The steep, copper-clad, châteauesque roof of the Fort Garry boldly announced that a new first-class hotel had arrived on the prairies. The roof, and the use of light-coloured Indiana limestone—stylistic elements borrowed from the Laurier—identified the Fort Garry (and the Macdonald) as part of the Grand Trunk's "illustrious" family.

The new hotel's compact form suited the flat spreading prairies beyond the city, and its bold silhouette stood out dramatically on the horizon. The *Winnipeg Free Press* opined, "The Citizens of Winnipeg can look upon this stately building with admiration akin to that of the Greek, who…viewed with pride the Parthenon, the crowning beauty of the Acropolis, and the most beautiful building in the World."

The Fort Garry was located near the recently completed Union Station, which served both the Grand Trunk Pacific and the Canadian Northern railways. In contrast to its Canadian Pacific competitor, the Royal Alexandra, the Fort Garry had the advantage of being located on fashionable Broadway Avenue, close to the impressive Manitoba Legislative buildings and the gate of old Fort Garry, the Hudson's Bay Company post. At some distance from the noise and dirt of Winnipeg's commercial centre, it towered over the neighbouring mansions of Winnipeg's elite, many of whom donned their fur

Fort Garry Hotel on Broadway Avenue, with Union Station in the background. Fort Garry chefs once prepared the meals for all transcontinental trains headed west out of Winnipeg. Hidden tunnels supposedly exist from these years when the hotel supplied the trains.

coats and stoles on December 10, 1913 to head to the social event of the year: the Fort Garry's opening ball hosted by the Victorian Order of Nurses. The extraordinary, two-storey ballroom and banquet hall were situated high up on the seventh floor, giving guests a sweeping vista over city and prairie. The next day's headlines declared the event a "Brilliant Success." The story reported that "Winnipeg's social world was agog, last evening, over the first ball to be given in the sumptuous new Fort Garry hotel…which in elegance of setting, and arrangement, eclipsed anything yet given by this worthy society." It went on to describe the striking gown worn by a Mrs. Cameron, an "exquisite gown of deep violet ninon and rose point lace, bordered with diamante, touches of sable, and diamond ornaments." Most men wore evening dress, although officers from various regiments, "in the full regalia of picturesque uniforms supplied the necessary dash and colour." That night, the Lieutenant-Governor addressed the assembled gathering, "In such a building as this we cannot claim any longer to be pioneers…."

The Palm Room (now the Oval Room), a curved lounge with tall banks of windows through which light streamed in. In the 1970s, this dramatic room had an unfortunate stint as the Drummer Boy Lounge.

Bands performed sedate music for "tea dances" between four and six on weekend afternoons.

(Left) Fort Garry waiters. Waiters stood in line for hand inspection prior to their shift. (Below) Early advertisement promoting Winnipeg and the hotel to the United States. The Fort Garry was the first château-style hotel on the Prairies.

The following day, the general public was invited to view the marvel. That night, a celebratory banquet was held for GTP officials. Upon entering the hotel, guests were first struck by the impressive Rotunda finished in Caen stone with floors of inlaid Napoleon gray marble. It was a welcoming space. The architects had sought "home-like comfort" and claimed that there was not to be a dark or uninviting chamber in the entire building. The wife of the GTP's president, Mrs. T. W. Bergman, who designed the rugs, furniture coverings and colour schemes, also aimed to create a feeling of warmth that would attract per-manent residents to the Fort Garry. Before the hotel's opening, the *Canadian Municipal Journal* reported that "suites of different sizes will tempt those who are tired of housekeeping to avoid its worries."

Since opening night, the Winnipeg landmark has played a role in the city's social life—more intimate than one might have liked on occasion. Apparently, if one sat along the curved wall of the Palm Room lounge, one could hear conversations from across the room quite clearly!

Formal dining took place in the elaborately panelled Provencher Room that stretched the full depth of the main floor. Tea dances were held from four to seven o'clock and featured sedate live music. One group of fashionable Winnipeg ladies, the "Mezzanine Minks," met regularly at such functions. During World War II, Saturday night supper dances in the seventh floor ballroom were the thing.

The Fort Garry in the distance as seen through the doorway of GTP's Union Station, 1914.

With so many men training at the nearby Commonwealth air base, the dances were spirited affairs (although with the War on, liquor could not be served in public, so one had to sneak in one's own bottles.) There was also a rumour that the exclusive Manitoba Club across the street was planning a tunnel link to the hotel, to avoid the winter slush.

Naturally, the Fort Garry also played a role in Manitoba's political life. In fact, the oak master clock in the lobby was synchronized with the Legislature's clock, so that its chimes could summon dining politicians back to the House.

In time, the Fort Garry's glory dimmed. During the 1960s and 1970s, the Rotunda's dramatic marble floor was carpeted; in the 1980s, the lobby was painted blue and pink. A 1979 architectural report says it all:

The heavy Tudor style bar with its rich red oak panelling now functions as the Country Kettle Coffee Shop decorated in a farm-kitchen theme. The oval Palm Room, which would have provided the early 20th century guest with a leisurely luncheon or afternoon tea to the sound of music drifting down from the Musicians' Gallery, has retained all its Adamesque Revival detail although with its conversion to the Drummer Boy Lounge all this delicate ornamentation has been painted over in a dark chocolate brown; the windows have been boarded up and the high domed ceiling has been obscured by brightly coloured streamers.

Fortunately, the seventh floor ballroom and banquet rooms survived the make-over.

With their old hotel out of vogue, its owners began sinking into arrears for hundreds of thousands of dollars in property taxes. In order to protect the building from demolition, the château-style Fort Garry was declared a National Historic Site in 1980. Despite this designation, after the City threatened to seize the Fort Garry in a dispute over the tax arrears, the *Winnipeg Free Press* reported on August 23, 1983:

"Fort Garry Hotel ready for wrecker unless tax relief obtained." The hotel's owners were applying for a demolition permit and threatening to bring in the wreckers in order to exert pressure on the City and get it to help solve their financial woes. Eventually, this prolonged uncertainty led to the Fort Garry's undoing. As companies began cancelling major conventions, the historic hotel faced ruin.

It was finally compelled to close its doors on January 26, 1987. Guests were moved to alternate accommodations and the locks on the hotel were changed. The City took possession of the building, but was unable to find a buyer. The cost of the necessary renovations was prohibitively high at a time when many people doubted that running old hotels was financially viable any longer.

But unlike the Royal Alexandra, the Fort Garry has survived. New owners are once again lavishing attention on the hotel, with renovations designed to respect the building's original look. In the words of one employee, "It's like the sheet was lifted off the building, and it's come to life."

Fort Garry chefs, 1922

Saskatchewan Dairy Association "Annual Ball" F

Saskatchewan Dairy Association annual ball, 1940. "The Hotel" was the scene of many elegant social functions, luncheons and meetings of musical societies, women's clubs, and such service clubs as the Rotary, Kinsmen, Gyro and Lions.

HOTEL SASKATCHEWAN

Regina, Saskatchewan

In the boom years before 1914, the Grand Trunk Pacific Railway began building a grand hotel in Regina, the Château Qu'Appelle. However, the project was abandoned when the outbreak of World War I signalled the start of troubled times (see p. 279). This left Regina, the "Queen City of the Western Plains" and Saskatchewan's capital, still in need of a grand hotel. Finally, in 1927, the Canadian Pacific Railway opened the Hotel Saskatchewan. Affectionately known in Regina as "The Hotel," it very quickly took centre stage.

When planning the building, CPR officials rejected the old GTP site in Wascana Park and chose instead a more central location on Victoria Avenue, facing Victoria Park. General contractors Smith Brothers & Wilson from Regina supervised over 25 sub-contractors. Steel and other building materials from the old GTP site were absorbed into the new building, while the earth removed from the site of the Hotel Saskatchewan was dumped into the ruined basement of the hapless Château Qu'Appelle. Construction ran right through the exceedingly bitter winter. In spite of canvas windbreaks around the work site, temperatures within sank to between minus 20 and 30 degrees Celsius. Before the hotel boilers and furnace could be installed, stonemasons carried around fire pots to keep frost out of the mortar until it set.

Every night for a month after the structure was completed, furniture and fixtures were hauled from the railway station up Scarth St. to the hotel. Much was shipped from Canada's manufacturing centres in Ontario and Montreal: fixtures from the T. Eaton Co., printing type from the

HOTEL SASKATCHEWAN

Location: Victoria Avenue facing Victoria Park, Regina, Sask.

1927: Opened May 23

Initial Owner: Canadian Pacific Railway

Architects: George Ross and R.H. Macdonald

Style: Modern Classical

Principal Materials: Faced in Tyndall stone and brick

Number of storeys when opened: 12

Prominent Guests: Queen Mother, François Mitterand, Harry Belafonte, Liberace, Tommy Douglas

Named After: The province of Saskatchewan (derived from the anglicized Cree word *Kisikatchewan*, meaning "swiftly flowing river."

(Above) One thousand men worked in shifts day and night to complete the Hotel Saskatchewan in less than 11 months. (Above right) The Hotel Saskatchewan's second floor was fitted with sample rooms where commercial travellers brought clients to see the new season's fashions. The upholsterer's shop was on the 11th floor. Apart from repairing rugs and furniture, the upholsterer looked after the beleaguered 12x18-ft. flag atop the hotel, which would sometimes last less than a day before being ripped to shreds by the prairie winds.

Toronto Type Foundry, linens from Dominion Linens in Guelph, and carpets from The Brenton Carpet Co. in Peterborough and the Toronto Carpet Company. Canadian Fairbanks Morse, Ltd. from Montreal set up the telegraph facilities. A few items came from the U.S., such as the towels from the Independent Towel Service in Chicago.

Towering above neighbouring buildings, the hotel's terraced silhouette stood alone on the skyline of the Prairie city. Assessment of the building was mixed. Some called Regina's new landmark hotel regal and opulent; others likened it to a grain elevator. Its design was "modernist classical," the style popular at the time. Ornament was restrained. The lower façade featured a row of arched windows with stone Corinthian pilasters between them surmounted by a stone balustrade. The three lower storeys were faced in Tyndall stone (quarried near Winnipeg and full of beautiful fossil forms) and the nine floors above in grey brick. Stone courses ran along the terraced roofline.

The elaborate interior featured a foyer that ran the entire length of the main floor. The foyer and rotunda had a "Spanish character," with walls treated in antique plaster effect, decorated wood beams and a panelled ceiling. Terrazzo floors and marble thresholds were found throughout. The ceiling in the main dining room had

remarkable hand-painted designs depicting the agriculture, wildlife and fauna of Saskatchewan: the bowl of plenty, wheat, the prairie chicken and wild duck, the whooping crane, Canada goose, prairie wolf, bear, fox—even the gopher.

On May 23, 1927, *The Morning Leader* crowed: "HOTEL SASKATCHEWAN IS READY." The kitchen garnered most attention. Headlines read: "Hotel Saskatchewan has 'Last Word' in Kitchen Equipment"; "Devices Mrs. Regina Never Dreamed of Are to be Seen In Kitchens of New Hotel"; and "There Are Instruments that PEEL VEGETABLES and BOIL EGGS TO THE EXACT SECOND." According to the last story, the vegetable peeler was a pan about ten inches deep, lined with rough stone. One of the forty cooks would have the job of putting the vegetables in the pan, covering them in water and opening the lid after twenty seconds to find the vegetables peeled by a fast spinning motion against the rough stone.

The hotel's opening was occasion for celebration. In preparation, the pastry chef from Lake Louise had spent ten days creating an eighty-pound model of the hotel in sugar. In his address, E.W. Beatty, president of the CPR, hailed the Hotel

(Inset) From the Hotel Saskatchewan one had an unobstructed view of the Legislature, the parks, and the spreading prairie beyond the city.

(Above) Mart Kenney and his Western Gentlemen perform at the hotel, 1934.

as evidence of the "progressive development of Western Canada on a sound and permanent basis." There was good reason for pride. The Hotel Saskatchewan was the province's first grand hotel, and the first grand city hotel built in the West since the Macdonald in Edmonton and the old Hotel Vancouver, constructed during World War I.

The Hotel was designed as a self-contained unit that could operate even if nothing else in Regina was working. Originally, water was pumped from the Hotel's private well in the basement. A refrigeration plant was equipped to manufacture pure—not cloudy—ice and there was a separate steam-driven pump for fire protection purposes. The hotel also had its own steam plant for heating and hot water. Huge boilers in the basement devoured 18 to 29 tonnes of coal a day to produce steam for the power generators that created electrical energy. Porter Norm Brooks recalls that, when they could get away with it, the men who shovelled the coal opened a door into the elevator shaft to release some of the heat—although they well knew this would cook the guests and elevator operators. Even in the days of coal dust, however, the engine room was always kept spotless.

When the hotel converted to gas in the 1950s, a backup diesel motor was installed that is widely rumoured to have been from a German U-boat. However, according to an inquisitive guest, naval historian John Harbron, it was more likely one of the engines of the type used in the CP ships. Either way, to this day, if the hotel's current natural gas system stops working for any reason, the diesel (which

(Right) The library (Below right) Storeroom located below the main kitchen. Estimated amounts of food to be bought at one time included 500 lbs. of turkey, 500 lbs. of chicken, 1,000 lbs. of fish, 1,000 lbs. of beef, 3,000 lbs. of flour, and 1,000 lbs. of sugar.

has enough fuel to run for 36 hours) will kick in within 38 seconds.

Between 1945 and 1984, the Hotel Saskatchewan served as the official residence of the province's Lieutenant Governors. This is because Tommy Douglas's CCF government closed Government House in 1945. It was deemed inappropriate for the Lieutenant Governor to be living in such luxury after the people had just undergone years of depression and war. In 1981, *The Globe and Mail* reported that Lieutenant Governor C. Irwin McIntosh had a modest three-room suite at the Saskatchewan, one room of which was his secretary's office, another a drawing room, and the third, his own office, where he slept on a cot. He also entertained in one of the hotel's larger suites, inviting cabinet ministers along so they would pick up the tab on their departmental budgets.

The moderation shown by her representative did not extend to Elizabeth II. Records at the hotel state that, during her 1978 visit, the Army moved 4.5 tonnes of the Queen's luggage and her retinue took up two entire floors. The Hotel Saskatchewan's protocol for Royalty includes a dry run one month before the visit in which everything is checked and the meals tested, a medical checkup for all food handlers, and security clearance for all staff that come in contact with the Royal retinue. The red carpet is rolled out each time Royalty enters or leaves the hotel, and, while the greeting "Welcome to Regina" is permitted, one may not ask the Queen any questions that require an answer. On hand are both Buckingham Palace and local police, as well as the RCMP. An Otis Elevator repair crew must be in attendance with machinery, along with the Health Department and the bomb squad. During their stay, the Royals have direct telephone communication with Ottawa, and the Royal Suite is secured until the plane they are on is certain not to turn back.

However, it is not the Queen who made the Saskatchewan "The Hotel." It is generations of Regina residents and social clubs who have chosen this distinctive building as their place to meet for tea, cocktails, suppers, and elegant social functions. It is also the people who have worked here—people like orchestra leader Mart Kenney, who began his long career in Canadian broadcasting at the Hotel Saskatchewan in 1934. Mart Kenney and his Western Gentlemen did live dance remotes from the hotel for broadcast on the Canadian Radio Commission (the predecessor of the CBC). They also collaborated on another radio show in which actors dramatized the lyrics of such popular songs of the time as "Two Cigarettes in the Dark" and "Love in Bloom." Meanwhile, Louis Vallee and Adolfo Lionetti, who worked in the barbershop for 43 and 20 years respectively, brought in some of the hotel's most loyal clientele, while John Fefchuk (in years past) and Dale Bowes (currently) were reputed to be the finest shoe-shiners in the country, leading commercial travellers to bring along cases of shoes when they stayed at the hotel.

Like almost all the grand Canadian hotels, however, the Hotel Saskatchewan began falling into disrepair during the 1960s and 1970s. When renovations were eventually undertaken for the Hotel's golden anniversary in 1977, many were not kind to it. As with other public rooms in the hotel, the dining room wall coverings, drapes, carpet and upholstery were redone in textured and patterned brown, beige, orange and yellow, and mirrors were prominent.

Upgrading facilities and competing with the newer hotel chains was expensive. The Hotel changed hands a few times, and renovations continued, but bad luck struck in March of 1982 when a fire gutted the Qu'Appelle ballroom (formerly the Colonial Ballroom) and closed the convention floor for months. Lost revenue and costly renovations forced the owners into tax arrears, and in the late 1980s, the Hotel went into receivership.

In 1992, the Hotel was officially re-christened the Hotel Saskatchewan Radisson Plaza. The new owners undertook interior renovations to restore the hotel's original beauty. The removal of low false ceilings revealed hidden surprises—original chandeliers on the convention floor and damaged but beautiful plaster mouldings that served as models for the mouldings installed in the current Victoria Tea Room. The shoeshine parlour and barbershop remain in their original form, the latter complete with its six original barber chairs and black and white pedestal sinks from 1927.

In 1993, Regina City Council designated the hotel a municipal heritage site, and the public has once again fallen in love with the building's quiet elegance. "The Hotel" shines again.

(Opposite page) Ladies Tea Room (Above) The Lounge (Inset) President of the CPR, E.W. Beatty and Mayor Macara shake hands at the Hotel's grand opening in May, 1927. Beatty hailed the opening of the hotel as evidence of the "progressive development of Western Canada on a sound and permanent basis." The first guests arrived by airplane from Scobey, Montana, and included U.S. Senator J.W. Shnitzler.

Through the years, the Bessborough has remained one of Saskatoon's defining landmarks.
(Right) Bessborough Hotel seen through the Broadway Street Bridge, August 1953.

BESSBOROUGH HOTEL

Saskatoon, Saskatchewan

"The Bessborough stands as a monument to the resourcefulness of man, who takes from the natural resources of field and mines and forests, the stones, clays, marble, iron and various woods, and fashions them into castles of beauty." Thus rhapsodized the *Star-Phoenix* on December 7, 1935, three days before the Bessborough's grand opening. There was good reason for grandiloquence—the Bessborough was magnificent. And it had risen during some of the worst years the Prairies had known, when there was a powerful need to believe in better things ahead.

When Canadian Pacific opened the Hotel Saskatchewan in Regina in 1927, Saskatoon businessmen canvassed the Canadian National Railways for a hotel in their city. Saskatoon was a rail hub for CNR's western network, and in the late 1920s, it was prospering. To serve its population of over 40,000, Saskatoon had both an Eaton's and a Hudson's Bay store. It seemed a propitious time to build a grand hotel to attract the convention trade in the west, and CNR president Sir Henry Thornton took action. By 1929, the CNR had bought property on 21st Street, just down from their station in central Saskatoon.

The structure that was soon to be built near the bank of the South Saskatchewan River, on the site of what had been a garbage dump, would exceed the wildest imaginings of the city fathers. The last big château-style hotel built in the country, the Bessborough, as designed by veteran architect J.S. Archibald, was more a romantic revival of its Canadian prototypes than of the French medieval châteaux. Archibald did not live to see the opening of this, his last grand CNR hotel. After his death, construction was directed by CNR architect John Schofield and his assistant George Drummond.

When the Depression hit, there was widespread fear that the project would be abandoned, but the 1929 crash did not affect the local economy right away. Crops that

BESSBOROUGH HOTEL

Location: On the South Saskatchewan River, 21st Street, Saskatoon, Sask.

1930-32: Constructed

1935: Opened December 10

Initial Owner: CNR

Architects: J.S. Archibald and John Schofield

Style: Château

Number of rooms when opened: 256

Number of storeys when opened: 12

Principal Materials: Orange brick and Tyndall stone

1989: Purchased by Delta Hotels & Resorts

Prominent Guests: Princess Margaret, Governor General Ramon Hnatyshyn, Bill Cosby, Marie Osmond, Pierre Elliott Trudeau

Named After: The ninth Earl of Bessborough, Mr. Vere Brabazon Ponsonby, the Governor General of Canada from 1931-35.

(Above) Steel framework of the Bessborough, 1931. Built between 1930 and 1932 during the early years of the Depression, the Bess stood empty until its opening in 1935. (Opposite page) Plumbing and heating contractors, 1931-32. Over 3,000 people applied for construction work on the Bessborough. The hard times may have contributed to the hotel's fine workmanship as workmen were in no hurry to finish the job and enter the anaemic job market.

year were good and fetched high prices. Moreover, construction projects—the most significant of which was the Bess—kept people working and put food on the table. So, against the odds, a castle began to rise on Saskatoon's horizon in 1930.

Louie Ulrich, recently arrived from Austria, was put to work digging the foundation—ten hours a day with only a short break for lunch. He remembers how hundreds of men would hover around the building site ready to jump at the chance if a position became available, and how workers who stopped to have a cigarette were sometimes fired and immediately replaced. The hard times, however, may have contributed to the hotel's fine workmanship. As workmen were in no hurry to finish the job, the 12-storey structure was solidly built.

When construction finally came to an end in 1932, a party was held for all the contractors—a wild and raucous affair, with a snake dance through all the rooms. No one held back that night, for the morning would bring with it crushing uncertainty. Each man knew he was heading into an anaemic job market. Many of his neighbours were already on relief.

The hotel still awaited its grand public debut. It would be a long wait. The devastating Depression, combined with large debts that the CNR had accumulated, caused the building to sit empty for three full years. During this period, it was opened only three times: for a Shriners' charity ball, and for two visits by Canada's Governor General, the Earl of Bessborough. Saskatoon residents must have gaped incredulously at this empty, fanciful castle, so out of step with their current reality. The dramatic central tower, the steep Norman copper roofs, the impossible ornaments in light coloured Tyndall stone, the silhouette of turrets, dormers, oriels and quoins—all would have seemed like something out of a fairy tale.

Finally, in 1935, when life seemed hardest, when destitute men drifting by on the freight trains were commonplace and civic relief had run dry, the CNR announced the castle would open on December 10. The city was jubilant, its optimism renewed. The *Star-Phoenix* ran several full pages extolling the wonderful amenities and appointments of the hotel, such as the 14,400 yards of carpet on its floors and

(Above inset) Laying wooden floor. (Left inset) The finished "Bess." "Mr. Hockey," Gordie Howe, helped build the retaining wall around the Bessborough's garden when he was about fifteen years old. His father was foreman of the project.

(Above) A view into the parlour.

corridors, and the elevators that levelled automatically, sparing passengers "the aggravation of toe-stubbing." For efficiency, the building was equipped with a central vacuuming system, chutes that ran down from the bedroom floors to the laundry, and a pneumatic tube carrier system for the dispatch of written messages, telegrams, keys, and so forth. Every room had its own telephone and bath, with hot water regulated so there would be "no danger of scalding." Mattresses were nine inches thick and padded with lamb's wool on one side for winter and cotton wool on the other for summer comfort. Razor-blade receptacles in the bathroom wall were accessible to cleaning staff from a tiny crawl space running off the hall between rooms. The Vice-Regal Suite, created for the governor general, was specially fitted out with a fireplace and a canopied bed, and one of its rooms had an unheated closet for the storage of furs. The hotel kitchen had six coal-fired ranges and a charcoal broiler that could hold fifty sirloin steaks, a six-foot-tall cast-iron vegetable steamer with three separately ventilated sections, and the capacity to manufacture two tons of ice per day.

The opening went off splendidly. The first guest to sign the register was Horace N. Stovin, Western director of the Canadian Radio Commission, who had come from Regina to supervise the broadcast of the opening. A luncheon for 350 business and professional men, and a supper dance for over 1,000, ran so smoothly that guests commented that it seemed as if the staff had done this for years. According to a CNR advertisement when the Bessborough first

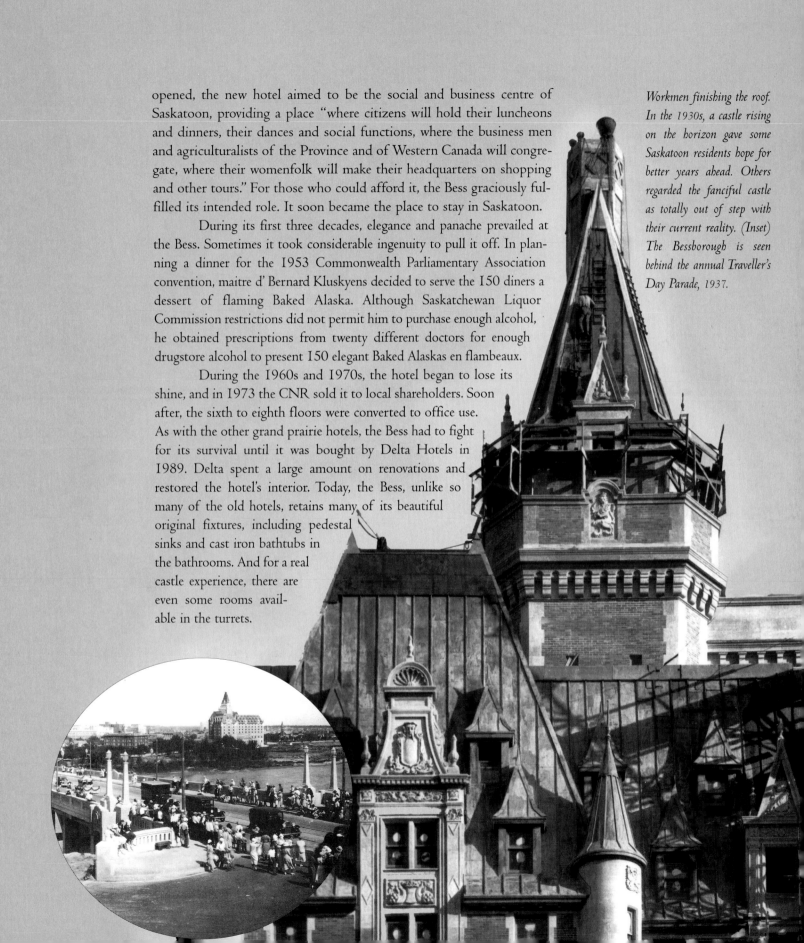

opened, the new hotel aimed to be the social and business centre of Saskatoon, providing a place "where citizens will hold their luncheons and dinners, their dances and social functions, where the business men and agriculturalists of the Province and of Western Canada will congregate, where their womenfolk will make their headquarters on shopping and other tours." For those who could afford it, the Bess graciously fulfilled its intended role. It soon became the place to stay in Saskatoon.

During its first three decades, elegance and panache prevailed at the Bess. Sometimes it took considerable ingenuity to pull it off. In planning a dinner for the 1953 Commonwealth Parliamentary Association convention, maitre d' Bernard Kluskyens decided to serve the 150 diners a dessert of flaming Baked Alaska. Although Saskatchewan Liquor Commission restrictions did not permit him to purchase enough alcohol, he obtained prescriptions from twenty different doctors for enough drugstore alcohol to present 150 elegant Baked Alaskas en flambeaux.

During the 1960s and 1970s, the hotel began to lose its shine, and in 1973 the CNR sold it to local shareholders. Soon after, the sixth to eighth floors were converted to office use. As with the other grand prairie hotels, the Bess had to fight for its survival until it was bought by Delta Hotels in 1989. Delta spent a large amount on renovations and restored the hotel's interior. Today, the Bess, unlike so many of the old hotels, retains many of its beautiful original fixtures, including pedestal sinks and cast iron bathtubs in the bathrooms. And for a real castle experience, there are even some rooms available in the turrets.

Workmen finishing the roof. In the 1930s, a castle rising on the horizon gave some Saskatoon residents hope for better years ahead. Others regarded the fanciful castle as totally out of step with their current reality. (Inset) The Bessborough is seen behind the annual Traveller's Day Parade, 1937.

Excursionists outside the Palliser, late 1910s. A travel writer from Utica, New York observed in 1915: "A hotel with kerosene lamps, boiled pork and potatoes for dinner, tin wash basins, and yellow soaps would about fit Calgary. Instead they have a palace." (Right) The Palliser's crest

PALLISER HOTEL

Calgary, Alberta

The Palliser Hotel opened without a formal ceremony on June 1, 1914, the celebration having been put off, the *News Telegram* explained, because the *Empress of Ireland*, a Canadian Pacific ship, had just met with disaster. In its splendour and scale, the Palliser, which was to become a central component of the city's self-image, stood alone in Calgary for more than half a century. A 1929 addition made it the city's tallest building; before World War II it was probably the most photographed structure in Calgary.

Two factors motivated the CPR to build the Palliser Hotel: its new-found confidence in Calgary's future, and a nationwide strategy to improve accommodations wherever its passengers travelled. Between 1901 and 1911, Calgary's population grew tenfold. Real estate prices soared as the 1890s cow town transformed itself into a 20th-century city. In proposing a large new depot for the city in 1907, CPR president Sir Thomas Shaughnessy observed that "Calgary itself will continue to grow and a building which at this time would appear almost extravagant will in the not remote future be quite warranted by the traffic." Shaughnessy judged that a Calgary hotel was an "almost essential" link to the CPR's mountain hotel system. Construction began in May 1911 on a CPR-owned site with two distinct advantages: access to the railway station and proximity to both the warehouse and shopping districts, making the hotel an excellent base for commercial travellers and tourists alike.

PALLISER HOTEL

Location: 133-9th Avenue S.W., Calgary, Alberta

1914: Opened June 1

Initial Owner: Canadian Pacific Railway

Architects: Edward and W.S. Maxwell

Style: Edwardian Classical

Principal Materials: Steel, reinforced concrete, Indiana limestone, buff-coloured brick

Number of storeys when opened: 8

1929: Addition of 4 storeys

Prominent Guests: R.B. Bennett, Prince of Wales (later King Edward VIII), Sophia Loren, Lord Louis Mountbatten, Cary Grant, Queen Beatrice of the Netherlands

Named After: Captain John Palliser, who led a British scientific expedition that explored the prairies from 1857 to 1860. Other proposed names included the Adanac, Crowfoot, Pride of the West, and even the Swastika—an innocent suggestion at the time. In 1913 it appeared the hotel would be called the Piedmont, an appropriate name for a hotel at the edge of Alberta's foothills.

The eight-storey hotel followed an "E" pattern.

Montreal architects Edward and W.S. Maxwell departed from the CPR's château tradition. The eight-storey structure was designed in Edwardian classical style, with a glistening, light-coloured façade. Service floors followed an "E" pattern, forming two window wells that ensured each room an outside window. *The Morning Albertan* expressed Calgary's booster mentality: "To a man flying far above it in an aeroplane, as will be common someday, it will look like a gigantic letter 'E' with the flanges of the letter without which the word 'energy' could not be spelled…."

The hotel's impact on the city was immediate. In a congratulatory telegram to the CPR, a group of prominent citizens captured the sentiment of thousands who toured the Palliser on opening day. "We can hardly realize we are in a Calgary hotel," they wrote. "The magnificence and splendour of the Palliser is beyond the wildest dreams of the ever-optimists who came here thirty years ago."

The "Castle by the Tracks," 1939. The 1929 addition of four floors is clearly visible. After a major oil discovery in 1947, the Palliser swarmed with oilmen. Staff could distinguish them from ranchers by the size of their Stetsons. "Ranchers wore the biggest hats," recalled Bellman Joe O'Neill.

Less impressed was a group of about one hundred disappointed job seekers from a nearby employment agency, who had heard a rumour that drinks at the Palliser were "on the house." Visitors admired the lavishly decorated public spaces, including the rotunda, with its candelabra lighting, fumed oak panelling and grey Tennessee marble floor; the dining room (later renamed the Crystal Ballroom) with its semicircular conservatory that extended towards the railway tracks; and the café (the future Grill Room, eventually renamed the Rimrock Room), where a massive stone fireplace and carved wooden mantle were illuminated by "electroliers" made from stag antlers.

The product of boom times, the Palliser aimed to become the social and cultural centre of a large cosmopolitan city. By the time it opened, however, Calgary's real estate bubble had collapsed. The Turner Valley oil boom, which gripped Calgarians in an oil-stock frenzy just as the Palliser opened its doors, only briefly disguised the gloom. While it lasted, talk in the hotel's public spaces focussed obsessively on oil. Facetious rules posted in the rotunda included "No well shall be drilled in a tone of voice which is audible within the three mile zone and causes the skylight to flutter." To discourage disruptively loud transactions, management removed the tableside telephones that had recently been installed in the café.

Many thought the Palliser simply too good for such a small city. A travel writer from Utica, New York, passing through Calgary in 1915, observed:

> The only thing in Calgary worth looking at or being interested in is the hotel. It is called the Palliser and its ten [sic] magnificent stories rise above the surrounding hovels and shacks and homely frontier town like a Grecian statue on a clam flat. It seems incredible that it could be there after you once step out and look at Calgary. A hotel with kerosene lamps, boiled pork and potatoes for dinner, tin wash basins, and yellow soaps would about fit Calgary. Instead they have a palace.

C.P.R. S & A. Club. Calgary.

One of the CPR's clubs. During World War I, social clubs donated their proceeds from functions to causes such as the purchase of Christmas gifts for men in the trenches.

During World War I, the Palliser took on a decidedly wartime flavour. Dinner speakers addressed the progress of war and the prospects for victory. Ballroom dances served as farewell parties for departing officers. Social clubs contributed the proceeds from their Palliser functions to such causes as the Red Cross, the Soldiers' Tobacco Fund and the purchase of Christmas gifts for men in the trenches. In response to wartime rationing, the management introduced a twice-weekly "meatless" menu. And in February 1916, armed sentries briefly guarded the Palliser—as well as City Hall, the post office and the brewery—following anti-German riots. When Prohibition came to Alberta later that year, the empty barroom was converted into headquarters for the Patriotic Fund and, later, the Victory Loan committee, which even the worldwide 1918 Spanish Influenza epidemic could not deter. In a week otherwise devoid of public functions, authorities allowed masked citizens to gather for a Victory Loan appeal in a disinfected room at the Palliser.

Memories of the war lingered at the hotel long after the armistice of November 1918. The Great War Veterans' Association (a precursor to the Royal

Canadian Legion) staged an Amputation Banquet in March 1919. The yearly Armistice Ball, held each November, became a Palliser tradition. And for half a century after the war's end, members of the 10th Battalion, Canadian Expeditionary Force—veterans of one of the first German gas attacks of the war—held an annual reunion at the Palliser.

The Roaring Twenties finally saw the Palliser assume its place as Calgary's fashionable address for entertainment and hospitality. At the hotel's Supper Dances, well-heeled guests danced

Watching the Calgary Stampede Parade outside the Palliser, 1963. The annual "Cowboy Ball" at the Palliser was a Stampede tradition, one that earned the Palliser the nickname, "the Paralyzer."

to the strains of Frank Henderson's Palliser Hotel Trio or Ma Trainor's Calgary Hillbillies. Although these functions were officially dry, helpful waiters served ginger ale while ignoring hip flasks and bottles hidden behind evening gowns or floor-length tablecloths. When Prohibition ended in 1924, the Palliser opened its basement beer parlour, becoming the first licensed hotel in the province after eight dry years.

The Palliser also became the locus of Calgary's intellectual and cultural life. Social clubs and service organizations held their regular functions at the hotel; music appreciation groups enjoyed concerts of local talent and visiting performers; and meeting rooms became temporary studios for art and photography exhibits. In 1930, the Palliser hosted the Great West Canadian Folk-dance, Folk-song, Handicrafts Festival—a CPR-sponsored event that toured the nation, marketing Canadian culture as a tourist attraction.

For Calgary, the cultural event of the year has always been the Stampede, first held in 1912 and an annual event since 1923. Dignity vanishes as people and places take on a western appearance and let loose for a bit of fun. The Palliser entered this tradition in 1924 with its Friday night Cowboys' and Old Timers' Ball, which accommodated two thousand western-garbed merrymakers in the ballroom and dining room. The party extended out to the street, where another three thousand dancers whooped it up well into the night. The Cowboy Ball became an instant

Elegant dining at the Palliser, c. 1920. Wartime rationing had been lifted, but Prohibition was still in force in Alberta.

tradition. Stampede revelry earned the hotel a new nickname: "the Paralyzer," and the Stampede board's hospitality suite in the hotel became known as the "Snake Room."

The Palliser's western connection extended beyond the Stampede, to those eternal archetypes of the Alberta tycoon: oilmen and ranchers. The newly formed Calgary Petroleum Club made the Palliser its headquarters in 1928, and for decades the powerful Western Stock Growers' Association held its annual meetings in the hotel. From 1929 to 1993, the Palliser hosted the venerable Old Time Range Men's Dinner, an annual tribute to Alberta's pioneer ranchers.

In January 1929, the CPR announced a $1.7 million addition to the Palliser. Three floors were added, with Italian, Spanish and Tudor-style suites. In addition, a new Penthouse

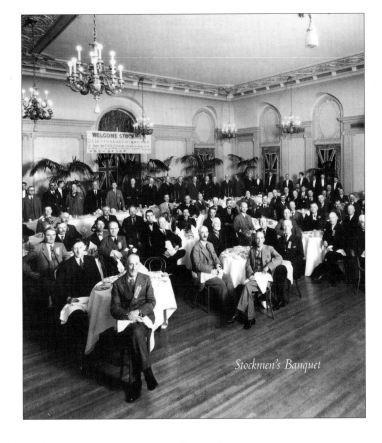

Stockmen's Banquet

replaced the Sun Room. The timing could hardly have been worse. According to lore, soon after the 1929 stock market crash, a ruined Calgary businessman stepped onto the open deck of the new Penthouse and leaped to his death. The hotel adapted to changing conditions, eventually replacing the Grill Room with a reasonably priced coffee shop. But the Palliser's standards of elegance remained, and those who had the means danced and dined through the 1930s to the music of Jerry Fuller's Orchestra. Among the hotel's resident guests during the Depression was the very man who epitomized it—R.B. Bennett, Conservative MP for Calgary West and prime minister from 1930 to 1935. Bennett kept rooms 759 and 760 at the Palliser from 1923 until 1939, when he retired to England. Though his tight fiscal policies angered the nation, he was loved by the hotel's 178 employees, to each of whom he sent a box of chocolates at Christmastime.

With recovery came another world war. From 1939 to 1945, military uniforms once more became a familiar sight in the hotel. Servicemen and air cadets came for supper or tea dances, graduation ceremonies, or to rent a room on a weekend pass. Officers and their families made the Palliser their temporary residence. "Something is being destroyed or broken up every weekend when those getting their 48-hour leaves start making 'whoopee'," observed a hotel inspector in 1942. Staff had to ask unruly soldiers to close their transom windows to cut down the late-night

Leaving the Palliser, 1962. The Palliser was a first stop for many families taking car trips through the mountains.

noise. One party included a young Pierre Berton, the future broadcaster and historian who was then stationed at Calgary's Currie Barracks. Berton and some fellow officers rented a room one Saturday night, started mixing Tom Collinses and ordered fifty pounds of ice to cool their drinks. The men were thrown out and permanently banned. "We created an awful noise," Berton recalls, but adds that all has been forgiven: "I've stayed there several times since then. They've forgotten all about it."

When the conflict ended, soldiers from Calgary returned to what was still a small city of barely 100,000, where the Palliser Hotel still dominated the skyline. The hotel offered an apprenticeship program for veterans, and returned servicemen found work in each of the Palliser's departments. Then in 1947, a major oil discovery ushered in a sustained petroleum boom that transformed Calgary permanently. The Palliser immediately swarmed with oilmen. Staff could distinguish them from ranchers by the size of their Stetsons. "Ranchers wore the biggest hats," recalled Bellman Joe O'Neill, who later became Bell Captain. American oilmen fell in love with the hotel's culinary specialties, and on occasion, the Palliser airlifted clam chowder and crusty French bread (baked in the hotel's 1914 brick oven) to Texas and Wyoming.

The invasion of oilmen proved a windfall for Bell Captain Cecil Heath, known to everyone as Harry the Horse. Heath made a fortune by using stock tips from oil-patch guests and reading the stock teletype machine in the lobby. He became a board member of Central del Rio, whose president, Texas oilman Neil McQueen, kept a permanent suite at the Palliser. On at least one occasion, Heath was summoned upstairs to a board meeting—in his bellman's uniform.

In 1959, the Palliser opened Calgary's first cocktail lounge in the Penthouse. But the hotel was aging, and by the mid-1960s it faced competition from a new convention hotel closer to the city's oil-patch district. Passing trains still shook the Palliser's south-facing rooms, but each year fewer guests arrived by

rail. To retain its position, the Palliser's management, in 1962, launched a renovation that modernized the building but masked its original grandeur. A massive new chandelier now dominated the lobby, and false ceilings, wallpaper and paint obscured original detailed work. Supper dances and their big band sounds receded into history, replaced by Calypso, Latin and rock-and-roll acts in the Big Top Lounge that replaced the Oak Room restaurant. The coffee shop was remodelled into the Rimrock Room, a western-themed restaurant decorated with hand-tooled leather panels and a 38-foot mural by famed western artist Charles Beil. In the basement tavern, jacketed, white-gloved waiters disappeared, and hostesses in mini-skirts made their debut in 1971, when the city's last men-only pub finally admitted women.

By the mid-seventies, CP Hotels was thinking of building a new Palliser nearby and replacing the original with an office tower. In the end, however, the company recognized the Palliser's irreplaceable heritage character, and began the first in a series of restoration efforts in 1978. The lobby returned to Renaissance Revival style, the Crystal Ballroom to Louis XIV and the Penthouse to Art Deco. The Palliser's selection as official host hotel for the XVth Olympic Winter Games, held in Calgary in 1988, signalled its return to glory days.

Though the world's elite—with its royalty, rock stars and billionaires—might come to its door, the Palliser has never forgotten its Calgary roots. To Ian Powell, who managed the hotel in the 1990s, Calgary's western flavour was what made the Palliser unique among Canadian railway hotels. People in one meeting room might be wearing business suits, while those in the next were sporting cowboy hats and jeans. "That's the thing about Calgary," says Powell. "Nobody would care if they ended up in the wrong one."

(Left) Bathroom phone service, 1965. Increasingly in the 1960s, the old hotels had to compete with newer hotels by offering modern amenities. (Below) Main entrance to the Palliser

Terrace dining, 1929. The Hotel Macdonald has a commanding view over the North Saskatchewan River. (Right) Image taken from early Hotel Macdonald letterhead

HOTEL MACDONALD

Edmonton, Alberta

The *Edmonton Journal* hailed it as "perhaps the most brilliant social event in the city's history." Just after 7:00 p.m. on July 5, 1915, Premier Arthur Sifton and Lieutenant-Governor George Bulyea sat down with three hundred of the city's elite to the inaugural dinner at Edmonton's magnificent new railway hotel. "Myriads of lights diffused their soft rays over women garbed in fashion's latest dictates," the *Journal* continued, "over men in conventional evening dress, officers in active service khaki and retired officers in uniforms of brilliant red and gold."

It wasn't supposed to be quite that way. First proposed by the Grand Trunk Pacific Railway (GTP) more than five years earlier, Edmonton's "Château on the River" was intended to open on Dominion Day, 1914. When construction began in 1913, the city was in the midst of a population and real estate boom, and a grand hotel had become a vital necessity. But by the time the "Mac" opened, almost exactly a year behind schedule, the economy had ground to a halt and World War I had begun. Opening night might well have been "brilliant," but the presence of so many in uniform served as a reminder that these were not ordinary times.

In its optimism, the GTP chose a 2.72-acre lot two hundred feet south of the major intersection of McDougall and Jasper avenues, at the edge of the river escarpment. With its commanding view of the North Saskatchewan River valley, the massive Hotel Macdonald towered over the city. In the decades that followed, depressed conditions put a virtual freeze on new construction, and the Macdonald alone dominated the skyline, a reminder of better days.

The Grand Trunk Pacific's Hotel Macdonald. When the Macdonald opened in 1915, steep château-style copper roofs and an Indiana limestone façade identified this hotel as part of the illustrious family of Grand Trunk hotels, most notable among them, Ottawa's Château Laurier.

Like the other GTP projects—Ottawa's Château Laurier (1912) and Winnipeg's Fort Garry Hotel (1913)—Montreal architects Ross and MacFarlane designed the Macdonald in Canadian château style, with a high copper roof and smooth Indiana limestone walls. The two wings formed by the hotel's L-shape aligned with the major avenues. Beyond the revolving doors lay the rotunda, featuring pink Lepanto marble, an oak beam ceiling and a grandfather clock synchronized with the Greenwich standard. "Visitors may therefore compare their watches at any time and secure absolute accuracy of time," the *Edmonton Journal* noted. A separate outside entrance led to the ladies' reception room, and thence to the hotel office and elevators. Women could not enter the rotunda without an escort. From his office next to the marble stairway, manager Louis Low kept a watchful eye on his palatial charge.

Two lounges, finished in dark oak, stood across the rotunda from the main entrance. Both opened onto the terrace and gardens behind the hotel, which overlooked the river escarpment. These lounges have since been unified into the

Confederation Room, so named because of the national treasure that has hung above its fireplace since the day the hotel opened: Frederick Challener's reproduction of the *Fathers of Confederation* mural by Robert Harris that features Prime Minister Sir John A. Macdonald. The original mural was destroyed by the fire that razed the federal Parliament building in 1916, rendering the hotel's version—one of only two Challener reproductions—irreplaceable. The east wing originally housed the dining room, eventually renamed the Empire Ballroom. This beautiful space had a spring floor for ballroom dancing, a musicians' gallery, and a barrel-vaulted ceiling decorated with an elaborate hunt scene.

It took only two weeks for the war to reach the Macdonald, if only indirectly. In a referendum held on July 21, 1915, a majority of Albertans voted to prohibit the sale of alcohol. If the Empire was waging war to purify the world, prohibitionists argued, like efforts should be made to purify society at home. Effective Dominion Day, 1916, hotels across the province closed their barroom doors, or else remained open to sell only "temperance beer" (which had two percent alcoholic content). For the many hotels dependent on liquor sales, the Prohibition years were devastating. But the stately Macdonald was much more than a watering hole, indeed, it has always manifested the quiet reserve that traditionally has distinguished Edmonton from its more boisterous southern neighbour.

Cowboys on steps of the Macdonald, June 23, 1919. During Alberta's Prohibition years of 1916-24, provincial hotels could sell only "temperance beer."

War-time cafeteria. Items on the menu, each 25 cents, included shoulder of mutton with sauce and steamed finnan haddie. The octagonal cafeteria was originally the gracious Palm Room. Now, restored to its early splendour, it is known as the Wedgwood Room.

After Prohibition ended in 1924, the Macdonald was in no hurry to re-open its beer room. As one newspaper reported, "The management is of the opinion that the coffee room is a more valuable asset than the privilege to sell beer." By contrast, Calgary's Palliser Hotel was the first in the province to receive a beer licence. Even when the Macdonald obtained a licence in January 1925, the bar was given a low priority. "The coffee room is used in the forenoon for the serving of meals alone," wrote one *Journal* reporter, "but in the afternoon it is changed into a beer parlor." Eventually the bar turned into a "men only" tavern.

The Hotel Macdonald easily survived the war years. Its parent company, the GTP, was less fortunate. Ottawa nationalized the ailing corporation in 1919, and in 1923 it was subsumed within the government-owned Canadian National Railways. Overnight, the hotel's monogrammed GTP doorknobs became historical artifacts. Unaffected by the fate of its corporate master, the Hotel Macdonald in the 1920s was the site of art displays, stimulating lectures, table d'hôte dinners, cabarets and the "rhythmic music of the modern dance," played by John Bowman and his Eight-Piece Orchestra with "supreme skill and spontaneity."

As the decade drew to a close, it appeared it would end optimistically for the Mac. A building permit for $13,000 worth of floor repairs—possibly the first major upgrade since the hotel opened—was issued on Black Tuesday morning, October 29, 1929. In the miserable Depression decade that followed, a shantytown of Edmonton's homeless developed on the riverbank below the hotel. From their luxurious rooms high above, guests of Edmonton's finest hotel had only to look out the window to see the devastation the Depression had wrought.

The Depression heralded a sea of change in Alberta politics, which peaked with the 1935 election of Calgary's William "Bible Bill" Aberhart and his Social Credit party. Aberhart and his wife moved into Suite 301 at the Macdonald and remained there until the premier's death eight years later. In the early days of the Socred government, two of Aberhart's senior ministers lived just down the hall. One was Ernest Manning, who succeeded Aberhart in 1943 and governed the province for a quarter of a century. The government "colony" on the third floor fit in well with the Macdonald's dignified atmosphere. "No wild merry-making or lavish tipping enlivened the Macdonald on Aberhart's arrival," writes Aberhart biographer David R. Elliott, "and the only lamp burning late in the Aberhart suite was on Aberhart's desk. There he worked, between the tall windows that looked down to the North Saskatchewan River."

The economy had recovered sufficiently by 1937 for the Macdonald to embark on a four-year, $100,000 program of renovations. Some of the work was rushed to completion for the Royal Visit of June 1939, when King George VI and Queen Elizabeth dined at the Mac with the Aberharts and a roster of distinguished guests. By that time, war clouds had reappeared on the horizon, and within months, World War II erupted.

The war in the Pacific led to three major projects that affected Edmonton directly: the Alaska Highway, the Canol Pipeline, and the Northwest Staging Route, a

Decorated façade of the Macdonald, 1920. Each of the four stone pillars bears the shield of one of the four western provinces.

chain of new airstrips built across western Canada to link Alaska to the continental U.S. Suddenly, Edmonton's reputation as the "Gateway to the North" became reality. The city was "invaded" by thousands of Americans, military and civilian. Hotel accommodations were taxed beyond capacity. In one instance, five men had to share a single room in the Macdonald, with one of them sleeping on a mattress in the bathtub. Reservations for the supper dances now had to be made weeks in advance. A similar American "invasion" of both Edmonton and the Macdonald was to take place in the early 1950s, with the development of the Distant Early Warning Line.

The wartime experience highlighted the need for expanded facilities, but it was the 1947 petroleum discovery at nearby Leduc that jolted CN into action. The Leduc find ushered in Alberta's postwar economic boom. Oilmen—many of them Americans—descended on Edmonton, rousing it from its slow, sleepy growth and beginning its cosmopolitan transformation. The change was immediately noticeable at the Mac. "The lobby is alive with oilmen, ranchers, mining engineers, manufacturers," observed the author of a contemporary brochure, "a cross section of the people taking part in the rapidly expanding future of Alberta." Demand for hotel and convention facilities prompted plans for a 16-storey extension, complete with banquet rooms and a shopping centre. CN architect George F. Drummond, working with Chicagoan John Root, designed a flat-roofed, clean-line, functional building decidedly unlike the original château. The intention was to "combine the honesty of expression of contemporary design with a touch of the old world romanticism."

(Left) Banquet at the Mac. Roast beef and baked Alaska were hotel specialties.

The Macdonald Tower opened without ceremony in early 1953. Its lighted marquee beckoned arrivals to the sleek new lobby; the original entrance rotunda was subdivided into rental office space. The *Journal* now referred to the "New Macdonald" and the "Old Macdonald" and compared the contrasting ensemble to "a patient mother, sitting quietly on the high bank overlooking the Saskatchewan with her husky, tall daughter standing close behind." Others were less kind. According to local lore, photographer Gladys Reeves coined the derisive nickname that satisfied the tower's critics. "This is the Macdonald Hotel," she told an out-of-town visitor, "and that's the box it came in." Thereafter, the new section became simply "the Box."

In the mid-1960s, CN began another program of renovations at the Mac. Private rooms and public spaces were modernized, with dropped ceilings disguising the grandeur of much of the original building's design. In 1966 the Empire Ballroom became the Hearth and Hound, a supper club described as Edmonton's "swingin' singin' nightspot." For a time its English Baronial hall motif maintained the hotel's traditional reserve, but before long that reserve ebbed and then vanished. One 1968 act included belly dancers, and in 1971 the Hearth and Hound briefly introduced topless entertainment. "We're out to remove this image of the Macdonald of old with the mental scene of the dinner-jacketed manager standing in the lobby stuffily overseeing the guests as they arrive," manager Keith Murray told the *Journal*. "That era is over."

Flooding in Edmonton. Preparing for the Macdonald's gala opening must have been challenging, as the week it opened in July 1915, the North Saskatchewan rose to an alarming level, causing a terrible flood and a major electrical blackout. The train pictured here is actually stationary. Fully-loaded, its purpose was to keep the bridge from being swept away. It was kept under steam so that a fast escape could be made if necessary.

American air force plane over the Macdonald, c.1940. During the war, so many American servicemen and civilians invaded Edmonton, "the Gateway to the North," that in one instance, five men had to share a single room at the Macdonald, with one of them sleeping on a mattress in the bathtub. (Below) Progressive Conservative rally, May 18, 1967. The Macdonald hosted many political events over the years.

In 1978, the Macdonald was still sufficiently upscale for the visit of Princess Margriet of the Netherlands. During her stay, a special locked refrigerator was installed and Board of Health inspectors supervised and tasted her meals. Samples of her food were retained for 72 hours, for later testing if the princess fell ill. But by the early 1980s, both the château and the Box were showing their age. In 1982, CN announced a $200 million project to renovate the original château, demolish the Box and build a replacement compatible with the 1915 structure. The Macdonald closed its doors in 1983 for what was expected to be a two-year period, its staff reduced to a handful of office, maintenance and security personnel. CN laid off some 150 employees, with the promise they could return when the hotel reopened. Years passed and the project was postponed repeatedly.

One of the few who continued working was assistant accountant Marguerite Jacobs, who was also treasurer of the employees' social fund. When CN instructed her to forward the fund's remaining $2,500 to Montreal, she refused—the money belonged to the employees. In the months after the hotel closed, Marguerite processed the pension applications of four employees with long service records. She recalls that none received any special recognition from the company. To set things right, Marguerite, in January 1984, invited the former staff to one last party in the empty hotel. "I asked the women to bring the food and the men to bring the booze and the mix," she recalls. Maintenance staff laid spare carpeting on the bare floor of the Jasper Room, and set up a Christmas tree for the Macdonald's final fling. People who had worked together for decades were reunited, and that night agreed to make the staff reunion an annual event.

The Macdonald's restoration resumed after Canadian Pacific Hotels & Resorts acquired the CN chain in 1988. By then the Box had been demolished, and the Mac had been declared Edmonton's first Municipal Historic Resource, which guaranteed a substantial tax concession. Guest rooms were entirely redesigned, making them larger but fewer in number, so that the Macdonald became the smallest of CP's château-style hotels. Elaborate new suites were designed for the attic, where for decades Jack May had operated the hotel's in-house print shop. A health club replaced the basement laundry facility.

CP's $28 million "interpretive restoration" was completed in time for the hotel's reopening on May 15, 1991. An all-new staff welcomed 96-year-old Margery Clausen—formerly a long-time chambermaid and assistant housekeeper—as the Macdonald's first "new" guest. The hundreds of Edmontonians who toured the hotel that day experienced a flood of memories. The resurrected Macdonald is sure to witness the making of many more.

"The Box." For the over thirty years that the Hotel Macdonald's 1952–53 addition was standing, it dominated the original hotel building. The Box was demolished in 1986.

Once one of the most dramatic buildings in the country, architect Frances Swales' 1916 Hotel Vancouver was demolished in 1949 and replaced by a parking lot until an Eaton Centre mall was built.

HOTEL VANCOUVER

Vancouver, British Columbia

When Cornelius Van Horne, president of the Canadian Pacific Railway, visited Port Moody in 1884, he ordered its abandonment as the western terminus of the transcontinental railway. Located at the head of Burrard Inlet, Port Moody lay beyond the Second Narrows, a dangerous channel likely to prove hazardous to shipping. More to Van Horne's liking was land in the vicinity of Granville, the little town that had grown around "Gassy" Jack Deighton's saloon, near Hastings Mill on Burrard Inlet's south shore. Extending the line to Granville would require twelve additional miles of track. To cover the extra expense, Van Horne winkled a six-thousand-acre land grant out of the government, then got down to the job of turning the CPR lands into "the metropolis of the west, the London of the Pacific." He decreed that the new terminal city would be known as "Vancouver," a decision that brought howls of protest from residents of Victoria, who accused Van Horne of "snatching" the name of their island. Then, he ordered the construction of a hotel.

On May 23, 1887, the first regularly scheduled train from Montreal arrived in Vancouver. A year later, the CPR's Hotel Vancouver opened its doors to rounds of noisy criticism. Its location on Georgia Street near Granville—a stiff walk from the business district—was deemed to be "way out in the sticks." Its appearance was unprepossessing. "A solid rather plain structure," a Vancouverite opined, "a sort of glorified farmhouse." Van Horne agreed. Introduced to the architect, Thomas Sorby, he growled, "So you're the damn fool who spoilt the building with all those little windows."

But soon, the critics were eating their words. The Hotel Vancouver acted like a magnet, drawing the business district up Granville Street with the "excellence

The Hotel Vancouver's humble beginnings. People complained the hotel looked like a farmhouse and was located too far out of town.

HOTEL VANCOUVER (OLD)

Location: Georgia St. near Granville to Howe St., Vancouver, British Columbia

1888: Opened in May

Initial Owner: Canadian Pacific Railway

Architect: Thomas Sorby

Principal Material: Brick

Number of storeys: 1888, five; 1916, fifteen

Additions: 1893, architect Thomas Sorby with alterations by Francis Rattenbury; 1903, architect Francis Rattenbury; 1912, architect Walter Painter; 1916, architect Francis Swales

1939: Closed in May

1949: Demolished

Prominent Guests: Edward, Prince of Wales, Will Rogers, Sarah Bernhardt, Winston Churchill, Mary Pickford, Douglas Fairbanks, John Jacob Astor, Charlie Chaplin, Babe Ruth

Named After: The city

HOTEL VANCOUVER (NEW)

Location: 900 W. Georgia, Vancouver, B.C.

1928-1939: Under construction

1939: Opened May 25

Initial Owner: Canadian National Railways (co-managed by CPR)

Architect: John S. Archibald, succeeded by his associate, John Schofield

Style: Modern Classical (Château roof)

Principal materials: Haddington Island stone

Number of storeys when opened: 17

Prominent Guests: King George VI and Queen Elizabeth, Crown Prince Olaf of Norway, Edna Ferber, Bob Hope, Bing Crosby, Audrey Hepburn, Pierre Trudeau

Earlier Proposed Name: The British Columbia

(Above) Completed in 1903, the Italianate Howe Street wing (to the right) looked odd attached to the 1888 centre block and its 1893 addition. As one Vancouverite mused, "The whole reminded one of a plain farmer-like man who has married an aristocratic wife."

of the liquors" offered in the hotel's bar. Vancouverites gathered on the welcoming veranda to watch their city grow toward the hotel.

Despite its "homely look," the Hotel Vancouver provided a level of service calculated to satisfy its most demanding guests. Henry Scrivener, the lone bellhop, stood ready to haul buckets of water from the well in the basement should any guest require a bath. A notice, posted in every room, included the request, "Guests will oblige the Manager by reporting to the office any incivility or inattention on the part of the servants." In keeping with an elite clientele, rates were high, ranging from $3 to $4 a night for a room and three meals. Guests were spared the ordeal of eating with their children by the provision of a separate dining room for "Children and Maids." Butlers travelling with their gentlemen were consigned to one of the attic rooms. After fielding complaints from guests who objected to climbing the stairs, the manager wrote a desperate letter to CPR headquarters in Montreal pleading for an elevator.

In March 1890, when the hotel was not quite two years old, CPR vice-president Thomas Shaughnessy

One of the fire escape systems considered by the Hotel Vancouver. Fire was a constant threat at the early hotels.

received alarming news. "There are heavy repairs required all over the house," J.M. Browning of the CPR's land department warned. Large pieces of plaster had fallen from the ceilings. Exterior bricks were crumbling. Worst of all, "rats and cockroaches have got complete possession of the house causing in many places such an offensive smell as to be absolutely unbearable."

Thomas Shaughnessy winced—and approved the expenditures. It was important that the work be done before the "travelling season." Vancouver was booming, and more and more tourists were discovering the spectacular scenery through which the railway line passed on its way to the coast. The hotel was doing well—so well that, the following year, the CPR decided to enlarge the building by adding an extension along Granville Street.

As luck would have it, by the time the addition was completed in 1893, the city was in the grip of a continent-wide depression. Further, just as hotel patronage was falling, the CPR was faced with unwelcome expenditures prompted by a letter from the city fire inspector. "I feel more than ever, since the enlargement of the Hotel, that the means of Egress in Case of Fire are lamentably inadequate," the inspector insisted, setting aside the CPR's claim that, because the hotel was lit by electricity rather than gas, a fire was highly unlikely.

By the turn of the century, the depression had lifted, and in 1901, Francis Rattenbury was asked to prepare plans for a new hotel. A 25-year-old Yorkshireman with modest credentials, Rattenbury had arrived in Vancouver in 1892. In March of the following year, he had pulled off a stunning architectural coup by winning the design competition for the new Parliament Buildings in Victoria. That achievement had attracted the CPR's attention and Rattenbury was asked to make interior improvements to the 1893 addition. Now he produced drawings for an elegant château-style hotel, "a palace for the public." Work had

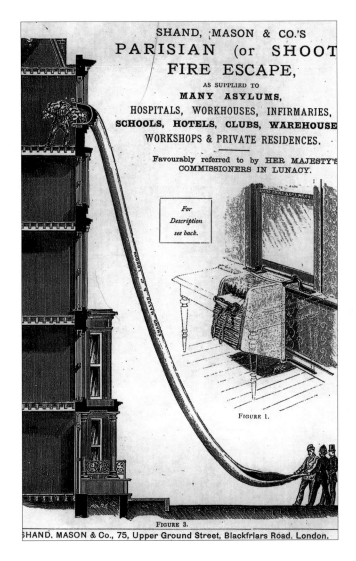

(Top right) Ornate detailing of the Rotunda ceiling in the old Hotel Vancouver demolished in 1949 (Above) Rotunda chandelier, old Hotel Vancouver

begun on the foundations when the CPR was overcome by caution and changed its plans. The new hotel would be built in stages as demand grew, and its design would follow the Italianate style—"Hotel-Renaissance," some people called it—that had proven popular for new luxury hotels in San Francisco and other American cities.

Rattenbury went back to the drafting table. Viewed from above, his new hotel would form an H. A five-storey wing would be built along Howe Street. Then, the old hotel would be demolished and replaced by a matching wing along Granville Street with a centre block, facing Georgia Street, forming the bar of the H. Expected to cost at least half a million dollars, the new Hotel Vancouver would be the "most modern on the Pacific coast." Every room would have a telephone and "nearly every room" would have an attached bathroom.

The Howe Street section was completed in 1903, but by then the CPR had had another change of heart. The old hotel would not be demolished. Instead, Rattenbury's grand new wing became an awkward appendage to the old building, with holes broken through walls to create connecting passageways.

In 1910, the CPR decided to resume construction but Rattenbury and the railway had parted company, the architect having resigned in protest over design changes to the Empress Hotel in Victoria. His place was taken by Walter Painter, who "improved on" Rattenbury's original scheme for the Hotel Vancouver by adding several floors to the Granville Street wing.

By 1912, a West Coast boom of unprecedented proportions prompted the CPR to resume hotel building on a grand scale. They commissioned the Ontario

(Left) The impressive old hotel was built in three stages, the work of three different architects. It was completed in 1916, serving until 1949 when it was demolished to make way for a parking lot.

architect Francis Swales to design a central section to connect the two existing wings. Although technically an addition, in reality the building was anything but. "A colossus," people gasped as it began to rise. Ambitious and flamboyant, it soared to fifteen storeys. Its turrets added a sense of play, leaving the older structures looking short and plain. Now the finest hotel in the city, its public rooms gleamed with polished granite and dazzled with lavish chandeliers.

In all its different configurations, the Hotel Vancouver served as a "Crossroads of the Empire." Among its guests were Edward, Prince of Wales, who "charmed everybody from the manager to the newest bellhop," and his brother, the Duke of Gloucester, who spent several days in his hotel bed recuperating from a polo injury. Sarah Bernhardt slept there. And so did Winston Churchill, Will Rogers, Mary Pickford, Douglas Fairbanks, John Jacob Astor, Charlie Chaplin, Edgar Rice Burroughs, Babe Ruth, John Barrymore, and Jack Dempsey—the list went on and on.

For Vancouverites, the hotel was the city's social centre. Business deals were concluded in the Spanish Grill. The roof-top garden was acknowledged as "the

257

most elegant place in Vancouver for afternoon tea dances." Hyman Lazarus sold the finest cigars in the city at the hotel's cigar stand.

Ten years earlier, Canadian National Railways had begun construction of its own grand hotel, the "British Columbia," on Georgia Street, only a block away from the CPR's hotel. However, the Great Depression brought construction to a halt and for almost a decade, the British Columbia remained an imposing, empty shell. By 1938, although economic conditions had improved, the CNR was still reluctant to proceed with the British Columbia's completion. Also, Canadian Pacific was known to be planning a major revamping of the Hotel Vancouver. Could the city support two large hotels? As it happened, the same question was plaguing the CPR. Finally, the CPR made a stunning announcement: they would abandon the old Hotel Vancouver. Rather than compete for clientele, the two railway companies decided to cooperate. The CPR would close the Hotel Vancouver. The name would be transferred to the CNR's hotel and the two companies would operate the "new" Hotel Vancouver jointly.

Afternoon tea at the rooftop restaurant, c. 1920. (Opposite page) Ballroom, old Hotel Vancouver. This building closed in 1939, and after World War II was taken over as a veterans' hostel. On their first night, veterans and their wives danced to the recorded music of Benny Goodman in the hotel's ballroom.

(Right) Sleek bar in the new Hotel Vancouver. (Inset) 1930s Moderne-style bedroom.

In May 1939, a thousand people attended a farewell luncheon in the old hotel's dining room. Vancouverites worried about the fate of "the greatest building of them all—the one where the heart of our city beat for half a century." Suggestions poured in. The hotel could be converted to a hospital, to an office building or apartment block, to a library and museum or to a civic centre and concert hall. All proposals found opposition from one side or another. Then, it was learned that the Eaton's department store chain was interested in acquiring the site. That made immediate demolition likely. "Wanton destruction!" roared Basil Gardom, the former superintendent of construction for CPR hotels. "The old CPR Hotel Vancouver is a comparatively new building of excellent design and of better construction than can be afforded today. It is good for 1000 years."

Before any decision was made, the old Hotel Vancouver was granted a reprieve due to the exigencies of war. In June 1940, it became a recruiting centre. "The old Hotel Vancouver is in the army now," the *Vancouver Province* announced. Luxurious suites were converted into barracks. Troops, training in the city, were billeted on the upper floors. When the war ended, the hotel was "demobilized" and its future once again became the subject of debate. Vancouver was bursting at the seams. For returning veterans with no place to live, the old hotel seemed an ideal solution. But under whose auspices should a veterans' hostel be run? For months, the federal, provincial and city governments argued against assuming responsibility. Bob McEwen, late of the Seaforth Highlanders, became impatient with the lack of action. On a snowy Saturday morning in January 1946, he led 36 veterans up to the lone man guarding the door of the empty hotel. "This would happen to me," the guard muttered as he stood aside. That night, veterans and their wives, including McEwen and his war bride, Eileen, were dancing to the recorded music of Benny Goodman in the hotel's ballroom. Soon, twelve hundred men, women and children were quartered in the building.

(Above) The impressive new Hotel Vancouver finally opened on Georgia Street in 1939. Construction had begun 11 years earlier, but because of the Great Depression activity came to a halt. For almost a decade it remained an imposing, empty shell.

In March 1948, Eaton's purchased the old hotel for $1,850,000 and announced its intention to demolish the building to make way for a parking lot. By May, most of the veterans had moved out, and the hotel was ready to fill its last role—a refuge for hundreds of people left homeless by the great Fraser River flood. Then it was over. In October, Eaton's called for demolition tenders. The following year, a wrecker's ball crashed into the old hotel and "the biggest wreckage in the city's history" was underway.

Bob McEwen's trucking company won the contract to haul away the rubble. Asked if he felt nostalgic about the old place, he shrugged, "No. It needs to be torn down." The city archivist, Major J.S. Matthews, was equally unsentimental. Asked if the archives were interested in hotel memorabilia, Matthews exclaimed, "Why, it's practically new-fangled!" and turned the offer down. Vancouverites, it seems, had transferred their affections to the new hotel.

The new Hotel Vancouver had opened its doors in May 1939, just in time to receive its most distinguished guests, King George VI and Queen Elizabeth. Breathtakingly different from the old, familiar building, it was decorated in the Moderne style popular in the 1930s. "We must keep pace with

Dal Richards' orchestra on the 13th-floor balcony of the Hotel Vancouver. Late afternoon tea dances like this one were made famous in London, England during the Blitz but were also popular in Canada during the war years when blackout regulations were in force at night. (Inset) Dal Richards and Lorraine McAllister performing at the Panorama Roof, 1962.

changing times," Lieutenant-Governor Eric Hamber declared at the hotel's opening. And Vancouverites were prepared to do just that.

During the war, the Panorama Roof on the fifteenth floor became Vancouver's favourite supper club. Band leader Dal Richards, whose orchestra played there for 25 years, remembered "A lot of uniforms. A lot of farewell parties, poignant moments. A lot of gaiety, some of it forced because you didn't know what was going to happen." On Saturday nights CBC Radio broadcast from the hotel. "CBC is bringing you the music of Dal Richards and his Orchestra from the Panorama Roof high atop the Hotel Vancouver overlooking the twinkling harbour lights of Canada's gateway to the Pacific," the announcer trilled, following a script that did not change even when the windows were shrouded with blackout curtains in the months following Pearl Harbor, when a Japanese invasion of the Pacific coast seemed a possibility.

Partial prohibition, introduced in 1920 and continuing until 1954, made it illegal to consume alcohol in a public place. Dal Richards developed a foolproof tactic for helping patrons avoid prosecution under the province's liquor laws. The hotel sold mixer and ice and looked the other way as people slipped their whisky bottles under the table or behind the drapes. "Occasionally the police would raid, so we had a system," Richards recalled. "When the doorman saw them coming, he'd call up to the Roof and we'd play 'Roll Out the Barrel,' the cue for everyone to get rid of their booze."

Like its predecessor, the new Hotel Vancouver became the centre of city life, "the only show in town," the home of broadcasting studios and "the" place for everything from wedding receptions to political rallies. But by the 1960s, attention

began to shift to newer hotels like the waterfront Bayshore Inn. After the Hilton hotel chain took over the responsibility for managing the Hotel Vancouver, the company embarked on modernization—lowered ceilings, plastic flowers, vivid colours. Head housekeeper Ethel Ferguson was appalled when she saw fine furniture—some of which had belonged to the old hotel—being removed. She managed to squirrel away into almost forgotten storage spaces, roomfuls of chairs, bureaux and other things that caught her eye.

The remodelled Panorama Roof, renamed the Roof Restaurant and Lounge, lost Dal Richards as well as its former cachet. A new restaurant, the Timber Club, turned its back on old-fashioned elegance. For its opening, the traditional ribbon cutting was replaced by a chainsaw roaring through a log. The room was lined with logs and decorated with axes, saws and other logging memorabilia. To become a High Rigger, a member of the unofficial "Timber Club," one had to throw back a "gut burner"—five liqueurs stirred into coffee and set ablaze.

Again, tastes changed. In the 1980s, after the Canadian National and later Canadian Pacific Hotels took over management, a long-term restoration project began. Once Ethel Ferguson was convinced that a genuine restoration was underway, she unveiled her cache—enough furniture to decorate thirty-five rooms—then retired, content that her hotel was again in good hands.

Lorraine McAllister performing with Dal Richards' orchestra in the Pacific Ballroom, early 1950s.

The Palm Court at the Empress, with its beautiful stained-glass dome. For a time it was the Tea Room. (Right) Former porte-cochère entrance at the south wing of the Empress.

THE EMPRESS

Victoria, British Columbia

By 1903, Victoria had become so desperate to be made "a CPR town" that the mayor and council were prepared to shower the Canadian Pacific Railway with civic favours if only the company would agree to build a tourist hotel in their city. Victoria had once been the centre of business and industry, the largest and most important city in the province. But by the turn of the century that role had been assumed by the CPR's western terminus, the upstart mainland town of Vancouver, and Victorians were uncomfortably aware that their city's economic health would now depend on the spending power of well-heeled tourists.

Since 1891, the CPR's sleek, white, Empress liners had been calling at Victoria's Outer Wharf and delivering to the city's doorstep just the kind of wealthy world traveller Victoria hoped to attract. However, there was little to encourage visitors to dally in the city—no tourist hotel to wrap them in the luxury they had experienced on the voyage across the Pacific from Shanghai or Hong Kong. The city's "hotel committee," which included the mayor and representatives of the Board of Trade and the Tourist Association, calculated that the hotel void could best be filled by the CPR.

In 1903, when CPR president Sir Thomas Shaughnessy visited Victoria, the hotel committee pressed their suit. "I want to say that our company is very much adverse to going into the hotel business," Shaughnessy warned. But Sir Thomas was playing hard to get. Not only had he decided to build a hotel but also he had a site in mind.

Two years earlier, Victorians had voted in favour of spending $100,000 to do away with the James Bay mudflats, a stinking tidal garbage dump at the

THE EMPRESS

Location: 721 Government Street, Victoria, British Columbia

1904-1908: Construction

1908: Opened January 20

Initial owner: Canadian Pacific Rwy.

Architect: Francis M. Rattenbury

Style: Château

Principal Materials: Brick

1910 & 1912: Additions by W.S. Painter

1929: Humboldt Wing by J.W. Orrock

1988-89: Addition by Steve Carruthers

Prominent Guests: King and Queen of Siam, Princess Margaret, Shirley Temple, Bob Hope, Spencer Tracy

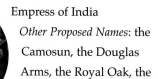

Named After: Queen Victoria, Empress of India

Other Proposed Names: the Camosun, the Douglas Arms, the Royal Oak, the Van Horne, the Alexandra

(*Above*) *The Empress Hotel was built on a tidal mudflat. The bridge spanning the inlet was replaced by a causeway. Then, the area behind the new roadway was filled with sand and gravel and mud dredged from the harbour bottom.* (*Inset*) *The Empress was built on a foundation of 50-foot-long Douglas fir pilings driven into the blue clay of the mudflats. If the 2855 pilings were laid end to end they would stretch 27 miles.*

head of the Inner Harbour. The bridge across the mudflats had been replaced by a permanent causeway, behind which the mudflats were now being filled with tons of silt dredged from the harbour bottom. The city had supposed that the reclaimed land might become a park or pleasure ground, but Francis Rattenbury, the brash young architect who had swept to prominence by winning the design competition for the provincial Parliament Buildings a decade earlier and who was now working as the CPR's western division architect, recognized the reclaimed mudflats as the most spectacular building site in the city. Built there, a CPR hotel would become the centrepiece of the harbour and the first building glimpsed by passengers on the CPR's coastal *Princess* boats as they sailed into the Inner Harbour from Vancouver and Seattle. It would become etched on visitors' memories as the one building they identified with Victoria.

Rattenbury had convinced Shaughnessy of the excellence of the site when the hotel committee came calling. But Sir Thomas, playing his cards close to his chest, allowed himself to be wooed. In the end, he "reluctantly" agreed to build a hotel—provided the CPR was granted, free of cost, five acres of land behind the newly built causeway.

From the moment it opened its doors in 1908, the Empress Hotel was a success. The latest thing in Edwardian style, the hotel had turned its back on the heavy, red plush interiors of the Victorian era in favour of cream and green with touches of rusty red. The Empress was something to behold, a destination in itself, and during the first summer, it was fully booked almost every night. Within a year, an addition, the north wing, was under construction. By 1912, a second addition, which included the magnificent Crystal Ballroom, was welcoming guests and the city fathers were congratulating themselves that the civic give-away had achieved its ends. Victoria, reaping the benefits of the CPR's world-wide publicity campaigns, was booming. As Emily Carr put it, "From London dock to Empress Hotel door was one uninterrupted slither of easy travel."

Hotel profits declined during World War I when the Empress liners were requisitioned for war work. The balance sheet improved in the 1920s, and in 1929, on the eve of the Depression, the CPR added the Humboldt Wing, a huge $2.5 million addition that nearly doubled the size of the existing hotel. The Empress struggled through the 1930s, but again sprang to life in World War II. Victoria filled with uniforms as the nearby naval base

(Above) The château-style Empress Hotel was the first impression of Victoria for thousands of travellers who arrived on the CPR steamships over the years.

267

Parade celebrating the 1911 coronation of King George V

expanded and the RCAF and RAF began training pilots at the airport. Many young servicemen and women were introduced to gracious living in the hotel's formal dining room. But when men in uniform booked a room, they were consigned to the Humboldt Wing—"Alcohol Alley"—a safe remove from the public rooms and the permanent guests.

The hotel became a "funk hole," a safe place for "fashionable refugees" to sit out the war. "Escapees poured in," the hotel's publicity director recalled. "Titled and untitled, they came from Europe, from the Orient and England itself." After Japan bombed Pearl Harbor in December 1941, coastal British Columbia suddenly seemed to be on the front line. Plans were made for the evacuation of the civilian population of Vancouver Island. A Japanese submarine shelled a lighthouse on the Island's west coast. At the Empress, blackout curtains appeared at all the windows; the front door was chained shut lest a chink of light escape onto the harbour, and public rooms on the lower level were converted into air raid shelters. But within a few months, fears of invasion eased and the Empress' refugees stayed on "for the duration."

Table setting for the Royal dinner for King George VI and Queen Elizabeth, May 30, 1939. The decorative pattern on the dining room ceiling looks like carved wood, but is actually horse-hair moulding.

By the 1950s, the Empress was looking decidedly dowdy. Other than converting the Library into a cocktail lounge in 1954, the CPR had spent nothing on improvements or upgrading. The hotel's wiring had become a serious issue. From the beginning, the Empress had generated its own power, delivered to the hotel as direct current. When electricity was required only for lighting, direct current had posed no problem. But now, people were travelling with radios, hair dryers and electric razors, all of which operated on alternating current and none of which could be connected to the hotel's power system without spectacular results. "You plugged your shaver in and, well, it just got fried!" a guest exclaimed.

During the 1960s, CPR management in Montreal, finally coming to grips with the problem of their "eccentric Empress," studied a number of options,

(Top) The Lounge had a wonderful view out to the harbour. Kate Reed did the interior decoration at the Empress as well as at many of the other Canadian Pacific Hotels like the Place Viger, and the Royal Alexandra. Her colour scheme in the Lounge was cream and green with rust-red accents. (Below) The Bengal Room's tiger was shot in India in 1966 by a Canadian doctor who was working at a mission hospital. By 1990, the doctor had lost his taste for trophy hunting and he offered the skin to the Empress. After $8500 changed hands, the tiger became part of the cocktail lounge decor.

including demolishing the hotel and building a modern motor hotel, or selling the vacant land. When news of the discussions leaked out, Victorians were aghast. Victoria without the Empress? The idea was unthinkable. Over the years, the "Grand Old Lady of Government Street" had come to symbolize the city—its Englishness, its eccentricities, its aura of shabby gentility. The city owed its identity to the Empress Hotel.

Victoria might never have become known as a "city of gardens" without the Empress. The CPR had added four acres to the land acquired from the city, and the hotel was set in a nine-acre garden. Head gardener Fred Saunders designed the Empress grounds to resemble those of an English country estate—clay tennis courts, wide perennial borders, arbours and pergolas heavy with perfumed roses, curving pathways winding through garden rooms, wisteria climbing over brick walls.

To lure visitors during the Depression years, the hotel decided to capitalize on its setting "amid this garden glory." In 1933, the Empress established Chrysanthemum Teas at which enthusiasts

Added to the hotel in 1912, the Crystal Ballroom featured a glass-paned ceiling. By day, sunlight sparkled on the crystal chandeliers; by night, dancers waltzed under the moon and stars. The great globe chandeliers were each made of 8,000 crystal beads.

displayed their prize specimens and Fred Saunders gave expert advice. The teas proved so popular that in 1936 the Empress began to sponsor a Spring Garden Festival—a four-day event that included tours of local gardens and drew guests from as far away as Dallas and Atlanta. By the 1940s, the hotel's promotional brochures were focussing on the gardens. "The ivy-clad Empress is the keynote of the garden city. Gardening and social life go together in Victoria. The pleasant city, its atmosphere that of an English country town, entertains in its gardens."

Visitors regarded the hotel's permanent residents as charming examples of Victoria's eccentricity. During the Depression, the Empress encouraged long-term guests by dropping the rate for the sixth-floor attic bedrooms, originally designed for live-in staff, to a dollar a day. The ladies of the sixth floor, the "Empress dowagers," lived in genteel poverty. To avoid the expense

(Inset) Billed as "the largest heated indoor salt-water swimming pool in the British Empire," the Crystal Garden pool was built by the CPR in 1925 on city-owned land. The pool and garden extended the Empress Hotel's tourist season into the winter while functioning as a year-round recreation centre for Victorians.

of eating in the dining room, some of the dowagers smuggled hot plates into their rooms. One lady was known to make strawberry jam on her hot plate and another was in the habit of filling the air of the sixth-floor corridor with the unmistakable aroma of liver and onions.

Long-term residents were creatures of habit. Used to having the hotel to themselves during the winter, they became most indignant if a summer guest settled into their favourite chair in the Lounge. One elderly lady became famous for her dining routine. Every evening she dined alone. After her meal, she dipped her fingers into the silver finger bowl then daintily patted them dry on a starched white linen napkin. Then, she removed her dentures, swished them in the finger bowl, and slipped them back in place before gliding elegantly into the lounge for Billy Tickle's evening concert.

The Empress Hotel suffered eccentrics gladly. One regular guest, a retired colonel, checked into the hotel several times a year with a box of lead soldiers. He would shut the door to his room and get royally drunk on his private supply of gin, stored for him between visits by the maitre d'hotel. While the colonel fought long-ago battles with his toy soldiers, the maitre d' kept him supplied with gin, carried his meals to his room and kept an eye on him until the old soldier checked out, refreshed, a few days later.

The Empress' indulgence of eccentrics extended to "lobby-sitters." John Rowland never booked a room at the hotel but every evening for over thirty years—from the end of World War I, when he had come to live in Victoria on his soldier's pension, until his death in 1951—he settled himself in the lounge in a comfortable armchair by the grandfather clock to listen to Billy Tickle's concert. As the years passed, Rowland became shabbier and shabbier, but his courtliness remained unchanged. Greeted by a hotel guest, he would stand and bow before extending his hand and exchanging the pleasantries of the day. He became a great favourite with returning guests. At Christmastime, cards and letters arrived from all over the world addressed to "John Rowland, By the Grandfather Clock, Empress Hotel." Asked why he made welcome a man

(Right) John Rowland was a lobby-sitter extraordinaire. Every evening for thirty years, he took up his position in the Lounge, in a comfortable chair by the grandfather clock, to listen to the Billy Tickle Trio's nightly concert. He became a hotel fixture, a great favourite with returning guests. (Below) Lorraine McAllister leading a group of ladies into the Crystal Ballroom for a British Columbia Pipeline Convention luncheon, c.1962.

who had never spent a dime in his hotel, the manager responded, "He was one of our characters—he loved music and he loved people. Why shouldn't he have sat in our lobby every night?"

Victorians had turned the Empress into the social heart of their city—afternoon teas in the Lounge, special-occasion dinners in the Dining Room, Saturday night dances in the Crystal Ballroom. At times, they made the hotel a rowdy place, but that was due to the strict liquor laws which prevailed from 1920 to 1954. Alcohol could be consumed only in private. No public drinking was allowed; even the Empress dining room was not permitted to serve wine with dinner. Guests could drink in their rooms and some of the Empress dowagers were known to keep a secret bottle of sherry hidden in their toilet tanks. When Winston Churchill dined at the Empress in 1929, his favourite tipple was placed prominently on his table, disguised in a china teapot. It was the custom of many Victoria organizations to hold annual for-

mal dances in the Crystal Ballroom. It was also customary for groups of friends to rent a hotel bedroom for drinking. Unfortunately, many dancers spent more time in the bedroom bars than in the Ballroom. "The Firemen's Ball and the Policemen's Ball; they were always the worst," page-boy Jack Ellett remembered. "Fire hoses pushed through the windows and turned on. Sheets tied together and people shimmying down from the third or fourth floor." The hotel detective turned a blind eye. He was on the prowl for bigger game. As a fellow employee recalled: "He used to creep along halls, pressing his ear to every door. He was determined that no room booked as a single was being used as a double."

(Left) The Empress' garden set the tone for Victoria, the "garden city." (Below) Gardener Art Sanders, Empress conservatory, 1946. When he retired in 1946, Fred Saunders, who had designed the Empress gardens, was replaced by his almost-namesake Art Sanders, who remained on the job for almost twenty-five years.

It was impossible to imagine Victoria without the hotel. As journalist Bruce Hutchison put it in 1950, the Empress had "distilled, bottled and preserved the inner essence of Victoria." The CPR was not impressed. "We are well aware of the affection Victorians have for the Empress," a railway executive commented in 1965, "but all we have here is a beautiful old building in the middle of a garden. It is costly to operate, it isn't functional, and it is losing the company a lot of money." Victorians waited in suspense for the company's decision. "Without this splendid relic of the Edwardian era, literally tens of thousands of tourists will never return," the *Victoria Colonist* worried. "This is the mecca, this is the heart and soul of the city."

Relief was palpable when the company announced that the Empress would not be demolished. Instead, the CPR launched a modernization programme, known as "Operation Teacup." The results were not to everyone's taste. Orange became the dominant colour. Dark mahogany doors replaced bevelled glass. The stained glass dome of the Palm Court disappeared above a false ceiling. The glass panes of the Ballroom's "daylight ceiling" were covered with plywood, and painted sky blue. The renovation stressed contemporary style rather than Edwardian character. "The Grande Dame of Victoria is wearing Hot Pants," a Seattle newspaper quipped.

But most changes were cosmetic rather than fundamental and they

allowed the Empress to survive its awkward middle-age to become truly appreciated in its eightieth year. In 1988, the Empress closed its doors for the first time in its history for the "Royal Renovation," an ambitious six-month project calculated to restore the building "to its original splendour."

Today, the Empress' public rooms present a picture of Edwardian opulence. But behind the scenes, the past lingers in very different ways. An almost forgotten tunnel, which once connected the hotel to its power house and laundry, still runs under Douglas Street. In the hotel's basement, the huge concrete piers that support the building rise above a dirt floor on which the height of the tide can be judged by the depth of the puddles. In the Humboldt wing, a locked door opens onto a stairway leading to the abandoned rooms on the uppermost floor. And above those rooms, unchanged since 1929, a maze of passageways connects hidden attic spaces, unexplored even by staff members who believe they know the hotel's every nook and cranny. A discreet "grand old lady," approaching 100 years, the Empress chooses not to reveal all the secrets of the past.

The Empress Hotel prided itself on impeccable service. According to the CPR's Manual of Service Rules: "Nothing is more repellent or offensive than an untidy waiter serving a guest. Not only the waiter's clothes, but his linen and his hands, finger nails, shoes and hair must be faultlessly clean and attended to." The same applied to waitresses, shown here in the uniform described in the Manual: "white dresses; white stockings and shoes; small white tea aprons; soft white collars and cuffs; white caps."

Lost City Hotels

Queen's Hotel (Toronto, Ontario)
1862–1927

Location: 100 Front Street West

For almost seventy years the Queen's was a meeting place for downtown brokers, bankers and businessmen, and hosted many of the city's most important social events and political gatherings. At the Queen's in 1864, Sir John A. Macdonald, George Brown and others worked out the terms of a coalition that later led to Confederation. Guests included HRH Prince Leopold, Grand Duke Alexis of Russia; Jefferson Davis, President of the Confederate States; and General Sherman, commander of the Union forces during the Civil War. It was the first hotel in Canada to have a hot-air furnace and running water in the rooms, and, according to an 1885 advertisement, its grounds were "both spacious and airy, with Croquet and Chevalerie lawns." The CPR bought the hotel for $2 million, demolished it, then spent $16 million to construct the Royal York Hotel on the same site. *(Left)* A mirror is being removed before the hotel's demolition.

Old Hotel Vancouver (Vancouver, B.C.)
1916–1939

Location: Georgia Street from Granville to Howe

The Canadian Pacific Railway's incredibly elaborate Italianate skyscraper hotel, designed by architect Francis Swales, was closed in 1939 when the CNR opened a competing hotel. During World War II, the empty old CPR hotel was used as a military recruiting centre and barracks. After 1945, it served in turn as a veteran's hostel and a refuge for victims of the Fraser River flood. It was demolished in 1949. (See p. 252 & 260) *(Left below)* The old Hotel Vancouver's ballroom

CLIFTON HOTEL (NIAGARA FALLS, ONTARIO) 1833–1932

Location: Now site of Oaks Garden Theatre, Clifton Hill
(*Above*) From its prime location near the bank of the gorge, the Clifton Hotel provided a splendid view of Niagara Falls. On June 30, 1859, thousands of spectators lined up outside the hotel to view the Great Blondin (Jean François Gravelet) cross the gorge on tightrope. The Clifton featured an outdoor concert hall where the Prince of Wales (later King Edward VII) danced at a ball during his 1860 visit, and where singer Jenny Lind performed. The hotel was at the centre of social activity in the area, inspiring A. Poppenburg to compose "The Clifton House Polka" in 1852. The first hotel was lost to fire in 1898 and was replaced by a stone building in 1905. After this new building burned to the ground on New Year's Eve of 1932, its land was donated to the Niagara Parks Commission.

RUSSELL HOUSE (OTTAWA, ONTARIO) 1864–1925

Location: Corner of Sparks and Elgin Streets
(*Above*) For years, Russell House was the social annex of Ottawa's House of Commons. Closed in 1925, it went up in flames on April 14, 1928. Seen here is the dining room.

QUEEN'S HOTEL (MONTREAL, QUEBEC) 1893–1978

Location: 700 Peel Street at Saint-Jacques
(*Above*) Porters from the Queen's Hotel would cross the street to the Grand Trunk Railway's Bonaventure Station as trains arrived. Attempting to persuade disembarking passengers to stay at the Queen's, they would point to the building to show how close it was. The Queen's claimed to be the only fireproof hotel in Montreal. As proof, the hotel advertised the story of a guest who blew himself up with dynamite in his room in the 1850s. The blast blew a hole in the floor, but the building lived up to its claim and did not catch fire.

When Bonaventure Station closed in 1948, the Queen's began to decline. Despite vehement protests from Montrealers, part of the building was torn down in 1988. In 1995, at 102 years old, the rest was demolished. On its facade, the building had two stone cartouches—one of Queen Victoria and the other of Prince Albert. As workers attempted to remove the one of Queen Victoria, the stone cracked right through her neck. The headlines ran, "We are not amused."

LOST CITY HOTELS

ST. LAWRENCE HALL

PRINCE EDWARD HOTEL (BRANDON, MANITOBA)
1912–1980

Location: 900 Block on Princess Avenue
(*Above*) Canadian Northern's "Prince Eddy" took two years to complete due to material shortages, strike action and bad luck. The original furnishings were shipped on the *Titanic* and lost at sea in April 1912. When the hotel was closed, a committee formed to save the "Prince Eddy." However, the committee was unable to prevent the building's demolition in 1980 and the transformation of the site into a parking lot. To this day, many Brandonites refuse to park there.

ST. LAWRENCE HALL (MONTREAL, QUEBEC)
1851–1910

Location: Corner of Saint-Jacques and Saint-François-Xavier Streets
(*Above*) St. Lawrence Hall was one of the most intriguing early Montreal hotels. In 1861, during the American Civil War, part of the hotel was converted into military barracks for British troops. Relations between the British government and the northern states were deteriorating and troops congregated in Montreal in preparation for possible deployment. Confederate agents on secret missions stayed at St. Lawrence Hall while in Montreal. John Wilkes Booth stayed here in 1865, just weeks before he assassinated President Abraham Lincoln. It has been said that he hinted at his murderous plans to a fellow guest during a game of billiards. In 1910, the Dominion Express Company's building was erected on the site.

THE ADMIRAL BEATTY (SAINT JOHN, N.B.)
1925–1982

Location: 14-22 King Square
(*Left*) Had it not been for the $131,350 raised by the Saint John Citizens Committee, the city would not have had a new hotel in 1925. The eight-storey hotel, designed by Ross and Macdonald, was named after Admiral David Richard Beatty, a British World War I naval commander. In 1985, the building was converted to seniors' housing.

GRAND IDEAS

CHÂTEAU QU'APPELLE, REGINA, SASKATCHEWAN

In 1910, the city of Regina granted the Grand Trunk Pacific Railway a 99-year lease on property diagonal from the GTP's proposed station site at Albert Street and College Avenue, on which to build the Château Qu'Appelle. The hotel was planned down to the last detail. It was to include a basement oyster pantry and a six-stool barber shop. Its exterior "streaky-bacon" horizontal banding at the cornice may have been inspired by other prominent Regina buildings like the King's Hotel and City Hall.

In 1913, the foundation was laid and five storeys of steelwork rose, but a prewar recession caused the project to be abandoned. When Canadian Pacific's Hotel Saskatchewan opened in Regina thirteen years later (see p. 219), the *Regina Leader* reminisced about the hapless Château Qu'Appelle: "[The] massive steel beams made ghost-like shadows across Wascana Park as the sun sank in the western prairies."

Steel and other building materials on the old site were used in building the Hotel Saskatchewan, and the earth removed from the site of the Hotel Saskatchewan was dumped into the ruined basement of the Château Qu'Appelle. The site became part of Wascana Park. Today, the Royal Saskatchewan Museum lies on the site of the old hotel foundation.

Proposed by: Grand Trunk Pacific, 1910–14
Location: Wascana Park, Regina, Saskatchewan
Architects: Ross & MacFarlane, then Ross & Macdonald
Style: Château
Construction materials: gray brick and stone trim

GRAND TRUNK PACIFIC HOTEL, VICTORIA, B.C.

Work was supposed to begin in the late spring of 1912, but like the other Grand Trunk Pacific hotels, this hotel was abandoned when the company went bankrupt by the end of World War I. In later years, F. M. Rattenbury provided Canadian National Railways (which had absorbed the GTP's assets) with a design for the "Campanile Hotel" to be erected on the old Victoria Hotel site. Due to the Depression that began in 1929, this plan also fell through.
Proposed by: Grand Trunk Pacific, 1909
Location: a site was purchased in 1910 for $291,000 at the former Douglas Gardens, between Government, Belleville and Elliott Streets, Victoria, B.C. The site was adjacent to the CPR's Empress Hotel.
Architect: Francis Mawson Rattenbury
Style: Château

CHÂTEAU MIETTE, JASPER NATIONAL PARK, ALBERTA

Francis Rattenbury designed what was meant to be Grand Trunk Pacific's answer to the Banff Springs. The site for the proposed hotel and "hydropathic establishment" was near the Miette Hot Springs in Jasper National Park. Rattenbury's plan called for a main building with two attached bedroom wings.
Proposed by: Grand Trunk Pacific, 1911
Designed: 1912–13
Location: near Miette Hot Springs, along the Fiddle River in Jasper National Park, AB
Architect: Francis Mawson Rattenbury
Style: adaptation of château style with pitched roofs and gables. Also inspired by English, Scottish and Dutch architecture of the 16th and 17th C.
Number of Rooms: to have accommodated 250 guests

CANADA WESTERN HOTEL, VICTORIA, B.C.

Victoria City Council had long been preoccupied with the idea of a grand hotel on James Bay. An 1891 issue of Victoria Illustrated printed an engraving of the proposed Canada Western Hotel. Although this five-storey building with a châteauesque roof was never built, the city finally got its grand hotel in 1908 with the opening of the Empress.
Location: on James Bay, Victoria, BC
Architect: believed to be Thomas Sorby

CHÂTEAU MOUNT ROBSON, CANADIAN ROCKIES

This hotel was to be GTP's signature resort. It was designed as a central block aligned to the northeast so as to face Mount Robson, the highest point in the Canadian Rockies. Bedroom wings were to have radiated out from this core.

Proposed by: Grand Trunk Pacific, 1911
Designed: 1912-13
Location: a valley beneath Mount Robson at the headwaters of the Fraser River, B.C. (near the Alberta border)
Architect: Francis Mawson Rattenbury
Style: Château
Number of Rooms: To have accommodated 500 guests

CPR HOTEL, WINNIPEG, MANITOBA

The Royal Alexandra was first planned as a château-style station hotel similar in design to the Place Viger in Montreal. The entrance was to have been located in a massive circular tower at the corner of Higgins and Main Streets. Flanking wings were to have extended along each street. The classically-inspired hotel that was actually built (see p. 153) represented the CPR's departure from the château style to one that was more influenced by contemporary grand American hotel design.

Proposed by: Canadian Pacific Railway
Location: Higgins Avenue, Winnipeg, Manitoba
Style: Château, combined station and hotel
Architect: Edward Maxwell

GRAND TRUNK PACIFIC HOTEL, PRINCE RUPERT, B.C.

The foundation trenches for this huge Grand Trunk Pacific terminal hotel were dug in November 1913, but no further work was ever done. The hotel was part of Grand Trunk's vision for a prosperous Prince Rupert, which also included a train station and steamship terminal. The GTP saw Prince Rupert's potential as the closest North American port to the Orient, and had the hotel designed to accommodate over one thousand guests. Because the GTP fell on hard times, Prince Rupert never became a "Metropolis of the North" and Rattenbury's million dollar château-style hotel was never completed.

Proposed by: Grand Trunk Pacific
Location: 2nd Avenue, Prince Rupert, B.C.
Style: château exterior, interior in Renaissance style
Number of rooms: over 600

BEHIND THE SCENES

Providing flawless service to guests means having an army of staff (up to 1,300) fulfilling an astounding array of tasks with great care and working to a schedule of military precision. Such an enormous operation, a grand hotel was regularly referred to as "a city within a city."

Château Frontenac doorman's cap

Château Frontenac waiter's jacket

(Above) Baker, Château Laurier. Old brick bread ovens like this one can still be found at the King Edward Hotel in Toronto, although they are no longer used. In the 1950s, Royal York bakers made 20,000 rolls per day.

(Left) From a 1950 article on the Royal York: "Chefs can only eat when they have time. Centre: Chef Henri Odiau. Left: Sous chef Perrault. Right: Assistant Didier. Odiau often has no stomach for anything except toast and tea." (Above) Kitchen staff of the Fort Garry, 1922

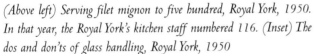

(Above left) Serving filet mignon to five hundred, Royal York, 1950. In that year, the Royal York's kitchen staff numbered 116. (Inset) The dos and don'ts of glass handling, Royal York, 1950

(Above right) The clock hovers as waitresses wait to pick up soup for a banquet party of five hundred at the Royal York, 1950. In the 1950s, the Royal York's kitchen served 25,000 meals per day, which involved preparing 6,000 lbs. of meat, 200 lbs. of fish, and 5,000 eggs.

(Below right) A new shift of bell staff parading for inspection before manager William Aylett in the marble lobby of the Château Laurier, 1954. A Canadian Pacific Hotels Manual of Service Rules of December 1922 includes these instructions to bell staff at the end of their shift: "On arrival of the incoming watch, the captain will give in succession the commands 'Stand,' 'Right turn,' 'Quick march,' and all will march off in step to the dressing room for dismissal, before which the captain will take up with any individual any point, error, disobedience or insubordination that has arisen during the watch."

(Above) Radio engineers, Royal York. Big band acts like Moxie Whitney and his Orchestra and Mart Kenney's "Sweet and Lo" were broadcast live across the country from the Imperial Room stage.

(Above left) Engineer A. W. Mason, 1929 at the Royal York. The Royal York was connected by a tunnel to the Toronto steam plant on Lakeshore Boulevard. The tunnel still exists, but has been blocked off.

(Middle) Every month in the 1950s, the linen room supplied, mended, and pressed all the uniforms for the Royal York's 1,300 employees, and repaired over 1,000 sheets.

(Left) Assistant Housekeeper Agnes Taggart and a member of the housekeeping staff in the Royal York's Presidential Suite, 1950. Housekeeping departments aim for perfection, and to be as unobtrusive as possible. They are one of the most important departments of any hotel. Attention to detail is crucial.

Upholsterers have to repair 1,000 of 7,200 pieces of the hotel's upholstered furniture annually. As the Royal York was the centre of Grey Cup celebrations, the management quickly learned to remove the lobby furniture before celebrations got underway.

Sommelier at the Château Laurier. Some of the hotels had the very best wine cellars in the country. The Ritz kept 5,000 bottles of the finest vintages, 60 brands of scotch, and 20 varieties of brandy, the oldest of which dated back to 1815.

Château Laurier print shop. The hotels economized by producing their own menus and other printed materials. The Fort Garry Hotel in Winnipeg still has an abandoned print shop up in a rooftop garret.

Svend Rasmussen and six assistants repaired, silver-plated and polished the silverware from all the CPR hotels. The silvering room was located under the roof of the Royal York on the 21st floor. Wear is so heavy that each piece of silverware is replated every three months!

Bruce Price   CP

Banff Springs Hotel	1888
Château Frontenac	1893
Place Viger Hotel	1893

Bruce Price's sketch for the first Banff Springs Hotel. The pyramidal central tower as depicted here was not built.

Francis Mawson Rattenbury   CP

Mt. Stephen House addition	1902-02
Glacier House annexes	1902-05
Château Lake Louise addition	1900-12
Hotel Vancouver west wing	1905
The Empress	1905

This preliminary sketch of the Empress Hotel by Francis Rattenbury appeared in the Victoria Colonist *on May 3, 1903.*

Walter S. Painter   CP

Algonquin addition	1908
Château Frontenac	1909-10
Mont Carmel Wing	
Empress Hotel additions	1900 & 1912
Banff Springs Hotel tower	1912-14
Chalet Lake Louise addition	1912-13

Painter's sketch for a new Banff Springs. Only the tower was built in the 1914 addition. Years later, different wings were added than those depicted here. Painter was given a tour of the Loire Valley in France before drawing these plans. (Note the sulphur pool in front.)

George Ross, D.H. MacFarlane & R.H. Macdonald   CN

Château Laurier (R&DM)	1912
Fort Garry Hotel (R&DM)	1913
Hotel Macdonald (R&DM)	1915
Mount Royal Hotel (R&RM)	1922
The Admiral Beatty (R&RM)	1925
Hotel Saskatchewan (R&RM)	1927
Royal York Hotel (R&RM)	1929

Edward and W.S. Maxwell   CP

Manoir Richelieu (EM)	1899
Royal Alexandra Hotel (E&WS)	1906
The Palliser (E&WS)	1914
Château Frontenac St. Louis Wing, service wing, central tower block (E&WS)	1920-24

John S. Archibald and John Schofield   CN

Jasper Park Lodge (main lodge) (S with Godfrey Milnes)	1923
Château Laurier east wing (A&S)	1927-29
Manoir Richelieu (A)	1929
Bessborough Hotel (A&S)	1935
Hotel Vancouver (A&S)	1939
The Nova Scotian (A)	1930
The Charlottetown (S with G.F. Drummond)	1931

(Top) Perspective view along Peel Street of Mount Royal Hotel, Montreal. (Middle) Maxwell drew his proposed tower onto a photograph of the existing Château Frontenac. (Bottom) Elevation drawing of the Bessborough Hotel

HOTEL VANCOUVER'S HIDDEN SPACES

Water Tanks, 19th floor

Attic, 20th fl.

Mechanical room, 17th fl.

Elevator Cables

Old Public Address Room 17th fl.

Royal Suite

Old Fire Alarm box

Hall on 14th floor

Laundry chute

Laundry, Sheet press

Elevator shaft

TIME LINE

1833	Clifton Hotel Opens	1906	GTP begins railway	1928	fire at Manoir Richelieu

1833   Clifton Hotel Opens
1851   St. Lawrence Hall, Montreal opens
1862   Queen's Hotel, Toronto opens
c.1878   Tadoussac Hotel opens
1878   Windsor Hotel opens
1886   Mount Stephen House opens
1886-1913   Richelieu and Ontario Navigation Co. cruise ships on St. Lawrence River (becomes Canada Steamship Lines in 1913)
1887   Glacier House opens
c.1887   Fraser Canyon House opens
1888   Banff Springs Hotel opens old Hotel Vancouver opens
1889   The Algonquin opens
1890   small Chalet Lake Louise built
1891   CPR begins Pacific maritime service from Vancouver to Asia with 3 ships: Empresses of *India, Japan, China* Canada Western Hotel proposed
1893   Château Frontenac opens Queen's Hotel, Mtl., opens Chalet Lake Louise burns
1894   new Chalet Lake Louise opens
1898   Place Viger Hotel opens
1899   Manoir Richelieu opens
Early 1900s Fraser Canyon House burns and is rebuilt
1901   Royal Muskoka Hotel opens
1903   Grand Trunk Pacific Railway (GTP), a subsidiary of Grand Trunk, is incorporated to complete a route to Prince Rupert on Pacific coast. CPR buys first ships for Atlantic route King Edward Hotel opens

1906   GTP begins railway Royal Alexandra Hotel opens Prince Rupert Hotel proposed
1908   Empress Hotel opens
1909   GTP Victoria Hotel proposed
1910   Château Qu'Appelle proposed St. Lawrence Hall, Mtl. closes
1911   Château Miette proposed Château Mount Robson proposed
1912   Ritz-Carlton Hotel opens Château Laurier opens Prince Edward Hotel opens
1913-66 Canada Steamship Lines Co. cruises on St. Lawrence River
1913   Fort Garry Hotel opens
1914   first Minaki Lodge opens Palliser Hotel opens old Algonquin burns down
1915   Hotel Macdonald opens new Algonquin opens
1919   CN is founded
1920   Bigwin Inn opens
1923   Grand Trunk Railway is amalgamated with CNR
1922   Jasper Park Lodge opens Mount Royal Hotel opens
1924   Chalet Lake Louise (Rattenbury addition) burns
1925   Glacier House closes Admiral Beatty opens new Château Lake Louise opens first Minaki burns down
1926   Hotel Newfoundland opens
1927   Hotel Saskatchewan opens Prince of Wales Hotel opens Reconstructed Minaki opens Queen's Hotel, Toronto, closes
1928   Lord Nelson Hotel opens

1928   fire at Manoir Richelieu
1929   The Pines at Digby opens Royal York Hotel opens new Manoir Richelieu opens Glacier House is demolished
1930   Château Montebello opens Nova Scotian Hotel opens
1931   Charlottetown Hotel opens
1932   Clifton Hotel burns
1935   Bessborough Hotel opens Place Viger Hotel closes
1939   old Hotel Vancouver closes new Hotel Vancouver opens
1940   Keltic Lodge opens
1941   old Hotel Tadoussac is demolished
1942   new Hotel Tadoussac opens
1949   old Hotel Vancouver is demolished
1952   Royal Muskoka Hotel burns main lodge at Jasper burns
1953   new lodge at Jasper opens Mount Stephen House is demolished
1958   Queen Elizabeth Hotel opens
1966   Bigwin Inn closes
1967   Royal Alexandra closes
1971   Royal Alexandra demolished
1978   Queen's Hotel, Mtl. closes
1980   Prince Edward Hotel is demolished
1981   Windsor Hotel closes
1982   new Hotel Newfoundland built
1983   old Hotel Newfoundland is demolished
1984   Mount Royal Hotel closes
1985   Admiral Beatty converted to seniors' housing fire at Lord Nelson
2000   Outlook Cabin burns down, Jasper Park Lodge

ACKNOWLEDGEMENTS

This book owes a large debt to the following people who offered their time, assistance, and memories to bring these stories to life:

Verna Alford; Brian Anthony, Veronica Vaillancourt, Heritage Canada Foundation; Peggy Archibald; Architectural Heritage Society; Didi Bartlett, Glenda Cornforth, Kathy Glenn, Jasper-Yellowhead Historical Society, Museum and Archives; Elinor Barr; Todd Battis; Grace Best; Don Boisvenue, Richard Martineau, Historic Sites and Monuments Board; Judy Boundy, Comstock Photo File Ltd.; Ila Bossons, Toronto City Council; Randy Brooks, Nova Scotia Tourism; Wayne Burley, New Brunswick Heritage; Wendy Bush; Elise Campbell; Laurie Carlyle; Will Chaburn; Dominique Chapheau; Eric Charman; Paul Chenier, Helen Malkin, Françoise Roux, Megan Spriggs, Canadian Centre for Architecture; Charlotte County Archives; Nicolas-Hugo Chebin, Centre d'histoire de Montréal; City of Ottawa Archives; City of Toronto Archives; Jo-Anne Colby, Steve Lyons, Canadian Pacific Archives; Janet Denis, Montreal City Archives; Jeremy Diamond; Luca Di Nicola; Alan Doyle; Susanne Dubeau, York University Archives; Ted Elfstrom; Manny Estralla; Colleen Field, Bert Riggs, Centre for Newfoundland Studies; Betty Findlay; John Fitzgerald; Mitchell Franklin; Elmer Gallant; George Gamester; Patrice Geroux, Musée de Charlevoix; Lyn Goldman; Bill Graham, M.P.; Sandra Head, Daly House Museum; Heritage Regina; Peter Herschorn; Alfred Holden, Toronto Star; Gordie Howe; Colleen Howe; Marg Hryniuk; Jamie Hunter; Les Hurt, Alberta Historic Sites; Yousuf Karsh; Alec Keefer; Mart Kenney; Joannie & Peter King; Robert Klein, Heritage Montreal; André Laframboise, Scott Shortliffe, Canadian Studies Program; Dane Lanken; Laurier LaPierre; Henri Lauzière; Paul Litt, Ontario Heritage Foundation; William Little; Eric Longley; Barb Lorenzen; Lorna Luke; Wanda Lyons, Provincial Archives of New Brunswick; Lois Mackenzie; Mabel MacDougall; Manitoba Historical Society; Heather McNabb, Suzanne Morin, Stéphanie Poisson-Dutoy, McCord Museum; Metro Toronto Reference Library; Ruth Millar, Saskatoon Public Library; Helen Miller, City of St. John's Archives; Pat Molesky, Glenbow Museum and Archives; Jacques Morin, Archives nationales du Québec; Patrick Nagle; National Archives of Canada; Phil Norton, Montreal Gazette; Tim Novak, Saskatchewan Archives Board; Jeff O'Brien, City of Saskatoon; Michael O'Neill; Antony Pacey, Museum of Science and Technology; Anne Pennington Mayer; Marla Preston; Harold Price; Tony Price; Al Purdy; Gary Ramsay, Charlottetown Confederation Centre Public Library; Del Reddy; Janelle Reynolds, Provincial Archives of Manitoba; Dal Richards; Mario Robert; Heather Robertson; Scott Robson, Nova Scotia Museum; Jeff Rogstad; Daniella Rohan, Blackader-Lauterman Library of Architecture and Art, Canadian Architecture Collection, McGill University; Tom Rooney, Ottawa Public Library; Robert W. Sandford; Fotios Sarris; Saskatchewan Archives Board; Herman Schaad; Robert Scott; Erez Segal, Kerry-Anne Smith, Pier 21 Museum; Geoff Shifflett and family; Sharon Shipley, National Library of Canada; Garry Shutlak, Nova Scotia Archives and Records Management; Ken Smith; Sean Smith, York University Archives; George Smitherman; Yvonne Snider-Nighswander, Manitoba Legislative Library; Mark Thompson; Vancouver Public Library, Special Collections; Gabie Villeneuve, Musée Maritime Tadoussac; Willa Walker; Lynette Walton, Glenbow Museum and Archives; Susan Wanamaker, Parks Canada; Sheila Washburn; Mary Haime Williams; Harold Wright.

Our gratitude also goes to the hotels for opening their doors and their archives, and to the many people who shared their time:

The Fairmont Algonquin:
Michele Facey, Lila Haughn, Tony Scammell, Andrew Turnbull

The Fairmont Banff Springs:
Holly Wood, Barbara Heimlich

The Delta Bessborough:
Mary Bazylevich, Stephan Deprez, Gloria Erikson, Hashem Melhem

The Rodd Charlottetown:
Bernie Carragher, Gary Craswell, Matt Malone, Gary Ramsay, David Rod, Jim MacMicken Wilson

The Fairmont Chateau Laurier:
Thom Ouellette, Deneen Perrin, Denis Perron, Claude Sauvé

The Fairmont Empress:
Kevan Cooper, Samantha Geer, Suzanne Girard, Jonatan Gomez, Paul Jeffery, Jason Jew, Guy Mac, Martin Repicky

The Fort Garry:
Ida Albo, Rick Bel, Charlene Petrash

Fairmont Le Chateau Frontenac:
Gaston Balduc, André Bowles, Anne Géry, Michael Henderson, Roger Martel, Nancy Murray, Patricia Rocheleau, Nathalie Samson, Lionel Verret

The Fairmont Jasper Park Lodge:
Charlene Petroskey

The Keltic Lodge:
Ken Donovan, Ian and Penny Green, Dorothy Irwin, Jim Mackeigan

Le Royal Meridien King Edward:
Al Betke, Pauline Cook, Tony Cousens, Don Jacinto, Mike Macdonald, Beth McBlain

The Lord Nelson Hotel & Suites:
Bobby Burns, Dave Clark, Lindsay Downie, Ralph Medjuck, Miriam Regan-MacNeil, Lauren Savary, Anne White

The Fairmont Hotel Macdonald:
Debbie Panas-Arrotta, Norm Kronemann, Karen Reichenbaugh, Moira Steward, Serena Veevers, Jay Wright

Fairmont Le Manoir Richelieu:
Adolf Frizzi, Alex Kassatly, Geneviève Parent, Caroline Samson

Fairmont Le Chateau Montebello:
Francine Cloutier, Katia Dalpe-Charron, Alain Daigneault, Mike Kuziniack, Marie-Marthe Lambert, Vincent Lavoie, Lorraine Nault, André Ratel, Werner Sapp

The Fairmont Newfoundland:
John Whelan

Westin Nova Scotian Hotel:
Virginia Bell, Roy Clorey, Diane Rose

The Fairmont Palliser:
Nancy Jackson, Heather Macaulay

The Pines Resort Hotel:
Kevin Crossley, René Leblanc

The Prince of Wales Hotel:
Gale Jensen

Fairmont The Queen Elizabeth:
Caroline Des Rosiers

Ritz-Carlton, Montreal:
Marie-Josée Allaire

The Fairmont Royal York:
Melanie Coates, Frank Daly, Kolene Elliott, Nancy Hall, Wally Jenkins, Julie MacNeil, Tom Smith

Hotel Saskatchewan Radisson Plaza:
Verna Alford, Dale Bowes, Norm Brooks, Robyn Fletcher

Tadoussac Hotel:
Claude Brassard, Alain Dufour, Paulette Dufour

The Fairmont Hotel Vancouver:
Donna Fisher Abadiano, Jill Killeen, Alfred Leung, Nick Macras, Eugene Mensch, Emory Szabo

Windsor Ballrooms:
Gordon Grégoire, Valérie White

Thanks to Ann Layton, Laura Fairweather, Janet Eger, at Fairmont Hotels and Resorts; to Nancy Williate-Battet and France Gagnon Pratte for their help with research and picture collection related to the Canadian Pacific Archives; and to Robert Kennell at the CP Archives for his kind assistance. Thanks also to John Lindsay for generously contributing his research and photo collection to this project.

At Lynx Images, I would like to thank Ginny Chau, Regan Clarke, Ian Copeland, Katharine Knowles, Susan Lee and Bruce for their assistance.

My deepest appreciation goes to the many talented writers who contributed to this project; to Joan Campbell, for her tireless efforts and clarity in editing the manuscript; Steve Gamester for dedicated hours of research, picture collection and indexing; Beth Yarzab for enthusiastic research and site organization; Barbara D. Chisholm and Amy Harkness for their excellent proof reading; R.W. Chisholm for his support; Deb Wise Harris for her wizardry; Russell Floren for producing the project and Cameron Taylor for launching it; and to Andrea Gutsche for photo and design brilliance.

And finally, thank you to Janet Looker, Charles and Benjamin Harlton, and Tom Miller for your patience and your love.

PICTURE CREDITS

Key:
Inset (i)
Bottom (b)

Top (t)
Middle (md)
Main (m)

Right (r)
Left (l)

Alexander Graham Bell National Historic Site: 80(b)

Algonquin Hotel Collection: 70, 72, 73, 74, 75 (t), 76(t), 77(t)

Appalachia Volume VIII: 45(i)

Architectural Forum, Vol. 39, plate 87 (Nov. 1923): 167(l,r), 168

Archives nationales du Québec: 135, 169(i)

Banff Springs Hotel Collection: 33, 34, 35(t, i), 36(bl), 233

Barney Lane: 269

Bell Canada Historical Collection: 160

Bessborough Hotel Collection: 287(b)

British Columbia Archives: 271(m, i), 272, 274(t, i)

Canada Steamship Lines Collection: 84(i), 86, 87, 89(t)

Canadian Centre For Architecture, Montreal: 287(t)

Canadian Pacific Archives: 6, 11(i), 12, 13, 18, 19, 20, 24(i), 28, 40, 43 (tl), 48, 49(t), 69, 78, 102, 130, 133, 134(t,i), 136, 137 (t), 138 (t, b), 140 (r), 141(t, i), 152, 153, 188 (t), 191, 192(t), 196 (i), 197, 206, 235, 237, 238, 252, 254, 256 (r,l), 257, 258, 259, 264, 265, 267, 270(t), 281(b), 282(itl,itr), 284(tl,tr), 286(b,t,md,i)

Canada Science and Technology Museum: 54, 59(t,b), 109, 110(tl, tr, bl), 111, 116, 117(t), 122(m), 125(t, b), 126, 127, 128, 129(t), 171, 173(t,i), 174, 213, 214, 217, 226, 229(b), 241(t), 246, 260(t), 282(tr), 285(tr, bl)

Cape Breton Highlands National Park: 80(t), 81(t)

Charlotte County Archives: 75(i), 76(t)

Charlottetown Hotel Collection: 129(i)

Château Frontenac Collection: 131

Château Laurier Hotel Collection: 175, 179, 180(t), 182(t r, l, md r, l, bl, r), 183(t), 283 (tl)

Château Montebello Collection: 94, 96, 97, 98(t), 99(t, i), 100(m, i), 101(l, rt, b), 103(t, b), 104(t, i), 105(t, b)

City of Montreal Archives: 161(i)

City of Toronto Archives: 276(t)

City of Victoria Archives: 266(it), 268, 280(b), 281(t)

Collection of the Heritage Canada Foundation: 234

Dal Richards: 262(t,i), 263, 273(b)

Daly House Museum: 278(tl)

Empress Hotel Collection: 265, 270(t), 275

Fort Garry Hotel Archives: 211, 215(i)

Glenbow Museum and Archives: 16, 17, 32, 39, 53, 232, 236, 239

Hotel Macdonald Collection: 243, 248, 249(t)

Hotel Newfoundland: 122(i)

Hotel Saskatchewan Collection: 219, 220, 221(m, i), 223(t, b), 224, 225(m, i)

Hotel Vancouver Collection: 260(b), 261, 277 (bl), 288(m)

Jasper Park Lodge Collection: 52, 55 (b), 57, 59 (t, b),60, 61(t, i)

Jasper-Yellowhead Museum and Archives: 55(t), 56(t), 58

John Lindsay Collection: 14, 114, 118, 122(m), 173, 180(t), 181, 184, 185(t) 196(m), 282(tl), 276(b)

John W. Gibson Collection: 231(i)

King Edward Hotel Collection: 200, 201, 203(m, i)

Lila Haughn: 76 (b), 77(i)

Lynx Images Inc.: 15, 42, 278(bl), 302 (r), 288(i)

Mart Kenney: 222

Maclean's Magazine, June 15, 1954: 183(b), 283(bl)

McCord Museum of Canadian History: 142, 145, 146, 147(t, br), 151, 165

Metro Toronto Reference Library: 9, 10, 42(ir), 63(i), 86(i), 92(i), 106(b r), 119, 128, 132(i), 156(i) 172(i), 176(m), 208(i), 228(i), 255, 266(i), 277(tr,tl), 278(t,r)280(t, r, bl), 281(md), 286(it,imd), 287(it,ib), 279

Minnesota Historical Society: 63, 65(b)

Montreal Gazette: 150

Montreal Standard article, Jan. 7, 1950, National Library of Canada: 283(tl,tr,i) 283(tl,tr,i), 282,(bl), 284 (bl, md), 285(tl,br)

Musée de Charlevoix: 82(m, rl, i), 83, 85, 88, 89(i), 92(t)

Musée Maritime Tadoussac: 91, 93(m, i)

Muskoka Lakes Museum: 107

National Archives of Canada: 22, 23(t), 24(t), 27, 31, 38, 43(tr, md, b), 65(i), 66, 84, 90, 98(i), 112, 113, 139, 140(l), 144, 148, 149, 164, 167, 169, 176(it, ib), 177(t, i), 178(l, r, i), 184, 198,199, 202, 216, 244(i), 249(i), 253, 277(bl)

No Hay Fever & A Railway: Summers in St. Andrews, Canada's First Seaside Resort, Goose Lane Editions: Fredericton, N.B.: 75(i)

Nova Scotia Public Archives and Records Management: 121

Nova Scotia Museum: 79

Nova Scotian Hotel Collection: 117(i)

Palliser Hotel Collection: 241, 248

Prince Edward Island Museum and Heritage Foundation Collection: 68

Private Collections: 195, 273(t)

Provincial Archives of Alberta: 44, 240, 242, 245, 250(t,i) 251

Provincial Archives of Manitoba: 8, 207, 208, 209(l, r), 210(m, i), 212, 215(t)

Public Archives of British Columbia: 254

Ray Djuff: 62, 67

Ritz-Carlton Hotel Collection: 154, 155, 156(r), 157, 158(l, i), 159(r, i), 161(t), 162, 163(t, b)

Royal York Archives: 186(m, i),187, 188(b), 189(i, r), 190(tr, tl, b), 192(b), 193, 194(t, b, i)

Saskatchewan Archives: 218, 219, 227

Saskatoon Public Library: 218(m), 229(m, ti), 231(m), 284(m)

Shifflet Family Collection: 106(t, i, bl), 108(t, b i)

Tedd Church/*Montreal Gazette*:170

Terry Reksten: 266, 270 (b)

The Globe and Mail: 205(md)

Toronto Star: 204, 205(t)

The St. Pierre and Miquelon Affaire of 1941, University of Toronto Press: 120

Toronto Telegram: 205(b)

University of McGill, Maxwell Archives, Blackader-Lauterman Library: 132(i, t), 287(md)

Vancouver Public Library: 11(t)

Victoria Times Colonist, 1903: 286(md)

Whyte Museum of the Canadian Rockies, Banff: 21, 23(i), 25(t, b), 26, 30, 36(tr, t l), 37, 45(t), 46, 47(t, b), 49(b), 50, 51(t, i), 55(t)

Yousuf Karsh: 180(b)

INDEX

SELECTED READINGS

Anglin, Douglas G. *The St. Pierre and Miquelon Affaire of 1941.* Toronto: University of Toronto Press, 1966.

Anne Géry Inc. "Documents des Visites Guidées au Château Frontenac."

Archibald, Peggy. "A Vacationers' Dream or A Political Scheme? The Evolution of Tourism in Ingonish, Nova Scotia." B.A. Thesis, Saint Francis Xavier University, 1999.

Armstrong, Martha. "Big plans for Bigwin." *The Muskokan.* Sept 14, 2000, p.A6

Baldwin, Douglas. *Land of the Red Soil: A Popular History of Prince Edward Island.* Charlottetown: Ragweed Press, 1990.

Barnes, Christine. *Great Lodges of the Canadian Rockies.* Bend, Oregon: W.W. West Inc., 1999.

Barrett, Anthony A. and Rhodri Windsor Liscombe. *Francis Rattenbury and British Columbia: Architecture and Challenge in the Imperial Age.* Vancouver: University of British Columbia Press, 1983.

Beattie, Benny. *Tadoussac: The Sands of Summer.* Montreal: Price-Patterson Ltd., 1994.

Berton, Pierre. *Niagara: A History of the Falls.* Toronto: McClelland & Stewart, 1992.

Billinkoff, Arlene. "The Royal Alex: A Reminder of the Past." *Winnipeg Free Press.* March 6, 1971.

Blyfield, Ted, ed. *Alberta in the 20th Century: Vols 1-3, 5.* Edmonton: United Western Communications Ltd., 1991, 1992, 1994, 1996.

Brennan, Brian. "Calgary's grande dame of hotels," *Calgary Herald Sunday Magazine,* May 28, 1989, pp. 16-20.

Broadway, Michael J. "Urban Tourist Development in the Nineteenth Century Canadian City," *The American Review of Canadian Studies* (Spring 1996), pp. 83-99.

Camp, Dalton. *An Eclectic Eel.* Ottawa, Ontario: Deneau Publishers and Co. Ltd., 1981.

Cavell, Edward. *Legacy in Ice: The Vaux Family and the Canadian Alps.* Banff, Alberta: The Whyte Foundation, 1983.

Choyce, Lesley. *Nova Scotia: Shaped by the Sea.* Toronto, Ontario: Viking, 1996.

Churchill, Winston S. *The Second World War: Closing the Ring.* Boston: Houghton Mifflin Co., 1951.

Churchill, Winston S. *The Second World War: Triumph and Tragedy.* Boston: Houghton Mifflin Co., 1953.

Corbin, Carol and Judith A. Rolls. *The Centre of the World at the Edge of a Continent.* Sydney, Nova Scotia: University College of Cape Breton Press, 1996.

de Caraffe, Marc and Wright, Janet. "Les hôtels de style Château des compagnies ferroviaires," Agenda Paper, Historic Sites and Monuments Board of Canada, June 1980.

De Jonge, James. "Banff Springs Hotel, Spray Avenue, Banff, Alberta," Historic Sites and Monuments Board of Canada Agenda Paper, 1988.

D'Iberville, Luc-Moreau. *Lost Montreal.* Toronto: Toronto University Press, 1975.

Djuff, Ray. *High on a Windy Hill: The Story of the Prince of Wales Hotel.* Calgary: Rocky Mountain Books, 1999.

Donzel, Catherine, Alexis Gregory and Marc Walter. *Grand American Hotels.* New York: The Vendôme Press, 1989.

Eagle, John A. "Shaughnessy and Prairie Development, 1899-1914." *The CPR West: The Iron Road and the Making of a Nation.* Hugh A. Dempsey, ed., Vancouver: Douglas & McIntyre, 1984, p. 124-148.

Evans, Lewis. *Tides of Tadoussac: The Golden Age of a St. Lawrence Resort.* Finch, David. *Glacier House Rediscovered.* Revelstoke, British Columbia: Friends of Mount Revelstoke and Glacier, 1991.

Garceau, Henri-Paul. *Chronique de l'hospitalité hôtelière du Québec de 1880 à 1940.* Montreal: Les Pionniers Méridien, 1990.

Germain, Jean-Claude. *Le Feuilleton de Montréal.* Les éditions internationales Alain Stanké, 1994.

Gournay, Isabelle and France Vanlaethem, eds. *Montreal Metropolis: 1880-1930.* Toronto: Canadian Centre for Architecture/Stoddart Publishing, 1998.

Grayson, L.M. and Michael Bliss, eds. *The Wretched of Canada: Letters to R.B. Bennett, 1930-1935.* Toronto: University of Toronto Press, 1971.

Grover, Sheila. "The Hotel Fort Garry." 1979.

Gwyn, Richard. *Smallwood: The Unlikely Revolutionary.* Toronto: McClelland & Stewart, 1968.

Hart, E.J. *The Selling of Canada: The CPR and the Beginnings of Canadian Tourism.* Banff: Altitude Publishing, 1983.

Inglis, Pat. "Divinely delicious delicacies please Palliser patrons," *Calgary Herald Sunday Magazine,* May 28, 1989, p. 19-20.

Hutchison, Bruce. "The Eccentric Empress of Victoria," *Maclean's,* 15 December 1950.

Jenish, D'Arcy. "Rescue of the grand old ladies," *Alberta Report,* August 9, 1982, p. 22-27.

Kalman, Harold D. *The Railway Hotels and the Development of the Château Style in Canada.* Victoria: University of Victoria Maltwood Museum, 1968.

Lamarche, Jacques. *Rêves et Splendeurs au Château Montebello.* Saint-André-Avellin, Quebec: Les Éditions de la Petite-Nation, Inc., 1997.

Lanken, Dane. "Summers down the St. Lawrence" *Canadian Geographic.* April/May 1987, pp.54-63.

Lapointe, Lise and Phillipe Dubé. *Charlevoix et le Manoir Richelieu.* Cap-à-l'Aigle, Quebec: Exploracom Inc., 1996.

Marsh, John. "A History of Mount Stephen House, Yoho National Park." *Alpine Journal* 65 (1982) : 33-34.

Marsan, Jean-Claude. *Montréal en évolution: historique du développement de l'architecture et de l'environnement urbain montréalais.* Méridien Architecture: Laval, 3ième édition, 1994.

McKee, Bill and Georgeen Klassen. *Trail of Iron: The CPR and the Birth of the West.* Vancouver: Glenbow-Alberta Institute and Douglas & McIntyre Ltd., 1983.

McKenna, Brian and Purcell, Susan. *Drapeau.* Toronto: Clarke Irwin, 1980.

McNeil, Bill and Morris Wolfe. *Signing On: The Birth of Radio in Canada.* Toronto: Doubleday Canada, 1982.

McVicar, Don. *Ferry Command.* Shrewsbury, England: Airlife, 1981.

Mead, Robin. *Haunted Hotels.* Nashville: Rutledge Hill Press, 1995.

Melnyk, Bryan O. *Calgary Builds: The Emergence of an Urban Landscape 1905-1914.* Alberta Culture /Canadian Plains Research Center, 1985.

Mills, Ted. "The Bungalow Trail: Rustic Bungalow Camps in the Mountain Parks." *Heritage.* Ottawa: Heritage Canada Foundation, Vol. III, No. 3, Summer 2000.

Muir, Allan and Doris with Nymark, Victor. *Building the Château Montebello.* Gardenvale, Que.: Muir Publishing Company Ltd., 1985.

Murphy, Gavin. "Titanic Disaster Claims Canadian Railway Legend Charles Melville Hays." Boston: Titanic Historical Society, 1992.

Nash, Knowlton. *The Microphone Wars: A History of Triumph and Betrayal at the CBC.* Toronto: McClelland & Stewart, 1994.

Neary, Peter, Ed. *White Tie and Decorations: Sir John and Lady Hope Simpson in Newfoundland, 1934-1936.* Toronto: University of Toronto Press, 1996.

Newman, Peter C. "Pier 21: the place where we became Canadians." *Maclean's.* 109.30 (July 22, 1996) 56.

Pearce, Sharon. "The Palliser," *Alberta Report,* October 23, 1989.

Peers, Frank. *The Politics of Canadian Broadcasting: 1920-1939.* Toronto: Ph.D Thesis, 1966.

Pole, Graeme. *The Canadian Rockies.* Altona, MB: Friesen Printers, 1999.

Pratte, France Gagnon. *The Banff Springs Hotel: The Castle in the Rockies.* Quebec: Éditions Continuité Inc., 1997.

————. *The Manoir Richelieu.* Quebec: Éditions Continuité Inc., 2000.

————. *The Royal York.* Quebec: Éditions Continuité Inc., 1996.

Pratte, France Gagnon and Éric Etter. *Le Château Frontenac.* Quebec: Éditions Continuité Inc., 1996.

Pratte, France Gagnon and Robert W. Sandford. *Château Lake Louise: A Diamond in the Wilderness.* Quebec: Éditions Continuité Inc., 1998.

Prévost, Robert. *Montréal: A History.* Trans. Elizabeth Mueller and Robert Chodos. Toronto: McClelland & Stewart, 1993.

Pryke, Susan. *Explore Muskoka.* Erin, Ontario: Boston Mills Press, 1999.

Putnam, William L. *The Great Glacier and Its House.* New York: American Alpine Club, 1982.

Raddall, Thomas H. *Halifax: Warden of the North.* Toronto: McClelland & Stewart, 1971.

Rankin, Joan E. *Meet Me At The Château: A Legacy of Memory.* Toronto: Natural Heritage Books, 1990.

Rees, Ronald. *St. Andrews and the Islands.* (Nimbus Publishing Ltd: Halifax), 1995.

Reksten, Terry. *In the Grand Style: The Empress Hotel.* Vancouver: Douglas & McIntyre Ltd., 1997.

Reksten, Terry. *Rattenbury.* Victoria: Sono Nis Press, 1978, 1998.

Robertson, Heather. "Minaki Lodge as an Indian Art Centre." *The Globe and Mail.* Dec. 15, 1979.

Robertson, Heather. "Minaki Ontario: The Magic and the Madness." *Equinox.* No. 18 (Nov./Dec. 1984): 105-118.

Robinson, Bart. *Banff Springs: The Story of a Hotel.* Banff, AB: Summerthought, Ltd., 1988.

Rogers, Irene L. *Charlottetown: The Life in its Buildings.* Charlottetown: The Prince Edward Island Museum and Heritage Foundation, 1993.

Rose, David. "The Canadian Railway Hotel Revisited: The Château Style Hotels of Ross & MacFarlane," *Bulletin.* Society for the Study of Architecture in Canada. Volume 18, No. 2, pp. 32-42.

Rosenvall, L.A. and S.M. Evans, eds. *Essays on the Historical Geography of the Canadian West.* Calgary: University of Calgary, 1987.

Rossiter, Sean. *The Hotel Georgia: A Vancouver Tradition.* Vancouver: Douglas & McIntyre, 1998.

Rostecki, Randy and Wright, Janet. "Fort Garry Hotel, 222 Broadway, Winnipeg, Manitoba," Historic Sites and Monuments Board of Canada Agenda Paper, 1979.

Sandford, R.W. *Hotels: The History of Alberta's Hospitality.* Edmonton: The Alberta Hotel Assoc., 1995.

Schull, Joseph. *The Great Scot.* Montreal: McGill-Queen's University Press, 1979.

Shutlak, Garry. "The Nova Scotian Hotel and Union Station." *The Griffin.* 20.2 (Summer 1995): 5.

Silversides, Brock V. *Waiting for the Light: Early Mountain Photography in British Columbia and Alberta, 1865-1939.* Saskatoon: Fifth House Publishers, 1995.

Smallwood, Joseph. *I Chose Canada: The Memoirs of the Honourable Joseph R. "Joey" Smallwood.* Toronto: Macmillan of Canada, 1973.

Smith, Cyndi. *Jasper Park Lodge: In the Heart of the Canadian Rockies.* Canmore, AB: Coyote Books, 1985.

Stevens, G.R. *History of the Canadian National Railways.* New York: Macmillan, 1973.

Taylor, Cameron. *Enchanted Summers: The Grand Hotels of Muskoka.* Toronto: Lynx Images Inc., 1997.

"The Algonquin History" Canadian Pacific Hotels & Resorts, 1992.

Walker, Willa. *No Hay Fever & A Railway: Summers in St. Andrews, Canada's First Seaside Resort.* (Goose Lane Editions: Fredericton, New Brunswick), 1989.

Waller, Adrian. *No Ordinary Hotel: The Ritz-Carlton's First Seventy-Five Years.* Montreal: Véhicule Press, 1989.

Weintraub, William. *City Unique: Montreal Days and Nights in the 1940s and '50s.* Toronto: McClelland & Stewart, 1996.

White, Robert and Sarah Baxter. *The Mac: Edmonton's Historic Hotel Macdonald.* Edmonton: Tree Frog Press, 1995.

Whyte, Jon and Harmon, Carole. *Lake Louise: A Diamond in the Wilderness.* Banff: Altitude publishing, 1982.

Williamson, David. *Debrett's Kings and Queens of Britain.* Great Britain: Webb & Bower Ltd., 1986.

ABOUT THE CONTRIBUTORS

Frances Backhouse is a Victoria-based freelance writer, author of *Women of the Klondike* and *Hiking With Ghosts: The Chilkoot Trail Then and Now.* She writes regularly for magazines on subjects including history, wildlife, environmental issues, interior design and business, and is an active member and past president of the Periodical Writers Association of Canada. Frances first became acquainted with the Glacier House story while working at Glacier National Park as an interpretive naturalist.

Barbara Chisholm has been a partner with Lynx Images for seven years. As a writer and filmmaker, she has completed many best-selling projects, including *Superior: Under the Shadow of the Gods* (Producer/Director/Writer) and *Mysterious Islands* (Producer), both of which received the Silver Screen Award at the U.S. International Film & Video Festival. She has co-authored other best-selling books including *Alone in the Night* and *The North Channel and St. Mary's River.* Barbara lives in Toronto.

Ray Djuff is a newspaper copy editor who has never forgotten his first summer as a bartender at the Prince of Wales Hotel in Waterton Lakes National Park. His twenty-year-long fascination with Great Northern Railway's hotels in Waterton and Glacier National Park, Montana, has resulted in three books on the subject; a fourth is pending. Ray lives in Calgary with his wife and two children.

John C. Lindsay is a Toronto writer and freelance broadcaster intrigued by North American hotels and theatres, both the buildings and the life around them. His most recent book, *Palaces of the Night: Canada's Grand Theatres,* is his most comprehensive. John is a lifetime member of the Writers Guild of Canada.

David Macfarlane is a freelance writer who currently contributes a weekly arts column to *The Globe and Mail.* He began his career as a writer and editor with *Weekend Magazine* and his work has appeared regularly in *Saturday Night, Toronto Life* and *Maclean's.* He is the winner of six gold and five silver National Magazine Awards. In 1987 David was given the Sovereign Award for Magazine Journalism; in 1995 he won the Author's Award for Magazine Writing, arts and entertainment category. David has written and produced a documentary, *Where is Here?,* for a PBS series on Canada. His remarkable memoir of Newfoundland, *The Danger Tree,* won the Canadian Authors' Association Award in 1992. In 1999 his best-selling novel, *Summer Gone,* was short-listed for the Giller Prize, and in 2000 it won the Chapters Award. Born in Hamilton, David now lives in Toronto with his wife and two children.

France Gagnon Pratte is an architectural historian who has written books on the history of the Château Frontenac, the Banff Springs, the Château Lake Louise, the Royal York and the Manoir Richelieu hotels. She is also the author of books on 19th-century villas in the Quebec City area and on the work of architects Edward and W. S. Maxwell. Since 1985 she has been President of the Conseil des monuments et sites du Québec and the Heritage Quebec Foundation. She has been president and vice-president of Les Editions Continuité since its creation in 1986. In 1999 France Gagnon Pratte received the Order of Canada for her contribution to the protection of Quebec and Canadian heritage. She lives in Quebec City.

Terry Reksten is the author of *Rattenbury, "More English Than The English": A Very Social History of Victoria* and *The Empress Hotel,* among other works. She was awarded the B.C. Book Award in 1979 and was chosen as an Honorary Citizen of the City of Victoria in 1985. Terry has recently completed an illustrated history of British Columbia.

Harry M. Sanders is a Calgary-based freelance writer and historical consultant. His work has been published in *Avenue* magazine, *Alberta History* and the *Calgary Herald Sunday Magazine.* From 1996-99, Harry's Looking Back column appeared weekly in the *Calgary Sun.*

Robert W. Sandford is a naturalist, historian and author who has been working to celebrate the nature, history and culture of the Canadian Rockies for more than 25 years. He is currently Historian-in-Residence for Fairmont's mountain resort hotels.

Adrian Waller is a British-born journalist and author who has earned a living on three continents from 15 published books, numerous newspaper columns, and some 600 articles in magazines including *Time* and *Reader's Digest,* where he was a roving editor. Adrian, who holds a Ph.D. in English, has also taught journalism, non-fiction writing and theatre arts at universities across Canada and in the United States, directed and acted in plays and sung with the Canadian Opera. He is now based in Montreal.

William Weintraub is the author of *City Unique: Montreal Days and Nights* in the 1940s and '50s, as well as two novels set in Montreal. As a writer, director and producer for the National Film Board, he has been involved in the making of over one hundred documentary films, the most recent of which was *The Rise and Fall of English Montreal.*

CANADIANS DON'T BRAG ABOUT THEIR LIVES. SO WE WILL.

The Great Farini:
Daredevil.

Bobby Rosenfeld:
Olympian.

Wilf Carter:
Country Legend.

Jay Silverheels:
The Real Tonto.

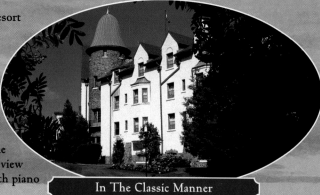
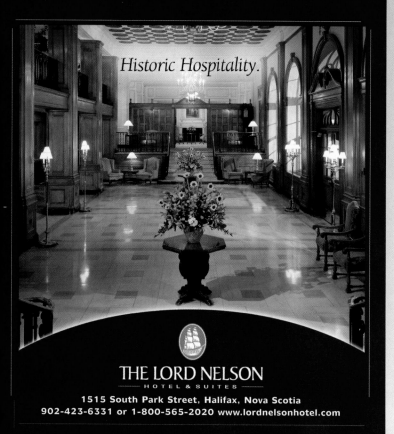

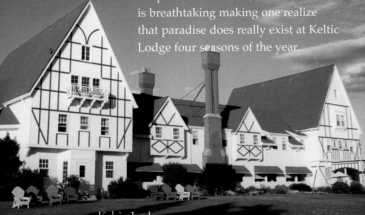

LYNX IMAGES

OTHER BOOKS & FILMS BY LYNX IMAGES

MYSTERIOUS ISLANDS:
FORGOTTEN TALES OF THE GREAT LAKES

An island ruled by a king who declared it his own country, an island used as a hideout by a notorious pirate, an island mined by pre-historic copper miners... these are only a few of the stories in this remarkable collection.

The book and film *Mysterious Islands* is a fascinating historical journey to islands in the vast basin of the five Great Lakes. Islands have been central to some of the Lakes' most important, outrageous and tragic events.

296 pages, over 500 b&w photos and maps
Video: 70 minutes

ISBN 1-894073-12-6 Book and Video $49.95
ISBN 1-894073-11-8 Book (6"x9") $24.95
ISBN 1-894073-10-x Video $29.95

"You are in for adventure and entertainment that will only leave you ready to read the book again."
 –Great Lakes Cruiser

"The video takes your breath away...because it's so all-encompassing and so beautifully done."
 –Thunder Bay Chronicle

PALACES OF THE NIGHT:
CANADA'S GRAND THEATRES

By John Lindsay

There was no place like it. With its towering marquees, majestic lobbies and magnificent auditoriums, the North American movie palace was right out of a fantasy.

Palaces of the Night chronicles the history of these impressive landmarks, from the birth of vaudeville theatres and grand opera houses, through the rise and fall of the beloved movie palaces, and finally to the contemporary phenomenon of the mega-theatre. Contains entertaining anecdotes and little-known facts about the famous actors and actresses, infamous businessmen and theatre owners, and forgotten inventors and architects who have graced the stage of Canada's rich theatre history.

296 pages, over 270 b&w and colour photographs
ISBN 1-894073-17-7 Book (8 1/2"x11") $29.95

"an enchanting read"
 –Muskoka Today

ENCHANTED SUMMERS:
THE GRAND HOTELS OF MUSKOKA

By Cameron Taylor

An engaging film and book package that brings its audience back to Muskoka's romantic era and the heyday of the grand hotels, when Muskoka was one of the premiere summer destinations in North America.

In the documentary, viewers are carried back in time through fascinating archival film footage and photographs, and a soundtrack which includes gramophone recordings from the 1920s through to the most popular names of the Big Band era. The present is linked with the past through beautiful 16mm footage of both the hotels and the captivating surroundings of Muskoka.

162 pages, over 250 photos
Video: 70 minutes

ISBN 1-894073-01-0 Book & Video $49.95
ISBN 1-894073-04-5 Book (10"x8") $24.95
ISBN 1-894073-05-3 Video $29.95

Write or email for your free catalogue
WWW. LYNXIMAGES.COM

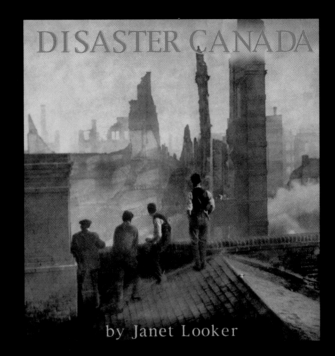

LYNX 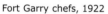 *Time*

Lynx Images is linking Canadians to their past through books and films filled with engaging stories and dramatic photography.

LYNX 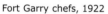 Place

Our projects are journeys of discovery, expeditions to intriguing places where the past still resonates.

Fort Garry chefs, 1922

Royal York chefs, 2001

LYNX 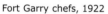 IMAGES

a small, dedicated group of writers and filmmakers who believe that history is something for all of us to explore.

Since 1988, **Lynx Images** has been creating books and films that help deepen appreciation of this country's history. After several years exploring the Great Lakes, we are now crossing the country with our current projects. Thank you for your input and support—revenue from each book and video goes directly towards future Canadian history projects.

–Russell Floren, Andrea Gutsche and Barbara Chisholm

Here's to a future of bringing you more of the past.

LYNX
IMAGES
lynximages.com

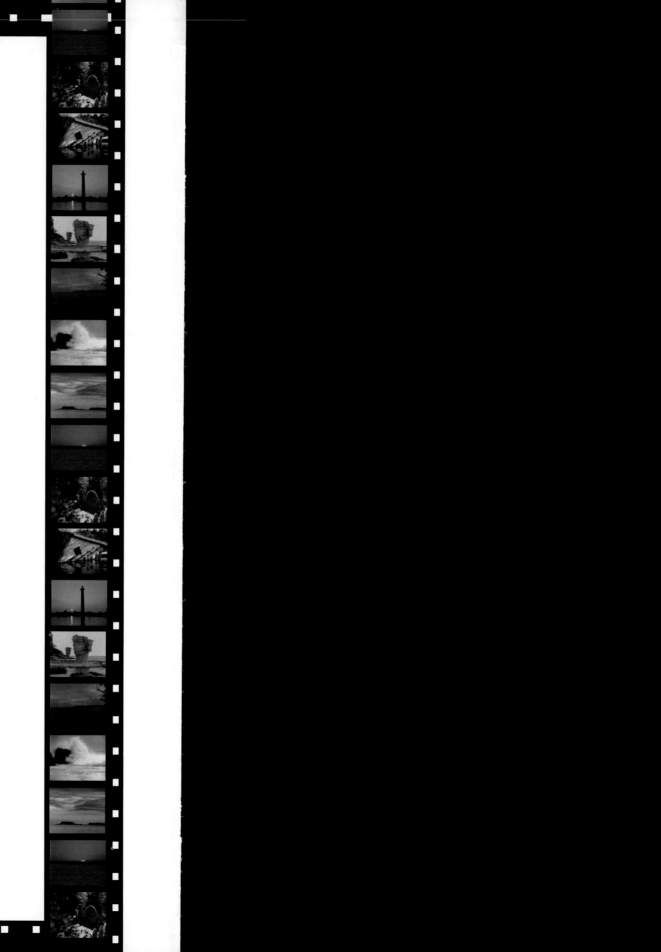